REBELLION IN BLACK AFRICA

REBELLION

IN BLACK AFRICA

Edited and with an Introduction

by ROBERT I. ROTBERG

OXFORD UNIVERSITY PRESS

London · Oxford · New York

1971

In memoriam

Eduardo Chivambo Mondlane,
scholar and revolutionary
(1920-1969)

In this volume proper names, foreign titles, acronyms, and Bantu usage conform to a pattern set—for the sake of consistency and intelligibility —by the editors, the publications staff of the Harvard Center for International Affairs, and the publishers. Pronominal concords are omitted from nonterritorial and nonlinguistic forms of Bantu nomenclature; genitival and adjectival agreement has been sought between nominals and their objects; and short titles rather than initials have been preferred for even the most well known African political parties in order to avoid readers' confusion. The imposed usage departs from the preferred style of some of the contributors but has the merits (and some of the defects) of simplicity and uniformity.

PREFACE

The six essays which follow, together with twenty-eight others, were originally commissioned for and published in Robert I. Rotberg and Ali A. Mazrui (eds.), *Protest and Power in Black Africa* (Oxford University Press, 1970). Rebellion was one of the dominant themes of that volume, and, in order to make the essays more widely available to students and teachers, the publishers suggested that at least that part of *Protest and Power* should be issued separately as *Rebellion in Black Africa*.

The essays in the present book are published without their original, rather extensive, footnotes, which may be found in *Protest and Power*. Similarly, interested readers will find a detailed bibliography on rebellion in Africa in *Protest and Power*. Otherwise, the essays have not been altered or revised. The relevant maps, charts, and graphs have been included, too, and a new index prepared.

The acknowledgments of the editors and the authors are contained in *Protest and Power*.

R.I.R.

Chocorua
August 1970

CONTENTS

LIST OF MAPS

MAPS BY VAUGHN GRAY

INTRODUCTION

To rebel is to refuse allegiance to and forcefully oppose an established government or any ruling authority. This is a syndrome of behavior which exactly fitted the needs of Africans during and after the era of colonialism and the six essays that follow discuss movements of rebellion which, at different times and in different places, dramatized the perennial quest of Africans for freedom from externally imposed restraints. Together, they exemplify some of the many important ways in which Africans sought to cope with the strains of colonial and post-colonial society. Each used the cement of religion and ritual to fashion a following and sanctify violence. Each served as an expression of the psychological stress of the particular society, and, although two of the movements (the Mumbo of Gusii and the Nyabingi) sublimated as often as they attacked, each proved a vehicle for the mutation of hostility into violence, thus becoming a definable movement.

Africans were angry and aggrieved, if for different reasons and against different authorities. They had in many areas (but not necessarily corresponding to the regions of later rebellion) bitterly resisted the forcible introduction of Western norms and power by the several European occupiers. They had resented European-imposed controls and constraints. But when they fought, whether in a desultory manner or on a major scale (for example, in Northern Nigeria, the Western Sudan, Angola, Malawi, Rhodesia, Somalia, South Africa, Tanzania, and Eritrea), only the Ethiopian kingdom ruled by Minilik possessed the unity, integrity, and technological expertise to forestall European domination. In Southern Africa, by comparison, the indigenous inhabitants were unable to cope completely with the expansionist designs of the Anglo-Afrikaner attack. Although the Zulu blocked the British advance at Isandhlwana and the Sotho managed, as a result of a number of campaigns, to prolong an otherwise untenable position between advancing Afrikaners and the British in Natal, both peoples lacked the technical and organizational abilities necessary for sustained opposition to foreign occupation. Similarly, Abushiri and the Arabs on the coast of Tanzania, the Yao chiefs on Lake Malawi, and even Samori and the Tukolor in the Guinée forests and the Western Sudan could harass and postpone, but not ultimately forestall, the loss of their respective patrimonies.

Resisters rejected what they anticipated and perceived. Rebels, however, who by definition came later and had experienced the exactions of the earliest (if only brief) phase of colonial or, in the Congo case, independent rule, rejected what they knew. By rebelling they sought to reclaim their lost liberty and spiritual freedom, to bare the extent of their despair (as in the case of Chilembwe's rebellion), to reassert individual and collective dignities, and, in the milder cases of African rebellion, to reform the alien framework of their sad subordination. To do so they tried to oust the occupiers or, at least, to carve out — not always realistically — some kind of separate domain. In some cases, such as those of Nyabingi and Mumbo, rebellion was seen as an aggressive declaration of independence without any noteworthy territorial expectations. The spirit and the essence were more important for them than the actuality, a generalization which may also apply to the modern Congo. Several of the most widespread and violent rebellions, like the Maji Maji (Tanzania, 1905–1907), the Mahdiya, Nyabingi, the Mumbo, the *simba* of the Congo, and perhaps the Zulu of Natal, were profoundly conservative. They harked back to an earlier, simpler, golden age, when traditional virtues were rewarded and life was somehow more vital, less corrupt, and devoid of the disruptive intrusions for which Western colonizers or their independent successors were responsible. These rebellions were revivalistic, and had latent expressive, mystical, and non-secular goals as important as those which were manifested at the more obvious levels of instrumental aggression. The Mahdi proclaimed a vision which owed much of its content to the early, glorious days of Islam. The others responded to a remembrance of pre-colonial times past. They sought to recreate the freedom and tranquility of bygone days in a manner meaningful to the troubled present.

Disillusionment with authority was and is common phenomenon in African life, but the resulting energies were only infrequently devoted to overt expressions of antagonism. Consequently the actual number of real rebellions during and since the epoch of colonialism is limited and their incidence scattered. None of them succeeded in permanently reversing the fate of Africans or their indigenous rulers. Yet they are rightfully important components of the heritage of many African peoples and states, and, for the colonial cases, provide a foreshadowing of the later rise of eventually victorious movements of nationalism. As periodic assertions of African dismay, they also affected the reactions of colonial governments to their subjects and may, as in Natal, Malawi, Tanzania, and — conceivably — the modern Congo, have subtly curbed harmful excesses of authority. Fear of potential rebellion was a potent force, particularly in those areas which had experienced none. Of the rebellions discussed here, the Mahdiya was the most successful and transformatory of the character of its state. They ruled supreme in the Sudan for thirteen years, and left a permanent political and religious legacy. Recurrent episodes of Nyabingism between 1908 and 1928 demonstrated the refusal of the Kiga and Rwanda of British Uganda and German Ruanda to accept foreign domination without a struggle. The Gusii rebels similarly remained truculent for several decades as a means of fending off and dealing with the tentacles of British administration. By contrast, the Zulu and Chilembwe's Malawians sought boldly to protest and to lessen the burden of colonial servitude. They were desperate. And so were the Congolese rebels, many of whom denied the legitimacy of their independent government.

The Mahdiya, Nyabingism, Mumboism, and Chilembwe's rebellion were organized by or around religious figures and were sustained, as were the *simba,* by the mobilizing force of powerful supernatural observance. Even the Zulu uprising, the most avowedly secular of the six rebellions discussed in the following chapters, was probably to a large extent assisted by traditional para-religious loyalties to Zulu ancestors and their contemporary representatives. All, except that led by Chilembwe, were mass movements. Again with the exception of Chilembwe's rebellion, all demonstrated agrarian disaffection (with merchant participation and intervention) and were tied in many ways to basic economic grievances. They, Chilembwe's still excepted, each achieved a measure of success, if not in all cases territorial independence, before succumbing to stronger firepower.

The appeal of the Mahdi can be understood only within the hallowed framework of a revitalizing Sunni Islam. Leon Carl Brown does not deny the particularistic appeal of the Mahdi at a time of acute socio-economic tension, and suggests that the notion of puritanical Mahdism was especially congenial to the peoples of the Islamic fringe of North and sub-Saharan Africa. The Zulu responded to a far less spiritual evocation. They had fought the British and Afrikaners throughout the nineteenth century and had been defeated and sub-jugated. Zululand had been annexed in 1897, one year before the Mahidya was defeated by an Anglo-Egyptian expeditionary force. But it was the decision to introduce a poll tax, and the unfeeling measures used to enforce its collection, which heightened the misery of a people who had recently experienced increasing impoverishment and coin-cidental natural disaster. This combination of circumstances, when added to the always present individual tribulations, proved conducive to small-scale rebellion — to a kind of rebellion which was common to colonial Africa — and to the more disruptive insurgency led by Bambatha, a Zulu chief who, in the manner of Chilembwe, was resigned to revolt.

The Nyabingi cult provided a different focus for rebellion. As Elizabeth Hopkins intimates, it was a spirit possession movement which, by virtue of its ideological equation of supernatural power with material gain, offered a ready vehicle for secular and, in this case, specifically anti-European activity. For nearly three decades the notion of Nyabingi incorporated the types of antagonism which were endemic to a marginal border area the populations of which were in the throes of externally-induced social change. Problems concerning alien admin-istration, taxes, and land rights exercised the sensibilities of Africans here as elsewhere, and the various Nyabingi and Nyabingoid leaders added a new quasi-religious dimension to the kinds of disparate pro-test which characterized the other movements of rebellion. Like the Nyabingi movement, the Mumbo movement discussed by Audrey Wipper was a pre-colonial cult resurrected and redirected during the colonial period as a functional source of security and a refuge from stress. Like the Nyabingi, it played an important role in a society anxious to cope with the persons and institutions which had made the old order disappear. Even Mumbo, however, sought indigenous re-integration as much as conflict. It was not rebellious *per se,* although it did, on occasion, resort to force of arms. Utopian and eclectic, it represented an ingenious method of adapting to, coping with, and pro-testing against new, complex, and intrusive strands of social changes.

The European governments clashed with Mumbo, Nyabingi, and a number of similar revitalizing sects. They worried about and fought the Kimbangu movement of the lower Congo, the Watchtower, Mwana Lesa, and Lenshina disturbances of northeastern Zambia, the Prophet Harris movement in the Gold and Ivory Coasts, sects in Southern Africa and Nigeria, and Islamic brotherhoods in West Africa. These groups, however, and the more than 2,000 independent churches which had been formed in black Africa before World War II, were for the most part subversive of colonial rule more because of their separate, disaffected witness than because of their violent intentions. Although many, it is true, refused to obey constituted white and black authorities, and occasionally resorted to arms, most expressed their disaffection quietly, and by simply existing. Their importance to Africans was largely due to the fact that they were black-controlled during an era when whites dominated most spheres of activity, even the non-Islamic institutions of newly introduced religions. These independent churches epitomized a response to a psychological awareness of inadequacy as much as they were an expression of precisely delineated anti-colonial aspirations. But, of all these African religious manifestations, the Nyabingi and the Mumbo were among the most indigenously authentic in their origin and organization, and the most militant in their manifestation of hostility to white rule.

Chilembwe's church was, by contrast, very Western in inspiration, organization, and aspiration. He was a modern man, but, in ways which are indicated in a following chapter, his alienation and the alienation of his followers were as profound as those of the Nyabingists, the Mumboists, and the *simba*. Reform was acceptable to him when it might not have been to Bambatha and the Mahdi, and would surely not have been to the followers of Nyabingi and Mumbo. But the desirability of reform was less obvious to the colonial government of Nyasaland than it was to Chilembwe, and rebellion, for personal as well as social reasons, seemed the only acceptable answer, even if the short-lived rising was meant merely to chasten the authorities — as a despairing gesture of protest, the precise configurations of which continue to perplex students of African society and self-assertion.

The chapter on the post-independence Congo provides a fitting conclusion to a book on rebellion in Africa. Crawford Young shows how the disorders and rebellious activity of the Congo were derived from socially strained situations in which Congolese of various categories suddenly found themselves. The Congo's insurrectionary potential grew as a result of a number of socio-economic and psychological crises; urbanization, unemployment, inflation, perceived iniquities in the distribution of power, and the inability of the new state to govern all played a part in stimulating the various outbreaks of the only loosely coordinated warfare that was the rebellion. Young's essay reminds us of the continuity of change, especially of the large extent to which modern African methods of mobilization and sanctification of rebellion were similar across time and space. The *simba*, the Mau Mau of Kenya, the Maji Maji, the Shona/Ndebele of late-nineteenth century Rhodesia, the Nyabingi, and even the Zulu of Bambatha utilized forms and techniques of antagonism which were strikingly similar in inspiration and employment and, in the very short term, successful. For the *simba*, as for the earlier militants, rebellion was an orderly response to difficulty.

There is little that is unique about rebellion in Africa, but it has played a critical role in the recent history of the continent. As the following six essays should make perfectly obvious, it was a significant mode for the expression of Africa's integrity in the midst of a concatenation of hostile, Western-oriented influences.

MAPS

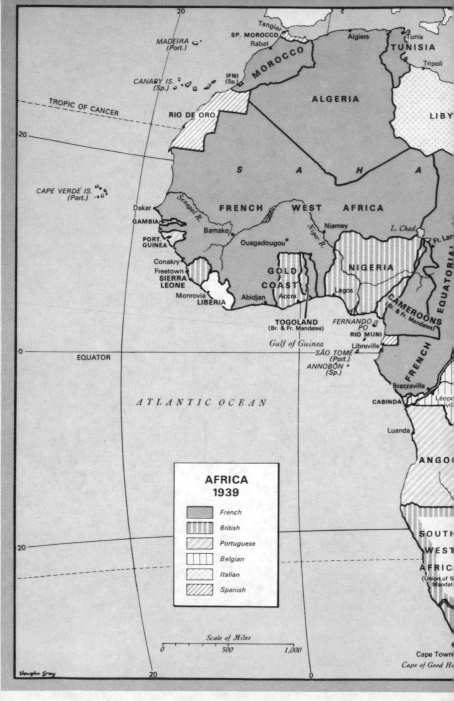

AFRICA
1939

	French
	British
	Portuguese
	Belgian
	Italian
	Spanish

Scale of Miles
0   500   1,000

20

MADEIRA
(Port.)

Tangier
SP. MOROCCO
Rabat

Algiers
Tunis
TUNISIA
Tripoli

CANARY IS.
(Sp.)
IFNI
(Sp.)

MOROCCO

ALGERIA

LIBY

TROPIC OF CANCER

RIO DE ORO

20

S   A   H   A   R   A

CAPE VERDE IS.
(Port.)

Dakar
Senegal R.
FRENCH   WEST   AFRICA
GAMBIA
Bamako
PORT.
GUINEA
Conakry
Freetown
SIERRA
LEONE
Monrovia   LIBERIA
Abidjan
GOLD
COAST
Accra
Ouagadougou
Niamey
Niger R.
NIGERIA
Lagos
L. Chad
Ft. Lam

TOGOLAND
(Br. & Fr. Mandates)
FERNANDO
PO
RIO MUNI
CAMEROONS
(Br. & Fr. Mandates)
EQUATORI

Gulf of Guinea
Libreville
SÃO TOMÉ
(Port.)
ANNOBÓN
(Sp.)
FRENCH

0   EQUATOR

ATLANTIC   OCEAN

Brazzaville
CABINDA
Léopo
vil

Luanda

ANGO

20

SOUTH

WEST

AFRIC
(Union of S
Mandat

Cape Town
Cape of Good He

Vaughn Gray

20

XX

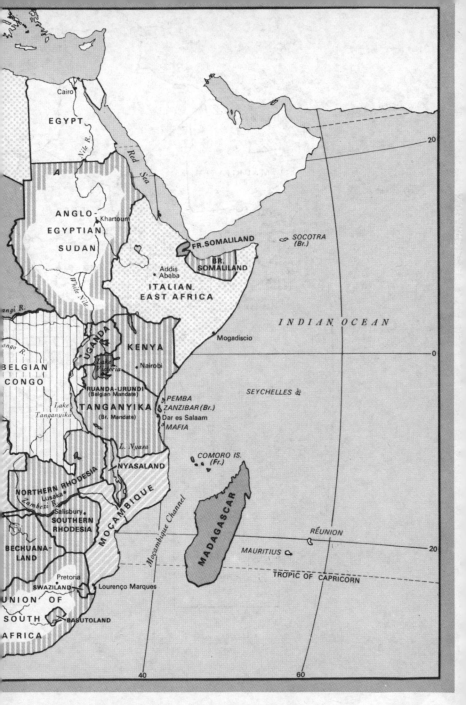

Cairo

EGYPT

Nile R.

Red Sea

ANGLO-
EGYPTIAN
SUDAN

Khartoum

White Nile

SOCOTRA
(Br.)

FR. SOMALILAND

BR.
SOMALILAND

Addis
Ababa

ITALIAN
EAST AFRICA

INDIAN OCEAN

angi R.

ongo R.

BELGIAN
CONGO

UGANDA

KENYA

Lake
Victoria

Nairobi

Mogadiscio

RUANDA-URUNDI
(Belgian Mandate)

Lake
Tanganyika

TANGANYIKA
(Br. Mandate)

PEMBA
ZANZIBAR (Br.)
Dar es Salaam
MAFIA

SEYCHELLES

L. Nyasa

NYASALAND

COMORO IS.
(Fr.)

NORTHERN RHODESIA

Lusaka

Zambezi R.

Salisbury

SOUTHERN
RHODESIA

MOÇAMBIQUE

Moçambique Channel

MADAGASCAR

RÉUNION

BECHUANA-
LAND

MAURITIUS

20

Pretoria

SWAZILAND

Lourenço Marques

TROPIC OF CAPRICORN

UNION OF

SOUTH

AFRICA

BASUTOLAND

40

60

20

0

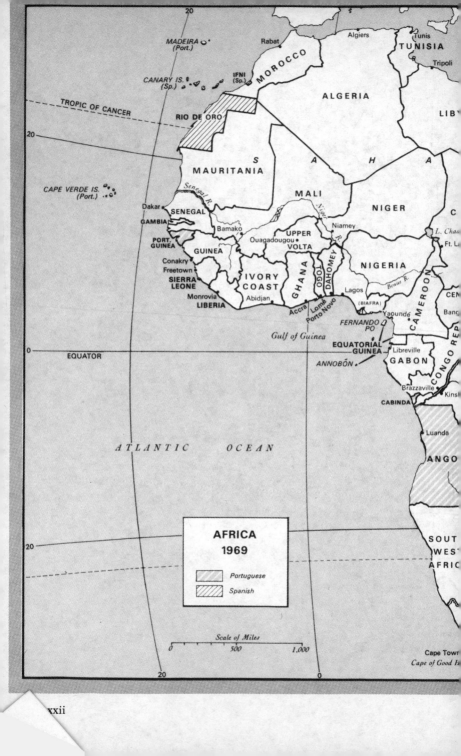

AFRICA
1969

Portuguese

Spanish

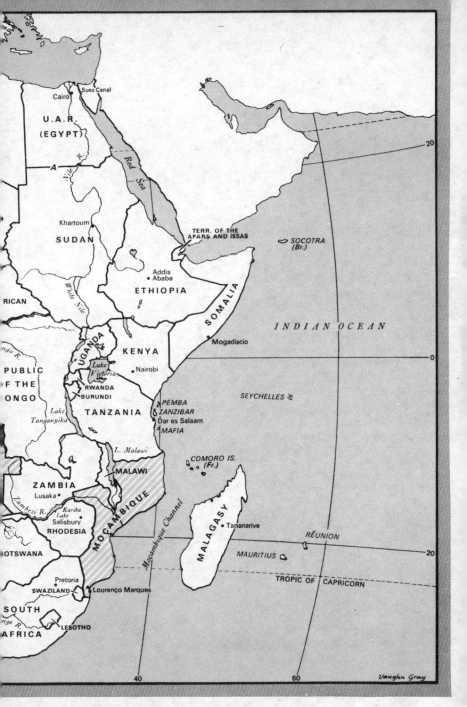

Cairo
Suez Canal

U.A.R.
(EGYPT)

Nile R.

Red Sea

Khartoum

SUDAN

White Nile

Addis
Ababa

ETHIOPIA

TERR. OF THE
AFARS AND ISSAS

SOCOTRA
(Br.)

SOMALIA

INDIAN OCEAN

Mogadiscio

RICAN

UGANDA

KENYA

Nairobi

PUBLIC

Lake Victoria

OF THE

RWANDA

BURUNDI

ONGO

Congo R.

Lake Tanganyika

TANZANIA

SEYCHELLES

PEMBA
ZANZIBAR
Dar es Salaam
MAFIA

L. Malawi

COMORO IS.
(Fr.)

MALAWI

ZAMBIA

Lusaka

Zambezi R.

Kariba
Lake
Salisbury

RHODESIA

MOÇAMBIQUE

Moçambique Channel

MALAGASY

Tananarive

RÉUNION

MAURITIUS

OTSWANA

TROPIC OF CAPRICORN

Pretoria

SWAZILAND

Lourenço Marques

SOUTH

Orange R.

LESOTHO

AFRICA

Vaughn Gray

20

0

20

40

60

REBELLION IN BLACK AFRICA

THE SUDANESE MAHDIYA

L. CARL BROWN

Muhammad Ahmad, the Sudanese Mahdi, and the movement he created in the 1880's are well known in the Western world when compared with most major figures and events of African history. The period of the Mahdiya evokes memories of General Charles Gordon who died in January 1885 defending Khartoum against the Mahdists, of Kipling's fuzzy-wuzzies who "broke a British square," of Kitchener who won renown as commander in chief of the Anglo-Egyptian expedition which had successfully reoccupied the Sudan by 1898, and of an adventurous young man serving in the British army, Winston Churchill, whose *The River War* contains a thrilling account of the reoccupation campaign. The titles of books written by European contemporaries caught up in the Mahdist maelstrom—*Fire and Sword in the Sudan, Ten Years' Captivity in the Mahdi's Camp, or A Prisoner of the Khaleefa*—also suggest the romantic heroism and exoticism connected with the European image of the Mahdist movement. The inexplicable, wild Sudanese of the 1880's and 1890's were only dimly perceived as flesh-and-blood human beings wrestling in an intense and extraordinary fashion with recognizable problems of the kind likely to descend upon any society. Instead, these Sudanese assumed the impersonal role of Fate in a real-life drama wherein the manliness and religious convictions of a handful of Europeans were put to the test. To the extent that Europe was concerned with the other side, the Mahdi and his followers represented a doomed struggle of primitives against civilization, although their piety and amazing personal bravery were usually acknowledged. Only recently has sounder scholarship on the Sudan and

3

Islam—part of a generally more perceptive and sympathetic view of non-Western history—begun to modify the stereotype.

In Sunni Islam the Mahdi (literally "the guided one") is the man whom God selects and guides in order to restore the faith at a time of cataclysmic trouble. The Mahdi, it is said, will "fill the earth with justice even as it has been filled with injustice." It is true that in the orthodox doctrine of the theologians the role of the Mahdi is by no means clearly established. Even Sunni Muslim eschatology, which does provide for a final restorer of the faith before the end of time, does not clearly give this role to someone to be called the Mahdi. A more accepted Sunni Muslim version of the events preceding the Resurrection would have Jesus come to destroy *al-Dajjal* (the antichrist). Theologians aside, however, the masses of Sunni Muslims have for centuries been strongly attached to a belief in a divinely appointed redeemer known as the Mahdi who would set matters right just when the forces of evil in this world appeared to be at their strongest.

To put it in a more general way, belief in a Mahdi can properly be classified as the specifically Sunni Muslim type of a general human phenomenon—the messianic, millenarian expectation; a belief which should hardly be incomprehensible to anyone familiar with the Judaic or Christian tradition. The movement created by the Sudanese Mahdi, and other Mahdist movements in Islam, can usefully be compared with Christian and Jewish messianic cults of varying time and place such as the sixteenth-century millenarians anticipating the advent of Christ and the establishment of the true kingdom of saints, the Shakers, the American Millerites expecting the end of the world in 1848, and the Jewish messianic movement led by Sabetai Svei.

A paradigm of messianic movements in the Semitic tradition (Judaic, Christian, and Muslim) would include the following characteristics:

1. Cataclysmic: The change which is believed to be imminent will be sudden, violent, and total.

2. Charismatic: The movement will be led by a divinely appointed individual with power and authority not to be explained or circumscribed by customary human patterns.

3. Sectarian: The individual adherent will be "called out." He must make his personal commitment to a new message, a commitment which is total and replaces previous obligations. Those not making such a personal commitment (even if they were

co-religionists before the new message) are henceforth outside of the community, and in many
cases to be fought as enemies.

4. Revivalist: There will be a return to the primitive simplicity
of the "old time religion."

5. Puritanical: All frivolity and self-indulgence will be forbidden
(wine, tobacco, music, fine clothes, sexual liber-
tinism) and an unremitting seriousness will be
seen as the *summum bonum*. There are to be "no
more cakes and ale."

6. Revelationist: A simplified scriptural doctrine will be accepted
on faith. Previous theological formulations or at-
tempts to create a new theology relying in large
part on systematic reason are to be resisted.

The messianic, millenarian expectation is no rarity in human history, and it is especially marked in the Semitic religious tradition. The
Sudanese Mahdiya is firmly within that tradition. The Western man
who finds the Mahdi and his Sudanese followers odd betrays only an
ignorance of his own cultural heritage. The common traits found in so
many of mankind's millennial dreams deserve our attention if only to
keep us from stumbling into egregious errors of interpretation. One is
then less likely to assert glibly that this ethnic group, or that religion,
or people at a certain level of economic development are especially
prone to messianic movements.

On the other hand, the different patterns into which these movements fall according to the variables of time, circumstances, and cultural tradition are an essential next step in any serious analysis. The
paradigm of messianic movements in the Semitic tradition, suggested
above, applies perfectly to the Sudanese Mahdiya, and this, in itself,
is important and useful to know. There remains the task of discovering
what was specifically Sudanese, Islamic, and African about the Mahdiya. At the same time the problem of cause, or more precisely priority of causes, must be dealt with. Is the Mahdist impulse to be explained largely as a pattern of traditionally sanctioned responses to a
body of "real" social, economic, and political problems? In that case,
it might be argued, the historian would be advised to use the Mahdiya
as a clear signal that important transitions and convulsions, yet to be
determined, were taking place in Sudanese society. Or was the Mahdist impulse itself the major formative influence? Although obviously
provoked and also shaped by the specific Sudanese environment, did

the Sudanese Mahdiya by its own ideology and inner logic change Sudanese society?

It will be argued in this study that the Mahdiya can best be understood as another in a series of socio-religious movements on the Islamic fringe area of Africa, that the Mahdiya conforms to a recognizable historic type in Islamic Africa, arising in response to a distinctive set of social, political, and economic circumstances, and, finally, that the Mahdiya itself exerted a demonstrable influence on Sudanese society along predictable lines. Before illustrating these points it will be useful to present a brief sketch of Muhammad Ahmad, the Sudanese Mahdi, and of the messianic movement which he created.

Muhammad Ahmad was born in Dongola province in 1844, on a small island in the Nile River some five hundred miles downstream from Khartoum. His father and brothers were boat builders, but Muhammad Ahmad from an early age demonstrated an affinity for religious studies, a not inappropriate calling for one member of a family which claimed sharifian origins, that is, claimed to be descendants of the Prophet Muhammad. When Muhammad Ahmad was still a small child the family moved to a village located about twelve miles north of Khartoum. In terms of Sudanese history, these apparently mundane facts have considerable significance since within the Sudanese context itself there was a world of difference between the riverain peoples and the nomads to be found east and west of the Nile basin, not to mention the pagan tribes located in the Southern Sudan. To be from Dongola meant, therefore, that one's environment included sedentary agriculture, a limited degree of commerce and economic specialization, access to a modest urban culture, and a certain rudimentary educational system. Also, it was the riverain area which Egypt had been able to control and influence most effectively since Muhammad 'Ali had first turned his attention to conquering the Sudan in the 1820's. Beyond the accessible regions of the Nile basin, Egyptian control of the Sudan was slight and, in many cases, only established as late as the reign of Khedive Ismail (1863–79). It might be added that the "pagan" Southern Sudan was definitely not easily accessible even though the map shows the White Nile and its tributaries as intersecting the area. At about the ninth parallel the White Nile almost disintegrates into a great marshy swamp area without fixed watercourses.

As a child and young adolescent Muhammad Ahmad received the customary Sudanese education, which entailed memorizing the Qur'an and the simpler Islamic principles. This stultifying technique of rote learning at the feet of the village shaykh (religious teacher), who was himself the product of a hardly more formal education, was weak enough in such venerable centers of high Islamic culture as Egypt itself (where the traditional educational system was beginning to be attacked by Muslim reformers); one can imagine the intellectual level of such education in an Islamic fringe area such as the Sudan. Nevertheless, by the standards of the day Muhammad Ahmad would, like so many other Sudanese during the years of Egyptian rule, have been sufficiently prepared to attend the great mosque-university of al-Azhar in Cairo as an increasing number of Sudanese had come to do. It seems quite plausible to speculate that had he attended al-Azhar, Muhammad Ahmad would never have declared himself to be the expected Mahdi and that his intense religious commitment would have been expressed in other ways. Instead, when he was seventeen years old Muhammad Ahmad chose the more traditional Sudanese form of religious training by becoming the disciple of one Muhammad Sharif, a shaykh in the mystical Sammaniya religious brotherhood. After seven years Muhammad Ahmad was permitted to become a religious leader of the order in his own right, establishing his own residence and in his turn teaching new disciples—while still, in accordance with accepted Sufi practices, remaining subject to the overall discipline of Muhammad Sharif.

A brief discussion of Sufism or Islamic mysticism and the great Sufi *tariqa's* (religious brotherhoods) will clarify the later importance of Muhammad Ahmad's Sufi training. In theological terms Sufism can be seen as a reaction against the orthodox Sunni concept of a transcendent deity by Muslims seeking a more intensely personal relationship with an immanent God. The great Sufi brotherhoods which had begun to appear in the twelfth century A.D. had institutionalized the gnostic tendencies inherent in earlier Sufi mysticism through a hierarchy of shaykhs to whom blind obedience was due. This mass veneration of the Sufi shaykh—an aspect of saint worship in popular Islamic beliefs, to use the terminology adopted by early European ethnographers—was diametrically opposed to a major tenet of Sunni orthodoxy as expressed by its most uncompromising theologians throughout the ages, such veneration of a mere mortal being considered by them a derogation from God's unity and transcendent authority. Indeed, it was to them the cardinal sin of *shirk* (association of anything with the Deity).

On the other hand, the Sufi idea of finding the way to God through an inspired mortal bore close comparison to the idea of a Mahdi. Sufi doctrine tended to be illuminist, seeking the real and true by other than rational means. In this way, too, it approached Mahdism, which relies on the nonrational authority of revelation as interpreted by a

Mahdi to the exclusion of orthodox Muslim scholasticism. Although to a true Sufi, embracing the essential Sufi doctrine of *fana* (annihilation, that is, the state of losing one's imperfect individuality in the Divine Unity), the Mahdist concern with wordly revolution could only appear as a parody of true mystical religion, it can nevertheless be seen how Sufi training could predispose a religious activist toward Mahdism and how, at the same time, a general veneer of Sufi doctrine could predispose a Muslim population only lightly touched by the learned tradition into readily accepting a Mahdi. Thus, by his knowledge of the esoteric path to God and by his divinely inspired *baraka* (superhuman powers), the Sufi shaykh of a large brotherhood possessed an authority which, if he so chose, could easily be translated into political power.

To return to Muhammad Ahmad, in 1870 he moved to Aba Island in the White Nile south of Khartoum. Here, during the next few years, his fame as a pious mystic grew. He appeared to be well embarked upon a career destined to establish him as an important Sufi figure, at least within the confines of the Sudan. Instead, by 1881 Muhammad Ahmad had declared himself to be the expected Mahdi. What events can be adduced to explain or at least make somewhat more plausible this transition from Sufi leader to Mahdi? Some importance is usually attached to Muhammad Ahmad's break with his own shaykh, Muhammad Sharif, in about 1878. Among the varying accounts of the incident the most likely explanation would seem to be that in the best puritanical tradition, Muhammad Ahmad had protested against the luxurious festivities accompanying the circumcision of one of Muhammad Sharif's sons. Whatever the exact cause of the dispute, it is clearly established that Muhammad Sharif banished Muhammad Ahmad, who was then accepted as disciple by a rival Sammaniya shaykh, al-Qurashi wad al-Zayn. When the latter—already elderly—died in 1880, Muhammad Ahmad emerged as his successor.

Undoubtedly this split with Muhammad Sharif must have had a great impact upon Muhammad Ahmad, because the presence of human failings in his master no doubt forced him to begin again his quest for religious purity and excellence. It seems reasonable to assume that had Muhammad Sharif been more ascetic and pious, Muhammad Ahmad would have satisfied his religious yearning by emulating his master within the existing Sufi tradition. On the other hand, disputes between master and disciple leading to new groupings of adherents around a rebel were hardly unusual among Sufi brotherhoods. There was nothing out of the ordinary about Muhammad Ahmad's being forced to leave his original master and join another, in a short time becoming a Sufi leader in his own right with a small devoted following.

Therefore, more than this dispute with his shaykh is needed to explain the ultimate step of announcing himself to be the expected Mahdi. (This can properly be separated from the question of why there was such an enthusiastic response to the Sudanese Mahdi, which can more adequately be explained in terms of the prevailing socioeconomic situation.) Obviously Muhammad Ahmad was a fervent, intense, totally committed religious figure. Given a different education, a happier experience with his first shaykh or a more halcyon Sudanese environment, he might well have acted out his religious commitment in personal asceticism and pietism. Quite a different set of experiences was, however, to mold his religious fervor in another fashion. Muhammad Ahmad came to feel that he had been called out to lead an errant, confused, and threatened people back to salvation. Thus, in March 1881 he confided to a few of his closest followers that he was the expected Mahdi, and three months later, in June 1881, he announced his mission openly, enjoining his followers to undertake the *hijra* (flight or emigration) to join the Mahdi.

This summons to the *hijra* marks the first step in what might best be called a reenactment of the Prophet Muhammad's role in the creation of the early Muslim community. Thus, the appeal suggested the famous *hijra* of Muhammad and his small body of followers, from an increasingly hostile Mecca to a new base of operations at Medina, and the Mahdi interpreted his forced move from Aba Island to Jebel Qadir (to put some distance between himself and a central government which, having failed in its first attempt to arrest him, would, he presumed, surely move again) as a *hijra*.

The Sudanese Mahdi was to use other terminology borrowed from the golden age of Islam. The Prophet Muhammad had labeled those Meccans who had made the *hijra* to Medina *muhajirun* (emigrants). The Medinese followers of the Prophet were called *Ansar* (helpers). The Sudanese Mahdi used these terms as well—*muhajirun* being in this case those who had made the *hijra* with the Mahdi to Qadir as well as others such as the Baggara tribesmen who had emigrated to join him; but the most common term (which has survived to this day) for describing the followers of the Mahdi was *Ansar*. Then, as events made offensive action possible, these moves were depicted as *jihad* (holy war). Muhammad Ahmad also evoked the lifetime of the Prophet and the period of the first four caliphs—the "rightly guided caliphs," a period which might aptly be called the Muslim patristic age—in asserting that he was by divine election the "successor of the Prophet of God";

his three principal subordinates were designated successors of Abu Bakr, 'Umar, and 'Ali. The fourth lieutenant in the Mahdist movement, who would have rounded out the historical parallel with the title "successor of 'Uthman," was to have been Muhammad al-Mahdi al-Sanusi, but the son of the founder of the Sanusi order rejected the invitation.

The Sudanese Mahdi also claimed to fulfill many of the signs associated with the coming of the Mahdi. He was of the family of the Prophet, his name was the same as that of the Prophet Muhammad, he possessed some of the expected physical signs such as a mole on his right cheek and the space between his two front teeth, and, when obliged to withdraw from Aba Island to Jebel Qadir, he renamed that mountain Masa in order to fulfill the prediction that the Mahdi would come from Jebel Masa. Furthermore, the Mahdist rising was co-ordinated with the beginning of the fourteenth Muslim century (1882), and it was a venerable Muslim tradition that the restorer of the faith would appear at the beginning of a new century.

Muhammad Ahmad's efforts to establish a parallel between his movement and that of the golden age of early Islam, and his careful consideration of the traditional "signs" announcing the Mahdi's appearance serve to clarify several points about the movement. First, unlike several so-called nativistic movements studied by anthropologists, the Sudanese Mahdiya was a revolt within the framework of Islam, not a syncretistic movement which built on but nevertheless broke away from Islam. In addition, identification with primitive Islam also justified the tendency to deny most later theological tradition. When, for example, the Mahdi was asked which of the four schools of law accepted in Sunni Islam he wanted his adherents to follow, he replied that there was no longer any need for schools of law: "We have cast aside acting in accordance with schools of law and the opinion of learned men." In fact, most of the learned heritage was viewed with suspicion as a defiled obstacle between the true believer and the pure religion as set out in the Qur'an and the *sunna* (tradition). Thus, it should be no surprise to learn that many standard books were repudiated and even burned in the period of the Mahdiya.

As in all such total religious challenges to the existing systems, the first mundane steps were of crucial importance. Had Muhammad Ahmad been successfully seized on Aba Island by the authorities he would have been dismissed as a harmless fanatic or even a madman. Muslim chronicles reveal a considerable number of these "false Mahdis" who, apprehended by the authorities almost as soon as they declare themselves, never again appear in the historical records. A few early successes and a certain amount of time are needed to effect the process in which thousands of potential adherents are swept through the stages leading from doubt to detached interest to enthusiasm and finally to unswerving dedication. The Sudanese Mahdi survived these early challenges, and his first defeat—the abortive first siege of El Obeid from September 1882 to January 1883—came late enough for an already well established movement to absorb the blow to his power and prestige without undue difficulty. Needless to say, when, in November 1883, the Mahdi's forces annihilated the Egyptian expeditionary army under its British commander Hicks Pasha, it became clear that a strong, new political force had arisen in the Sudan. By this time both the religious and worldly bases of the Mahdiya had been set. In order to understand how and why such a movement could arise, and succeed, there is therefore little need to trace the period from Gordon's return to the Sudan in January 1884 until his death at the hands of the Mahdi's forces on January 25, 1885. Nor is it necessary to deal with the early death of the Mahdi in June 1885, his replacement by his principal lieutenant Khalifa Abdullahi al Ta'ashi, and the relatively long period of the Khalifa's reign until the Anglo-Egyptian reconquest of 1896–98. Instead, having briefly sketched the rise of the Mahdiya as seen from the career of its creator, Muhammad Ahmad al Mahdi, let us now retrace our steps, shifting emphasis to the Sudanese environment from which the Mahdiya sprang.

A brief reference to early Islamic history is required properly to distinguish the Sudan from the rest of the eastern Arab world. The Arab Muslim conquerors bursting out of the Arabian peninsula in the seventh century managed within less than a decade to conquer all of what now forms the Arabic-speaking world from Iraq to eastern Libya. From that time, in spite of countless political vicissitudes, this large region has served as the heartland of the Arabo-Islamic cultural world. By contrast, the remainder of what is now the Arabic-speaking world experienced a different development. The Maghrib—present-day Algeria, Tunisia, Morocco, and Mauritania—was absorbed into the Arabo-Islamic world at a much slower pace. The process in the Sudan was slower still, being only gradually accomplished in the northern portions of the country by the steady infiltration of Arabic-speaking tribes. Effective Islamization had also been delayed; portions of the country had not begun to be absorbed into the Islamic world until the fourteenth century. Even to the present day most of the Southern Sudan lies beyond Arabism and Islam. Therefore, the Sudan of Muhammad Ahmad's time was an Islamic fringe area, just as much of the Maghrib had been a few centuries earlier and just as portions of Africa farther to the south are today. Nothing more clearly indicates the inchoate nature of Sudanese Islam at that period (and even later) than the indiscriminate manner in which the Sudanese Arabic term *faki* (corruption of the classical *faqih,* scholar or jurist) was used to label all categories of Muslim religious leaders and scholars, mystics, and saints, right down the social scale to "the ignorant hedge-priest and to the dubious dealer in charms and amulets." Sudanese Islam still lacked an elaborate institutionalization and a long-standing, scholarly commitment to the Islamic learned tradition.

Nor was there a centralizing Arabic-speaking dynasty to accelerate the work of Arabization and social integration until the Egyptian conquest of the early nineteenth century. But in the 1820's the Egyptian conquest of the Sudan delivered the *coup de grâce* to the important Muslim Funj dynasty. In one sense the Egyptian occupation was—to use the emotion-laden modern terminology—a form of imperialism. The conquest was brutal, its later administration was often harsh, and for most of the period its major aim was to use the Sudan in a fashion which would help the mother country, Egypt. Nevertheless, Egyptian rule also brought the Sudan within the context of a larger and more "advanced" Islamic world. The Sudan became part of a stronger, more institutionalized political unit—Egypt, itself still formally part of the Ottoman Empire. The Islamic cultural tradition—even if it had fallen upon hard days by comparison with its more illustrious past—became more readily available with the appearance of Sudanese religious judges, teachers, and administrators trained in Egypt. Thereafter, a handful of Sudanese began to receive their higher education at al-Azhar in Cairo. The Egyptian period also witnessed the creation of the new capital city of Khartoum at the junction of the Blue and White Niles, the inauguration of a steamer service, the introduction of the telegraph, and somewhat hesitant moves toward a more expansive trade policy. Although contemporary European observers were almost unanimously critical of Egyptian rule in the Sudan, it is nevertheless true that, seen in the broad sweep of Sudanese history, the Egyptian period brought the most effective "bureaucratic empire" the Sudan had known for centuries.

The revolutionary changes brought by Egyptian rule had an unequal impact on the several strata of Sudanese society. Many of the riverain tribes (including many people from Dongola, the Mahdi's home region) who had traditionally controlled commerce now found opportunities for expansion radically increased, and by the time of the Mahdiya a large number of these people were domiciled in the western Sudan (Kordofan and Darfur), with even more in the south. The latter were active in the slave trade, which was greatly extended by Egyptian penetration southward, and they felt economically threatened when attempts at suppression of the slave trade began in the 1860's. These riverain "frontiersmen" proved to be among the earliest and staunchest supporters of the Mahdi.

The new political and economic activities connected with Egyptian rule also produced an increased urbanism. In addition to Khartoum, there was the completely new town of Kassala, the provincial capital of al-Taka (now Kassala) province in the eastern Sudan. Other towns such as El Obeid, Suakin, Berber, and Dongola experienced appreciable increases in size and importance. On the other hand, as invariably happens in periods of radical change, certain towns increased at a slower pace or even declined. For example, Shendi on the main Nile north of Khartoum never recovered from the destruction caused by the Egyptians in 1822–23.

What was the population of these Sudanese towns during the Egyptian period? To the modern world they now appear to have been derisively small, but the relative increase from what had existed before is impressive. Even if small, these towns now constituted a network of urban control over the much larger rural areas, both sedentary and nomadic—a control which readily made itself felt not only in administration and taxation, but also in commerce and education. A new class, largely foreign but with a sprinkling of Sudanese, was in charge.

The centralizing impulse of Egyptian rule also tended to distort the existing tribal and religious balances. For example, many of the Ja'aliyin, whose chief, Nimr, had assassinated Muhammad 'Ali's son, Ismail Pasha, in 1822, felt compelled to emigrate westward. Their riverain neighbors, the Shaiqiya, grew in political strength by serving as police and irregular soldiers for the Egyptian administration. The religious brotherhood of the Khatmiya under the Mirghani family cooperated with the Egyptians and achieved a marked growth in prestige and membership throughout the period. This rise in the fortunes of one brotherhood was not without its impact on others. The Majdhubiya, strong in the eastern Sudan, was among the brotherhoods most threatened by the rising fortunes of the Khatmiya. It is not surprising that its leader was soon found supporting the Mahdiya. Indeed, the greatest of the Mahdi's generals in the eastern Sudan, 'Uthman Diqna (Osman Digna), had been a member of the Majdhubiya order.

In addition to this inter-brotherhood rivalry which had been intensified by Egyptian rule, there was the incipient threat to the influence and position of all the brotherhoods with the arrival of al-Azhartrained shaykhs to serve as judges, legal advisers, and teachers in the new administration. It has already been noted that from the advent of Egyptian rule small but increasing numbers of Sudanese began to find their way to al-Azhar for religious training. The slow intrusion of a more orthodox Islam based upon the learned tradition, as jealously guarded by the *ulama* (priestly) class, did not necessarily mean the end of Sufism and mass religious brotherhoods. There is no doubt that during this period most of the *ulama* in Egypt itself were members of religious brotherhoods. After all, the reformism of Shaykh Muhammad Abduh and the Salafiya movement with its harsh strictures against the brotherhoods was, itself, just beginning at the time of the Mahdiya. Even so, there can be little doubt that the imposition of an *ulama* class offered a clear threat to the social and political power then enjoyed by the leadership of the several brotherhoods in the Sudan.

A final point of considerable importance about the impact of Egyptian rule on the Sudan in its relationship to the rise of the Mahdiya is that in the ten to fifteen years before 1881 Egyptian power was declining. A brief reference to events in Egypt proper should make this clear. The advent of a dynamic but rash Westernizer, Ismail, marked an activist policy of economic buildup at home and attempts at expansion abroad (penetration into the Southern Sudan and the abortive campaign against Ethiopia), but this policy was financed by a vicious cycle of foreign loans with increasingly onerous terms. As a result Egypt was soon plunged into bankruptcy, European financial control (from 1876), and, finally, outright European control in the form of British occupation beginning in 1882. Ismail's laudable attempts to curb the slave trade had also induced him to appoint an increasing number of Europeans, and even a few Americans, as officials in the Sudan.

The net result of all these policies for the Sudan was a growing imbalance between ambitious policies and the ability to perform. By 1882 the Egyptian hold over the country had been greatly weakened. Morale was undermined, pay often in arrears, efforts against the slave trade had been sufficient to disrupt and divert but not to destroy. In such a political climate the nomadic and semi-nomadic populations remotest from central control, and chafing under restraints imposed by Egyptian rule, began to sniff the telltale signs of *ma fish hukuma* (there is no government); the sedentary population began to wonder uneasily if the government would be able to mantain at least minimal public security—the implicit quid pro quo making even extortionate taxation bearable; certain groups began to hedge on their embarrassingly strong commitments to the regime; and other groups, bearing old grudges, waited for the time to strike.

The analysis above suggests that no monocausal theory will adequately reflect the complex totality out of which the Mahdiya arose.

Embittered and resentful slave traders, tribal and brotherhood rivalries, a confused combination of new emerging classes and of old declining groups—all these played an important role in a movement which, itself, was strongly marked and shaped by the venerable Sunni Muslim tradition of Mahdism. No neat, simple theory will suffice, but on the other hand there are several historical patterns with which the Sudanese Mahdiya can claim affiliation. It is important to select the most satisfactory. This chapter began by placing the Mahdiya squarely within the Semitic messianic tradition, but it was suggested that such a category was too broad to offer an adequate explanation. The Mahdiya might also be viewed as one of several traditionalist Islamic reactions to the impact of the Western world in modern times, for much that Egypt attempted to implement in the Sudan could be interpreted as surrogate Westernization. This view, quite useful up to a point, has certain disadvantages. It tends to exaggerate the importance of the Western impact as the dynamic factor and to discount the possibility of explaining the movement by reference to past Islamic history. A similar reservation should be entered regarding any attempt to depict the Mahdiya as an example of a traditional religious response by *any* premodern society (that is, characterized by near-subsistence economy, diffused political power, ascriptive social organization, and a single ethico-religious belief system—inflexible and theocentric—embracing all aspects of human behavior) to a body of challenges represented by the West. Such an approach would concentrate attention on its comparability with several other African movements being studied in this book, but, like the general Semitic messianic tradition, it is too broad a category. It would also squeeze out of proper perspective the extent to which Islam was an essential element in shaping the course of the Mahdiya.

What then of the possibility suggested in this chapter—the Sudanese Mahdiya as a socio-religious movement typical of the Islamic fringe areas in Africa? Such a theory could give the Islamic tradition its full importance. Further, by insisting on the importance of an historical *pattern* (which is to say, a variant on previous experience) there would be less chance of exaggerating the role of intrusive new factors. Without in any way overlooking new elements in the specific period of Sudanese history under consideration, one could avoid the anachronistic and illogical trap of pre-emptorily seeing the Mahdiya solely as another example of a general phenomenon, that is, the last-ditch fight of the pre-modern opposed to the modern world, or any similar moderno-centric fallacy.

The historical pattern which perhaps best embraces and clarifies the Sudanese Mahdiya possesses the following major characteristics:

It occurs on an Islamic fringe area which can be identified in two complementary senses. The Islamic fringe is, on the one hand, a physical border—the outer limits of *dar al Islam* beyond which lies the non-Muslim *dar al harb*. At the same time the fringe area is less fully integrated into the high Islamic tradition. The juxtaposition of Islamic and non-Islamic beliefs and values still prevails. The transitional nature of Islamization is usually to be explained by a variety of factors, including time (Islam introduced relatively recently into the area), intensity (the mode of introduction being often via a slow penetration of merchants and isolated groups or, at most, a military conquest leaving in its wake only a superficial political control system), and a low proportion of urban, or in some cases even of sedentary, population. This latter point calls attention to an important fact: Without a network of cities the fundamental educational and economic infrastructure creating and sustaining an *ulama* class is lacking. The Islamic fringe area is also, from the perspective of the urbanized Islamic high culture, an uncouth hinterland, a frontier.

The frontier motif suggests the next major characteristic of the Islamic fringe messianic movements: They usually partake of conflict, pitting the hinterland against the cosmopolitan centers. This is not to suggest a pattern of religiously led jacqueries. Nor would a Marxian framework positing non-urban groupings resisting more effective integration into larger economic units controlled from the cities offer an adequate description, although it would be quite useful up to a point. The underlying socio-economic tension in the Islamic fringe area is better depicted in political terms. These areas possess pockets of sedentaries, transhumants, nomads, and, often, mountaineers. Tribal organization is still intact. A considerable diffusion of political power is the norm, and at best the governments of the cites have made only tentative moves toward political centralization. In this situation of inchoate state structure and uncertain political stability the Marxian quest to isolate the progressive forces appears especially irrelevant. More important is the manner in which challenge to the existing power of the cities is mounted from the rude hinterland base. The townfolk and the sedentary agriculturalists closely tied to the towns, fearing anarchy most of all, adopt a wait-and-see policy. Then they come over en masse when the new challenger appears as the best candidate to restore order. Yet, the ultimate goal of the movement which appears to be directed against the towns, relying as it does upon forces of the hinterland seizing the opportunity to reassert their complete autonomy, is to create an even more effective centralization directed from the city. In all cases, the leaders of the movements are themselves products of the sedentary regions closest in touch with the Islamic high cultúral tradition.

The historical pattern also reveals revolts conducted in the name of Islam. They may be heretical or schismatic, but these movements always ensure that the socio-political and ideological conflict be within an Islamic framework. As a result, the particularistic tendencies which are undoubtedly represented in these movements—indeed in pure material terms these tendencies dominate—are kept under control, and syncretist new religions do not result. Instead, the ultimate result is to facilitate the process of integration into Sunni Islam of the high cultural tradition, because the heretical or schismatic nature of these movements is evanescent and the Islamic context in which they are presented results in a net increase in Islamization.

The classic examples of messianic movements on the Islamic fringe of Africa are the rise of the Fatimids and the Almohades in North Africa. In general Islamic history the Fatimid dynasty is connected with Egypt, the founding of Cairo, and the great challenge which an aggressive Shi'ism posed for Sunni Islam. Quite a different picture emerges, however, when attention is directed to that area in North Africa where the Fatimids got their start as a political power, for the missionaries from the Middle East preaching the revolutionary Fatimid ideology (itself a product of the social and theological struggles growing out of the urban-based Islamic high culture) in North Africa did not gather converts in the cities or sedentary area of Ifriqiya (roughly modern Tunisia). Instead the Fatimid missionaries relied on the Kutama Berbers from the Lesser Kabylia, that rugged mountainous region lying within the triangle bounded by Djidjelli, Setif, and Constantine in Algeria. The Lesser Kabylia was only partially Islamized in the latter years of the ninth century when Abu Abdullah al Shi'i began his propaganda work there in the name of the Mahdi who was to come. Equally important, the Lesser Kabylia had never been brought under the political control of the city-based Muslim dynasties. The Aghlabids ruling from Kairouan had never attempted more than a policy of keeping this area under surveillance. In regional terms, the Fatimid revolt was a successful political challenge by the Islamic fringe area against the existing government of the cities. Yet the ideology for which they fought was universal and centralizing in its aims, and nothing was more normal than for the victorious Fatimids to move into the cities and work for a more effective political unification.

The Fatimids remained "Eastern" in leadership and outlook, and after a successful military campaign, the dynasty moved its political

base to Egypt—establishing the new capital of Cairo in A.D. 969. Ifriqiya soon reverted to a staunch Sunni Islam and, in a sense, it might
appear that the Fatimid period in North Africa left no lasting imprint.
However, there can be little doubt that the imposing socio-political
upheaval occasioned by the Fatimid period in North Africa had advanced the frontiers of effective Islamization. The Kutama and the
other quondam supporters of the Fatimids did not remain Shi'i sec-
tarians, but they did emerge from the experience more effectively integrated into Muslim culture.

The Fatimids had been a Mahdist movement. The first ruler,
Ubaydallah, had assumed the title Mahdi and, as the name (from
Fatima, the daughter of the Prophet) implies, the dynasty claimed
descent from Muhammad. Emphasis was placed upon the Mahdi's
possession of esoteric knowledge and power, and blind obedience was
enjoined. In other respects, however, the Fatimid movement represents an intermediate stage between Mahdism as a political ideology
and Mahdism as a puritanical, apocalyptical, and millenarian movement. The full flowering of Mahdism as later seen in the Sudanese
Mahdi is connected with the Almohades. Here again the historical pattern suggested above is clearly in evidence.

The man later to become the Mahdi of the Almohades, Ibn Tumart, was born some time between 1077 and 1087 in a small mountain
town of the Anti-Atlas in southwestern Morocco. The many similarities
between his life and activities and those of the Sudanese Mahdi a full
eight centuries later are striking. Ibn Tumart was born into a family
known for its piety. He himself was from an early age fully absorbed
in religious studies. After a period of travels to further his religious
education in Muslim Spain and the Middle East he returned to North
Africa, and, as he made his way westward toward Morocco, he soon
gained a reputation as a stern, censorious puritan. The Muslim chronicles are filled with references to his breaking musical instruments and
wine jars and publicly rebuking highly placed officials for alleged religious laxity—often at the risk of his imprisonment or banishment. Near
Bougie the famous meeting took place between Ibn Tumart and the
man who was to become *caliph* (successor), Abd al-Mu'min. This famous warrior/administrator was to do for the Almohade movement
what Abdullahi al Ta'aishi did for the Mahdiya. Abd al-Mu'min, at
the time of his encounter with Ibn Tumart, was bound for the East
seeking religious training; but when Ibn Tumart saw him he immediately recognized him as his chosen successor, and exclaimed, "The
knowledge which you are seeking in the East is here. You have found
it in the Maghrib."

Later, still with only a handful of faithful disciples, Ibn Tumart arrived in Marrakech, the capital of the reigning Almoravid dynasty, where he sought to gain acceptance of his rigid puritanical ideas. Soon he realized that his stern preachings had placed him in some peril in Marrakech, and he retreated to his mountainous home in the Anti-Atlas. There the religious reformer took the ultimate step and declared himself to be the Mahdi. Again the pattern of conscious imitation of the Prophet's life is evident. His retreat into the mountains was deemed a *hijra* and those accompanying him were *muhajirun*. The term *Ansar* was also employed, and his later struggle to overthrow the Almoravid dynasty was depicted as a *jihad*.

At the same time it should be noted that the mundane base of the Almohades was tribal—the Masmuda Berbers, a hinterland mountain folk, were challenging the dynasty and the cities of the plains. Once victorious, however, these mountaineers moved to the cities and eventually established North Africa's most extensive empire.

Again, as with the Fatimids, superficial evidence might seem to suggest that nothing survived the Almohade experience. North Africa rejected the theological doctrines of Ibn Tumart, even in the mountain capital. "Ibn Tumart's grave still exists in Timmel, but his name and history is utterly forgotten." In fact, the Almohade dynasty not only left behind a legacy of a political structure destined to survive in part until early modern times (and, it might be argued, even longer in Morocco proper), it also advanced the effective Islamization of North Africa's remotest regions.

The Fatimids, the Almohades, and the Sudanese Mahdiya constitute the three major examples of a Mahdist movement in the suggested historical pattern. However, in socio-political terms the emergence of a self-declared Mahdi represents merely the ultimate step taken by certain puritanical protest movements. As Goldziher noted concerning Ibn Tumart, "the *mahdi* represents the summum of action to be taken to correct what is wrong in this world . . . It is the supreme application of the Muslim community's mission to 'command the good and prohibit the bad.'"

A number of intense, puritanical Muslim reformers stopped short of this ultimate step of declaring themselves to be the Mahdi, but in most other ways the movements that these reformers created also conformed to a historical pattern characteristic of the Islamic fringe area in Africa. In this sense attention should be called to the Kharijite activities in eighth-century North Africa, the nomadic-based Almoravid dynasty which sprang up in the eleventh century in the western Saharan region dividing North Africa from West Africa, the *chorfa* movements of sixteenth-century Morocco (properly *shurafa*—those claiming to be descendents of the Prophet Muhammad), and the reformist agitation of 'Uthman dan Fodio and later al hajj Umar in West Africa during the period extending from the late eighteenth century until the late nineteenth century. All of these, in spite of considerable differences in doctrine, are similar to each other and at the same time closely related to the three Mahdist movements cited. They were all rigidly puritanical, reformist movements relying on an essentially tribal base for major support and involving a challenge by the hinterland regions to the governments of the cities. All emphasized *jihad* even, in most cases, against nominal Muslims. Yet at the same time, in spite of the particularist nature of their mass support, all these movements extended acculturation into the high cultural tradition of Sunni Islam, just as in most cases they encouraged political centralization.

These are the more important examples which could be cited to justify the idea that there is a historical pattern of puritanical Muslim protest on the Islamic fringe areas of Africa. From what has been said earlier it should already be clear how completely the Sudanese Mahdiya fits into such a pattern. First, there can be little doubt that the Sudan in the period of the Mahdiya fits the dual definition of an Islamic fringe area. By comparison with Egypt and the Middle Eastern heartland of Muslim culture, the Sudan was still very much in the process of being effectively integrated into the high cultural tradition. And there can be no doubt that the geographical border dividing Muslims from non-Muslims runs through the Sudan. The importance of the pastoral Baggara tribe as the military backbone of the Mahdist movement can hardly be overlooked, and there is considerable evidence that the Mahdiya was in many ways a revolt of the hinterland against the political control of the cities and their satellite, settled areas. For example, the first major defeat of the Mahdi's forces was their failure to capture the fortified city of El Obeid. A contemporary European scholar summed up the Mahdi's military posture: "His strategy is elementary, but it is that which the country requires: no assaults on fortified towns, which are merely to be surrounded until famine opens their gates; no great battles, but a constant harassing of the enemy, surrounding him from a distance, then when he is exhausted, swooping down on him with all forces united to make an end of the affair." The tribal and hinterland base of the Mahdi's support clarifies the tactics which led to the crushing defeat of Hicks Pasha and his army, the long siege of Khartoum, and the inability of 'Uthman Diqna, one of the Mahdiya's best generals, to capture Suakin on the Red Sea. A description of the siege of Khartoum, based on the account of four Christian prisoners of the Mahdi, appeared in the London *Standard* of March 4, 1885. The article contained the following revealing passage:

The number of fighting men congregated before Khartoum seems to have been very fluctuating, sinking sometimes to seven or eight thousand, and again rising to forty and fifty thousand, according to the seasons and the requirements of agricultural pursuits, as no impediment was ever placed in the way of their going off, sometimes for weeks together—the fellaheen to look after their crops and harvests, the bedouins to graze their camels, and their flocks and herds. When in camp their time was wholly devoted to prayers, recitations from the Koran, and sham fights, often on a large scale. The actual number of properly drilled and disciplined troops, chiefly blacks from El-Obeid, was relatively small, nor did they seem to be implicitly trusted by the *Mahdi*. On the other hand, the enthusiasm of the Dervishes, as the *Mahdi's* true followers are styled, appeared to be wrought up to the highest pitch by the Prophet's fervent preachings, and to be in no way abated by the repeated checks they experienced before Omdurman.

Yet, as the later history of the Khalifa's rule makes quite clear, the ultimate victors were not the forces of tribalism and particularism. The Mahdist state of Khalifa Abdullahi represented an effort at more effective centralization. Even in the time of the Mahdi himself, something approaching a regular army and bureaucracy began to emerge.

Evidence of the long-term more effective Islamization set in motion by the Sudanese Mahdiya is to be found today in the Sudan. Certainly, if the period of the Anglo-Egyptian Condominium involved in one sense a reaction against the Mahdiya, it was in no way a reaction against Islam. Instead, just as has been the case with modern Western colonialism in other Muslim countries, great strides were made in integrating the Sudan into the Sunni high cultural tradition. The forces of the Mahdiya also survived, and the posthumous son of Muhammad Ahmad al Mahdi, Sayyid Abd al Rahman, became the leader of a major nationalist grouping—the Umma party. In 1966–1967 a great-grandson of the Sudanese Mahdi was Prime Minister of the independent Sudan. There is little doubt that the political power of the Mahdi's descendants is based in large measure upon the continued veneration felt for this family by the descendants of the original *Ansar*. Yet, there already is considerable evidence to suggest that the religious followers of the Mahdi's descendants are merging imperceptibly into the greater Sunni community. Already, the *Ansar* are for all practical purposes equivalent to a religious brotherhood living in harmony with other brotherhoods, all within the framework of Sunni Islam. In the long run the *Ansar*, like the Khatmiya and other brotherhoods, may well fade away or split into other groupings, but it is already clear that one result of their appearance will be a more effective Islamization.

It has been suggested in this chapter that the Sudanese Mahdiya can best be understood by reference to the historical pattern of puritanical Muslim protest movements on the Islamic fringe areas of Africa. A few reasons why it is preferable to place the Sudanese Mahdiya in *this* historical pattern as opposed to others which might claim serious consideration have also been mentioned. However, it can properly be asked if the entire approach—that of seeking the most appropriate historical pattern—has any special value to recommend it over other possible methods of analysis and interpretation.

First, it must be admitted that a correct classification of phenomena into a historical pattern, in and of itself, merely offers somewhat greater order to a welter of data. The question remains whether the historical pattern can do more. Does it offer useful insights helping to explain some of the major problems facing historians of the Sudan as well as other parts of Africa? Quite possibly it does. For example, the historical pattern indicates that these protest movements, in spite of their particularist base, move along certain channels and provoke a body of reactions, all of which in the long run serve to advance Islamization in the area concerned. The same pattern does not seem to prevail with non-Islamic protest movements of a religious nature in Africa. A careful study of these movements can help to clarify the question of how Islam has spread—and is spreading—in Africa. Of course, one would want to push even farther in seeking the elusive "why." One would want to know why a certain pattern of social activities in an Islamic framework would have coalescent tendencies whereas approximately the same social activities in another cultural tradition might prove disruptive. There will be no easy answer to this question but it does at least underline the importance of Islam in African history.

According to the historical pattern a Mahdist movement (or a movement similar in every other way except that the leader stops short of declaring himself to be the Mahdi) occurs only given certain social situations. This would include a genuine difference in way of life between the hinterland and the urban areas, an incomplete political control over the entire country by the central government, a low level of economic integration, and several other factors usually associated with traditional or premodern societies. This suggests that the historical pattern of Mahdism as described in this chapter is to be found only in traditional or transitional Muslim societies in Africa. To the extent that Muslim societies in Africa achieve a certain level of politi-

cal, social, and economic integration—that is, the process of "development" or "modernization"—movements such as the Sudanese Mahdiya
will become increasingly unlikely.

More important for the future, however, it is clear that the Sudan
—and other parts of Muslim Africa—will not move from one hermeti-
cally sealed epoch called "transitional" to another called "modern." Nor
will these societies by becoming "modern" move into an earthly paradise where there is no need for patterns of social protest. Instead, new
patterns of protest will evolve in response to new situations, and, if the
work of previous historians and sociologists has any value, it can be
predicted that there will be a certain lag between the changing situation and the institutionalized pattern of responses. The venerable historical pattern of puritanical Muslim protest movements on the Islamic
fringe areas of Africa will still be an essential point of departure for
the scholar attempting to assess the nature and direction of new traditions of protest in the several parts of Muslim Africa.

THE ZULU* DISTURBANCES IN NATAL

SHULA MARKS

Introduction

On 8 February 1906 the Colonial Office in London received a startling telegram from the Governor of Natal, stating that two white police officers had been shot in an attempt to arrest a group of armed Africans at Trewirgie, a farm near the village of Byrnetown, to the south of Pietermaritzburg. The colonists of Natal were as dismayed, if rather less surprised. The imposition of a poll tax in September 1905 on all adult males in the multiracial colony was widely opposed by the African majority. The long hot summer months of 1905-6 were full of disquieting rumors. Besides, the Africans had begun killing their white pigs, white goats, and white chickens, which many settlers feared to be a signal that white people would be next. Since the slaughter was said to result from an order by Dinuzulu, the son and heir of Cetshwayo, the last Zulu king, it appeared particularly sinister. Indeed, James Stuart, whose semi-official *History of the Zulu Rebellion* is still the essential starting point for any discussion of the disturbances, felt sure that the order had emanated from Dinuzulu and that "its underlying intention . . . was that the natives of Natal and Zululand should rise against the white man. Its purpose was to warn as well as to unite by use of a threat."

The course of the "Zulu disturbances" in Natal may be divided into

* The term "Zulu" today has a linguistic rather than a strictly ethnic connotation, though it is used in a loose sense to refer to all the chiefdoms and clans of Natal and Zululand. As a result of the conquest of Natal and Zululand by Shaka, the chief of the Zulu people at the beginning of the nineteenth century, the name became widely applied at least to those people actually incorporated into the Zulu kingdom. It fact the use of the term is fraught with difficulties. Many of the Africans

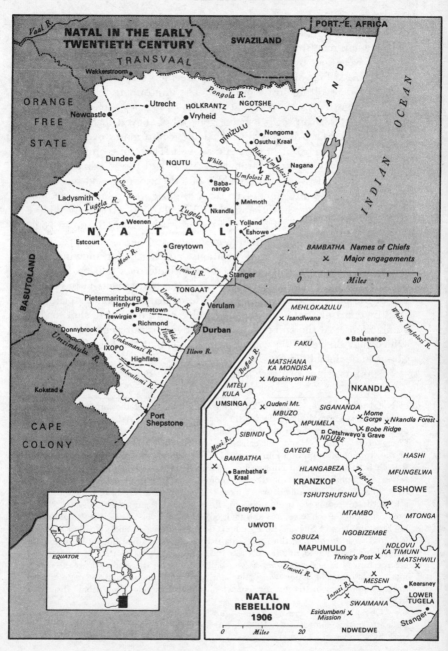

three stages, which will be briefly summarized here as an introduction to their more detailed description and analysis below. The first phase began when magistrates trying to collect the poll tax at the beginning of 1906 were met by angry Africans waving sticks and shouting war-cries. The killing of the two white policemen seemed the signal for widespread revolt against white rule. The atmosphere was further inflamed when it was learned that the armed men were members of an independent African sect, it being generally believed that the African separatist churches had as their goal the white man's overthrow not only in the church but in the state as well. Therefore, on 9 February martial law was declared throughout Natal and the military alerted.

For almost two months after this initial episode, armed forces under the command of Colonel Duncan McKenzie in the south and Colonel George Leuchars in the north marched through African locations, burning crops and kraals and confiscating cattle. As the result of summary trials, chiefs were fined and, in some cases, deposed and removed from their tribes for alleged "seditious intentions," for allowing their people to possess assegais, or for failing to hand over persons branded as rebels by spies. On 15 February two of the participants in the shooting of the policemen were themselves summarily shot; on 2 April after trial by court-martial at Richmond, twelve more men were shot for the same offense. At the end of March the Governor informed the Colonial Office that the rebellion was at an end and that the field forces were about to be demobilized.

The first signs of overt African resistance came on 3 April, when

_____

of Natal were refugees from the Zulu kings and for most of the nineteenth century would almost certainly have denied the appellation "Zulu." As late as the first decade of this century, the true "Zulu" contemptuously called the Africans of Natal "Amakafula" (Kaffirs) and still call them "Amalala" (apparently the name of one of the streams of migration into Natal). By the beginning of this century, however, it is clear that certain non-Zulu groups even in Natal were beginning to class themselves as "Zulu"—perhaps partly in response to a European tendency to classify them in this way. For some it was a more self-conscious assertion of nationalism, an attempt to overcome the tribal divisions which beset African society in Natal. Under pressure from the white settlers and their government, even Africans in Natal looked back to the days of Shaka with nostalgia. Both traditionalist and Christian Africans in Natal were turning to the representative of the Zulu royal house, Dinuzulu, to save them from white rule, as witness the many stories associated with his name casting him in a messianic role. As we shall see, during the disturbances the rebels made wide use of his name, war badge, and war cry, in an attempt to create a more unified opposition to the government which could transcend the "tribal" disunities in the colony.

The alternative term to Zulu—Nguni, or Natal Nguni—would be somewhat pedantic in the context of the 1906 disturbances and perhaps create as many problems as it solves.

Bambatha, a minor chief who had been deposed by the government, captured the regent who had been appointed by the government in his stead. On the following day, Bambatha fired on the magistrate who had been sent to investigate the situation and on 5 April he engaged in a skirmish with a police rescue force, killing three of its members. Then, accompanied by a section of his Zondi people, as well as by one Cakijana who was widely believed to be an emissary from Dinuzulu, he made his way into the fortress-like Nkandla mountains, where he set about raising an army.

Troops under the general command of Colonel McKenzie were immediately dispatched to the Nkandla area to ferret out the rebels. Through a series of converging movements on the rebel hideouts, McKenzie brought this second phase of the disturbances to an end on 10 June with the Battle of Mome Gorge. Bambatha and most of the important African leaders were killed, and a large number of the rank and file were also killed or captured. Once again the Governor believed that the disturbances were at an end.

Within a few days, however, reports were received that Africans in the Lower Tugela and Mapumulo divisions were disaffected, and troops were dispatched to that area. After several skirmishes and what were somewhat ambiguously termed "sweeping movements," this phase of the disturbances was also brought to an end. The long process of rounding up the rebels and trying them by courts-martial began. Martial law came to an end on 17 September 1906, well over a month after the last armed encounters. In all, more than three thousand Africans had lost their lives in these uprisings and some thirty whites were killed. Not a single white woman or child was harmed.

Despite the end of martial law and the appointment in 1906 of the Natal Native Affairs Commission to inquire into African grievances, the government continued to track down participants in the disturbances. Many had fled to Zululand; some found refuge at Dinuzulu's headquarters. The denial of a general amnesty contributed to the bitterness and poverty caused by the upheaval of 1906. In 1907 two chiefs who had fought on the government side were assassinated and other "loyalists" feared for their lives. Most whites, especially those with vested interests in Zululand—which had only just been opened up to white settlement—joined the "loyal" Africans in believing that Dinuzulu was behind the continued unrest in Zululand proper and that he was planning further rebellion. Finally, at the beginning of December 1907, martial law was again declared and Dinuzulu was arrested.

In November 1908, after a long, drawn-out preliminary examination, Dinuzulu was brought to trial before a specially constituted court, on twenty-three separate charges of high treason. The government of

Natal went to great lengths to prove that he had been the chief instigator of the disturbances of 1906, largely on the basis of evidence gathered while martial law had been in force in Zululand. It had been prolonged specifically for this purpose. He was found guilty on two and one half counts: hiding Bambatha's family during the rebellion, sheltering rebels during and after the disturbances, and possessing unregistered firearms. He was sentenced to a fine and four years' imprisonment. However, one of the first acts of the Union government in 1910 was to release him, at which time he was permanently exiled from Natal-Zululand.

The Poll Tax as a Cause of Rebellion

This then, in barest outline, was the Natal rebellion of 1906, "the last tribal revolt on South African soil" and the most severe crisis faced by self-governing Natal during its short history. Not surprisingly, these events were variously interpreted by contemporaries. The Governor of Natal, for example, had little doubt that the Christian Africans had been responsible, and that the rebellion had had as its mainspring the cry, "Africa for the Africans." This view was shared by John Buchan, who, some four years later, based his novel *Prester John* on the Natal disturbances, though curiously enough his tale bears a closer resemblance to the later Chilembwe uprising in Nyasaland. Stuart agreed that the part played by Christian Africans had been prominent, but felt that the outbreak was rather more the "inevitable" result of the "attempt made to impose the European character and civilisation on the native races" —a view well in accord with the social Darwinism of his day.

As for the military men in Natal, they had long prophesied a Zulu uprising. They saw the disturbances as "a golden opportunity" to inflict the most severe punishment on Africans who, they felt, had been "insolent" and "out of hand" since the end of the South African War (1899 to 1902). The Natal government and army were both convinced that the first outbreak of violence had to be dealt with as swiftly as possible, and that they were saving the whole of South Africa from "the nameless barbarities which the savage mind alone can conceive."

Other observers were less sure. From the Orange Free State, ex-President Martinus Theunis Steyn talked of Natal's "hysterical" handling of events, while other South African statesmen, none of whom could be accused of being overly sympathetic to the black man, all expressed concern lest the methods used by Natal to suppress the rebellion would only spur it on. Harriette Colenso, daughter of the famous Bishop John William Colenso of Natal, and an ardent protagonist of the Zulu people, went even further in suggesting that the Africans had been virtually goaded into revolt. A more moderate viewpoint was expressed by Archdeacon Charles Johnson, an Anglican missionary in Zululand, who declared that while the rebellion was the result of

> a combination of causes, among which were the attitude of the white man towards the black and the gradually growing antipathy of the black man towards the white . . . he thought that the last straw was the way in which the Government commenced to deal with the first indications of disaffection. He considered that the measures which were adopted were nothing more than an invitation to people who were irritated to go on to worse.

The African case was put rather more simply, albeit dramatically, by one Dhlozi, who was not himself a rebel, when he stated to the Natal Native Affairs Commission that

> The reason for the rebellion was that the Natives felt themselves overburdened and considered that they might as well fight and be killed straight away. . . . If any nation as strong as the British should appear, the natives would fly to it owing to the heavy troubles that afflict them.

A compatriot, Socwetshata, added: "Happy are those who fought and are dead."   No greater protest could be made.

The very diversity of interpretation suggests some of the many strands involved in the disturbances. Each view finds its echo in the events of 1906. With the passage of time, however, these views must be put into perspective: New questions are being asked about colonial rebellions. If the older interpretation of rebellions as the "inevitable" result of the contact between primitive peoples and civilization was an oversimplification and distortion, so probably was the over-ready inclination of the radical-humanitarians to see only the provocative actions of the army without considering the varied reactions of the Africans themselves to the military presence. Nevertheless a detailed examination of the actual course of the disturbances does support the view that in many cases the Government of Natal's handling of an already explosive situation did precipitate revolt.

It is also essential to point out that, even before the appearance of the field forces, there had been a deep undercurrent of hostility between black and white. In large measure this feeling is to be traced to the land and labor policies adopted by successive Natal governments and to the increasingly rigid and autocratic approach of the administration to the African population. Also, the rapid expansion of Natal's white population in the last decade of the nineteenth century and Natal's annexation of Zululand in 1897 had made the white man's presence far more obvious and far more onerous than it had been in the early days of the colony. At the same time the economic expansion of South Africa as the result of the mineral discoveries on the Rand had greatly increased the demands for labor of industrialists, farmers, and the government. While, however, settler and governmental pressures can be seen as the underlying and precipitating causes of African dissatisfaction prior to 1906, the imposition of the poll tax at the end of 1905 can be considered as an underlying, predisposing, and precipitating cause. In its relationship to the entire structure of land and labor policies it formed part of the underlying causation; in imposing a new and heavy burden of taxation on the shoulders of an indigent population (not all of whom rebelled against it), it was certainly a predisposing factor; finally, by providing the occasion for the defiance of governmental authority by certain groups and for the declaration of martial law, the poll tax was undoubtedly the precipitating cause of the 1906 disturbances. Despite Stuart's dismissal of the poll tax as "merely a contributory cause and not the most important of those that have been cited," most Africans at the time attributed the disturbances to the imposition of the tax. It was from that moment that "things began to go wrong."

Indeed, so close was the link between reaction to the tax and the 1906 disturbances, they have frequently been called the "Poll Tax Rebellion." Although the disturbances arose out of a number of complex causes which varied from tribe to tribe, and indeed from group to group within the African population, it was the poll tax which had set off the batch of nervous rumors about an impending uprising at the end of 1905 and which had led to the spate of white animal killing in the most densely populated rural districts of the colony—a reaction very similar to the cattle killing among the Xhosa in the Eastern Cape in 1856.   To take this up in greater detail, many Africans linked the tax with the unpopular 1904 census, which magistrates had promised would have no sinister repercussions: the poll tax was thus regarded as a distinct breach of faith on the part of the government.   The translation of poll tax into Zulu as a "head tax" was also rather unfortunate and led to wry remarks among Africans that a leg and arm tax would follow. However, in introducing the poll tax bill in the Natal Legislative Assembly in 1905, the Minister of Native Affairs had asserted that ". . . the natives of this Colony will hail the present Bill, if it is made law, with pleasure. . . . I can assure [members] . . . that if this bill is made law there will be no difficulties as far as the natives are concerned."   Magistrates in many parts of the colony were also initially sanguine as to the ease with which the tax would be collected.   Nevertheless, when, at the end of

January and February 1906, they actually attempted to collect the tax, they were generally met with passive resistance and even, on occasion, as has already been touched on, by open defiance. Thus, on 22 January, the acting magistrate of Mapumulo was met by angry gesticulating men of Ngobizembe's tribe, many of them armed with sticks; in the same district the followers of Swaimana and Meseni also refused to pay the tax. Furthermore, though in September 1905 the magistrate of Nkandla had stated that the reports of the forthcoming tax had not roused "the slightest sign of disloyalty" in any of the chiefs or headmen to whom it had been announced, in January 1906, Sigananda's people in that division maintained that they could not afford to pay the tax, apparently shouted their war cry, and did a war dance in front of the magistrate.

It is difficult to know how to interpret this early passive resistance to the tax, or indeed even the more violent expressions of hostility. Some of the protesting chiefs and their people were later involved in the disturbances and did fight against the white forces. But several others who also protested against the tax and at first refused to pay it later remained neutral, and some, like Sibindi and his followers, even remained conspicuously loyal to the government and provided men to fight on its side. Moreover, at the same time that the Africans were voicing their protests against the tax, its white opponents were holding several very noisy meetings in Pietermaritzburg and Durban. For Africans, however, there were few ways of expressing opposition other than by passive resistance. Whether Africans were allowed to express their views or not depended to a large extent on individual magistrates—as did the adequacy of the information they received as to when and by whom the tax had to be paid.

Partly as a result of the failure of the government to listen to their complaints, several chiefs in 1906 sent messages to Dinuzulu to find out what he was going to do about the tax. Nor were these chiefs only from Zululand; messengers came from prominent chiefs as far south as Tilonko and Sikukuku in the Ixopo division of Natal. Dinuzulu's replies to these messages would appear invariably to have been proper: He pointed out that his people had been the first to pay the tax, and completely denied the rumor, which was supposed to have emanated from him, that all white animals were to be killed. More than one witness at Dinuzulu's subsequent trial on charges of high treason affirmed that "If Dinuzulu had refused to pay the Poll Tax we would have fought and died" and that "Dinuzulu was the Peacemaker between us and the Government. He stopped what might have taken place. . . ." Indeed, Sir Charles Saunders, Commissioner for Native Affairs in Zululand, maintained throughout the disturbances that Dinuzulu's example in paying the tax had prevented the disturbances from spreading through Zululand, but his view as to Dinuzulu's participation became less favorable later.

Even overt signs of defiance were not taken equally seriously by all the magistrates. As will be seen later, some, if anything, overreacted; others took an opposite path. Chief Ngokwana's tribe, for example, was initially reported disrespectful and insolent; two weeks later it was apparently "paying well," after a simple reprimand by the Commissioner for Native Affairs. A. J. S. Maritz, the magistrate of Entonjaneni, who tried Sigananda's men for breach of the peace, thought so little of that episode that he dismissed the men with a caution. The conflict in magisterial views as to what constituted "rebelliousness" was to persist throughout the disturbances and to become even more marked once the troops were in the field.

The government was clearly in a difficult position over the collection of the tax, having imposed it with little consultation, even with those magistrates who were closest to African public opinion, and despite the advice of others who had pointed out that it would probably aggravate African poverty and undermine family life. It now found itself faced with widespread opposition. Apart from military preparations —and even in this respect at the beginning of 1906 the active militia had been reduced and the militia reserves were still disorganized—there is little indication that the government had considered what it would do if its authority were challenged over the collection of the tax. James Stuart, at that time First Criminal Magistrate in Durban and responsible for convening meetings of African urban workers to announce the tax, was one of the few to face the issue squarely. After a couple of turbulent meetings at which Africans had vigorously voiced their opposition to the tax, he wrote to the Minister for Native Affairs:

> On getting refusal, compulsion in some form or other may have to be resorted to, but is it desirable to resort to force when, as I think, the whole people are not only opposed to the tax, but regard it as oppressive and as calculated to disturb their social system. . . . I as one whose duties bring him into close contact with the natives venture to think that the passing of this act brings the Colony . . . face to face with a grave risk which cannot be too well considered beforehand.

Far from considering the risk, however, the sole response of the Minister was to reprimand Stuart for holding meetings of Africans and allowing them to get out of hand: his not proceeding through the traditional chieftainly authority (non-existent in the urban centers) was regarded as a far greater threat to the security of the colony than a possible explosion over the tax.

The Incident at Trewirgie: February 1906

One of the most important instances of early defiance over the collection of the poll tax occurred on 7 February 1906, when Chief Mveli of the Funzi tribe brought his people to Henly to pay their tax to the magistrate of the Umgeni division, T. R. Bennet. On hearing from the chief that some twenty-seven armed members of his tribe had taken up a position almost two miles away, the magistrate sent a European trooper, who spoke no Zulu, and two African messengers to discover the reason for their behavior. Both the African messengers were relatives of the chief; one of them, Jobe, was his brother.

On arrival, the emissaries addressed themselves to the leaders of the group, Makanda and Mjongo, and asked what was going on. According to Jobe, their reply was: "We have come to the Chief or magistrate who is collecting the money. We shall refuse our money for the Poll Tax." They were then asked why they were carrying assegais, and answered: "These assegais, it is our day today. There will be blood today." At this point the rest of the men moved forward suddenly—whether to hear what was being said or for some less innocent purpose is not clear—and the messengers fled.

Mjongo and his men then went back to their homes on Henry Hosking's farm, Trewirgie, near Byrnetown. The following day, 8 February, a detachment of fifteen policemen, including two Africans, was sent to arrest the twenty-seven men accused of being in unlawful possession of arms. Under Subinspector S. K. Hunt, the police arrived at dusk, having lost their way earlier in the day, and, despite Hosking's advice, decided to proceed with the arrests. At the huts, about a mile away from the farmhouse, they asked for the wanted men; Mjongo and two others were found immediately and handcuffed. The police then began their search for the others, who were some distance away from the kraals. According to the court-martial evidence of Mbadi, one of the accused,

After Mjongo had gone we decided to follow him. Then one police trooper saw us and turning round called the others. The police came and . . . said "Go home, go home."
We noticed that they had drawn their revolvers; they were in front of us, so we drew back to the rocks, saying that we had done no harm in the location. They said: "You have been carrying assegais." We said: "There is no harm in that. Mveli sent us back." We said, "Let Mveli come here, we will talk to him. It is no good your coming here

armed." . . . They told us to lay down our assegais and we said, "How can we do so when you have drawn your firearms. . . ." The others then shouted, "You have come for our money; you can shoot us. We won't pay," and "We would rather die than pay."

When Mjongo was released by the police to try to quiet the men who were flourishing small shields and assegais, he was pulled down among them. The police then apparently rode their horses into the group, who believed that they were trying to trample them down; this did nothing to improve the temper of the Africans. Eventually the police returned to the huts, followed by the men, some of whom, according to their evidence, had agreed to discuss matters there or at Hosking's farm, while others wished either to join or to rescue the two men already arrested.

However, they trooped down after the police in twos and threes, according to Stuart "jeering and taunting . . . [them] in the most insolent manner," and, according to some African witnesses, singing and praying as they had done outside Henly. Suddenly one of the Africans grabbed hold of the bridle of the policeman in charge of prisoner Ngcubu. Subinspector Hunt immediately fired his rifle, and the other police followed suit. In the ensuing scuffle, four Africans were wounded and two of the police, Subinspector Hunt and Trooper Armstrong, stabbed to death. The following day, 9 February, martial law was declared throughout the colony.

In what followed, the declaration of martial law played an important role, for in a sense martial law is the abrogation of law. Under it, any acts carried out "in good faith" by the Governor, the commandant of the militia, or their subordinates, in an attempt to put down the disturbances, would be indemnified later by an Act of Parliament. Once there was "no law" in Natal, the normal restraints of society could be loosened. The element of force took on a new significance. As well as being a response to aggression, whether overt or covert, it could in turn become its cause, although not, of course, its only cause. Reactions were varied. Thus, many tribes who witnessed troops marching through their locations took the government's advice and remained quiet—or even responded to appeals for aid from the whites. And the same was true of those tribes who found themselves attacked by the "rebel forces" in the second phase of the disturbances, when the rebels under Bambatha attempted to force other peoples to join them; some responded positively, others fled to the nearest magistracy or to the bush. Nevertheless, where there was a background of tension and conflict with white authority, administration, police, or settlers, fears were aroused simply by the appearance of white troops on the scene: Africans would arm and doctor themselves for war, sometimes, it would appear, purely in self-defense; such steps in turn aroused fresh apprehensions on the other side, and forces would be sent to deal with a new outbreak of "rebellion." In much of what follows there is something in the nature of a self-fulfilling prophecy: fearing, perhaps half wanting, rebellion, the colonists and their leaders by their actions gave substance to their fears. For, although the picture concerning the events on Hosking's property which emerges from the court-martial evidence is not absolutely clear and there are obviously great difficulties in interpreting the evidence of the accused, it would appear from this incident that the murder of the magistrate or the police officers had not been premeditated, nor was there any intention to massacre whites. Even if one follows the official account of what occurred, or Stuart's rendition, the Africans did not, despite their jeers and gesturing, strike first. The first shot had been fired by Hunt at a handcuffed prisoner.   On 7 February, the three messengers from the magistrate to the armed men had escaped unscathed; nor is it clear why, if, as was alleged, the group had intended murdering the magistrate, it should have taken up a position two miles away from the magistracy. Indeed, some of the group maintained that they had been ordered to stop there by Mveli himself—presumably because they were carrying assegais, although this was not illegal, and because he wished to stop them from voicing their opposition to the poll tax before the magistrate. According to both Nomkuba, the sister of Makanda, and Mantayi ka Mjongo, himself one of the accused, they were on their way to pay their taxes when they were ordered to stop. Had they gone on to the magistracy, it is conceivable that an incident no more serious than those already described as having taken place in Mapumulo and Nkandla might have occurred. Once it was reported, however, the magistrate could not ignore the fact that these men were armed, but his sending relatives of the chief as the only Zulu-speaking messengers was perhaps unfortunate, as they were likely to share the chief's views on the dissident minority in their midst.

The crucial mistake would appear to have been the sending of so small a detachment of police to arrest Makanda, Mjongo, and their supporters the following day. Furthermore, Subinspector Hunt was not well suited to his task. Knowing no Zulu, and apparently convinced beforehand that this was going to be the start of a widespread uprising, he felt that he had been selected as "bait" by the government.   His own somewhat extreme views on the "native problem" may have influenced his behavior. Thus, in a letter to his family shortly after his arrival in Natal in the early 1890's, he had written of "licking the niggers into shape" and "knocking hell out of them."   It is possible that ten years in Natal had mellowed Subinspector Hunt's approach to Africans. The tradition, however, that lives on of him as an autocratic, overbearing man seems to have been borne out by the African evidence at the court-martial.

Yet whatever the truth about the police handling of the matter, it can also be argued that after all twenty-seven armed men had appeared in defiance of the poll tax, and that such an act was in itself sufficient indication of hostility to the government.

Again, the picture is more complicated. While it would appear that the immediate reason for the group's defiance was their chief's order to join other members of the tribe in paying the tax, the fact that they were, as has already been mentioned, all members of an independent church, was significant. Although it did not mean that they were necessarily anti-white, it did mean that they were estranged from their chief and his other followers who were pagans.

Actually, there had been a fairly long history of antagonism between Christian converts and pagans in the Funzi tribe. Thus in 1896 a case had been taken from the Native High Court to the Supreme Court, in which tribesmen who were orthodox members of the European controlled Wesleyan Methodist church had alleged that they had been victimized by their chief, at that time Hemuhemu, Mveli's father. Apparently as a result of the complaints of some of the older members of his tribe that their wives and daughters "stayed out late" when they attended services, Hemuhemu had forbidden public services and private prayers. The penalty for infringing this command had been set at a £2 fine or a beast, and, when a local missionary came to hold services in the location, the chief had actually sent his private policeman to note the names of those who attended. While Chief Justice Sir Walter Wragg of the Supreme Court had found in favor of the Christians in this instance, the complaint of the chief that they were disrespectful of his authority is a familiar historical theme. That the conflict did not die down in 1896 was borne out by a letter written by Joseph Baynes, a member of the Legislative Assembly, to the magistrate of Richmond in the middle of 1904 in which he transmitted the complaints of "respectable kraalheads" in the area about the disruptive effects, especially on the women, of a Christian sect operating from Trewirgie under Mjongo, at that period a sawyer with Makanda in the Enon forests. By this time, however, the Christians who were complained of appear to have become members of the independent African Presbyterian church.

In some ways, the 1906 episode also suggested a continuance of this aspect of the conflict. It is difficult to say how much antagonism was directed against the chief as the representative of the government, and how much as the representative of rejected tribal tradition. Mbadi's statement—"Let Mveli come here, we will talk with him"—suggests that the defiance was primarily directed against the chief and not the government. Mveli's own prompt reporting of the incident to the magistrate—unlike Bambatha's subsequent behavior—and his alacrity and zeal in hunting out the rebels, as well as his expressed wish to remove their women and children,   may well have represented an attempt on his part to consolidate his hold over the tribe and to rid himself of an unruly and undermining element in its midst.

Whatever the complexities of the incident, the fact that it involved members of a separatist sect and that two police officers had been killed undoubtedly increased white fears and made the incident appear particularly ominous. Taken against the background of rumors and isolated incidents of resistance to the poll tax, this was the last straw. It led to the swift declaration of martial law over the entire colony within hours after an event which in normal circumstances would hardly have warranted more than the reinforcement of the local police force.

The participants in the killing of Hunt and Armstrong were soon to suffer dearly for their actions. On the day that martial law was declared, troops were mobilized and a column under McKenzie was dispatched to Thornville Junction, Richmond, and Elandskop. Together with Mveli and five hundred of his men, they searched the Byrnetown area and the Enon forest. On 15 February, just a week after the initial incident, two of Mjongo's men were captured and, after trial by drumhead court-martial, shot in the presence of Mveli and his men.   The remaining participants were rounded up in the weeks that followed and tried by a court-martial which sat from 12 to 17 March. Another twelve were sentenced to death and, after some delay as a result of protests from the Colonial Office, were shot before assembled tribesmen and chiefs from the Midlands and Southern districts of the colony on 2 April. Several others were sentenced to twenty years' imprisonment at hard labor, confiscation of property, and lashes.   Finally, three remaining participants, who had been too badly wounded after a brush with the troops hunting them out in February to be shot by order of the Richmond court-martial like the others, were put to death after a trial by the Natal Supreme Court in September 1906. Mjongo was hanged on this occasion.

These events undoubtedly had a profound effect on the people in the surrounding areas. According to Stuart, news of the drumhead court-martial on 15 February "which was regarded as just and proper by every loyal Native" spread at once far and wide.   Having dealt with these rebels, McKenzie then found it necessary to turn his attention to other chiefs and tribes in the district concerning whom "there had been many adverse reports." Interviews were held with chiefs regarded as defiant in some way, who were reported to have been reluctant to pay the poll tax, or who were said to have had their tribes "doctored" for war. From the evidence that he had received from settlers and military spies, McKenzie was convinced that his action had "nipped in the bud" a widespread conspiracy of the black man to rise against the white. Ultimatums were delivered to various chiefs to hand over their "rebellious" subjects and to search their tribes for assegais. Failure to comply meant the confiscation of cattle and, not infrequently, the burning of crops and kraals. "Rebels" were tried before specially constituted courts set up by McKenzie, and sentences of death, twenty-five years' imprisonment, and fifty lashes were not uncommon, although they were generally modified by the Governor in Council.

While some of the magistrates appear to have considered these proceedings essential to combat the growing restlessness of the tribes in their district, others were less sure. Thus, in a private letter to the Undersecretary for Native Affairs, J. Y. Gibson, the magistrate of Richmond, who was soon forced to resign from this position for being too sympathetically inclined toward Africans in general and for opposition to the Richmond court-martial in particular, wrote:

> Men are still being continually arrested under Martial Law, but I have no idea what the charges are against them. I have discovered the spirit of Titus Oates prevailing to a certain extent and it is not possible at present to determine the extent. . . . A large number of men were taken away from my division, I hear, and tried at Ixopo. I have not been informed who they were or what they had done. Only occasional information reached this office in regard to some individual said to have been seen with one or more assegais. . . . There is a general belief . . . too that it is intended to send the force to deal with Tilonko. In the meantime, complete peace appears to reign, the people being all most amenable and anxious to do right. . . . They are all poor people in this division and heavy fines and exactions are ruining them completely. . . .

As the troop movements were extended throughout the Midlands and the Southern districts of the colony, many chiefs and tribes began to feel apprehensive. These fears were perhaps most marked among members of Tilonko's and Msikofeli's tribes in the Ixopo and Richmond divisions. Both chiefs headed large and important peoples, and both were extremely unpopular with their white neighbors, who probably resented their independent attitude and coveted their land. Thus, from the outset of his career as head of the Kuze tribe in 1897, Msikofeli had been faced with the opposition of the magistrate and local settlers who for some years had been agitating for the breakup of his chiefdom. In the Richmond area, suggestions for deposing Tilonko because of his alleged reluctance to pay the poll tax came from white residents even before the declaration of martial law and before there was any evidence of his, or his tribe's, overt hostility to whites. On 12 February there were reports that members of Msikofeli's and Tilonko's tribes had taken up arms—according to Stuart, and even McKenzie—because they feared the arrest of their chiefs. The moving of all of the Europeans in the area into a laager further increased their apprehensions: according to the one local resident who did not join the flight from the farms, the African population now "seemed to have one idea and that was the troops were coming to kill them all." Now that the whites had moved out, Chief Msikofeli openly expressed the fear that the troops had come to wipe out him and his people.

Despite the reports that the two tribes had armed themselves, on the following day the Minister and the Undersecretary for Native Affairs risked meeting these chiefs to reprimand them for their unruly conduct before the magistrate collecting the poll tax. The meeting passed without incident, and both the tribes began to pay the tax without further ado. By early April the Embo people, including Tilonko's, had paid nearly all their taxes. Yet, though Tilonko and Msikofeli played no further part in the disturbances, whites continued to agitate for the break-up of their tribes. Five months later, when virtually all the troops had been demobilized and the disturbances were at an end, Tilonko was summoned before the Minister of Native Affairs. He went voluntarily to Pietermaritzburg, where he was tried by court-martial behind closed doors for sedition and public violence. He was found guilty, fined five hundred head of cattle (later reduced to two hundred and fifty by the Governor, who thought that the original sentence would inflict the punishment on his tribe), deposed from his position, and deported with the ringleaders of the disturbances to St. Helena. Msikofeli, who had handed over all the men wanted by the military in the early days of the disturbances, was not dealt with as harshly, merely being fined in cattle and having his chiefdom divided into three. Yet much of Natal's argument for a dangerous conspiracy—which could only be dealt with by martial law and military action—rested on the cases of Tilonko and Msikofeli. It is an interesting footnote to Tilonko's "rebellious and dangerous" character that, on the day following the arming of his men and their assembling at his kraal, he sent an apology to the neighboring white farmer lest his tribesmen had inadvertently trampled his tobacco during the night's activities.

Bambatha's Rebellion

During the first phase of the disturbances, when there was no overt resistance to the white forces, fear of punishment may well have cowed would-be rebels. It has been stated as a psychological "law" that, with "the strength of frustration held constant, the greater the anticipation of punishment for a given act the less apt that act is to occur." And certainly this dictum would appear to have been borne out in the early weeks of the "rebellion," when for nearly two months white forces were able with impunity to march through locations, fine and depose chiefs without trial, confiscate large numbers of sheep and cattle, burn crops and kraals, and flog all Africans whom the military men considered "insolent." Trials were held under martial law for offenses as vague as those of "insubordination or contempt or defiance of public authorities, or menaces or seditious language or acts inciting to insurrection." All this time the ordinary courts of the colony were functioning normally. By the end of March, McKenzie considered that he had sufficiently "impressed" the Africans in the Midlands and South Coast to be able to demobilize his forces.

In terms of the subsequent history of the disturbances, however, McKenzie's operations, and those of the troops under Colonel George Leuchars who were operating in the Mapumulo area principally against Chief Ngobizembe and his tribe, may well have been converting latent hostility into open aggression. There appears to be a point at which punishment intended to deter aggressive action can actually become its cause, where the punishment for minor offenses is so disproportionate that people feel they may as well commit major ones. Moreover, for punishment to act as a deterrent, people must feel they have something to lose—whether it be property, status, or family comfort and happiness. In the next phase of the disturbances, which saw the first open defiance of the government, there appears an element of despair and desperation, so well expressed before the Natal Native Affairs Commission by one Mvinjwa—not himself a rebel—when he talked of Bambatha, the chief of the Zondi people and the leader of the rebellion:

> They were like Bambata. He went to extremes simply because he was tied hand and foot by the network of troubles in which he found himself. He then strayed off in revolt. He was very much like a beast which on being stabbed rushes about in despair, charges backwards and forwards and, it may be, kills someone that happens to be in his path.

To modern African nationalists Bambatha has become a great national hero, and, of course, in the simple sense that he resisted oppressive European rule and attempted to unite behind him the chiefs and people of many tribes, he is rightly so regarded. Unfortunately, however, Bambatha himself left no record of what he was trying to do and therefore—in analyzing his motives and aims—we are dependent on the very imperfect assessments of administrative officials and the less imperfect but still inadequate views of his *induna* (headmen) and followers. From these records one does not get a picture of a man with a clear plan of action. Despite his frequent use of Dinuzulu's name, war cry, and war badge, and his attempt to bring the ex-king of the Zulu into the rebellion, one's predominant impression is that of a man goaded beyond endurance who was using the king's name as a centralizing device and making an appeal to Zulu national feeling, but who was prepared to die fighting—probably in the knowledge that his chances of success were slender in the extreme.

Already very unpopular with his white neighbors, who called him "Bellicose Bambata the Chief of Misrule," Bambatha was in the course of 1905 involved in two faction fights and, on being brought before the Undersecretary for Native Affairs at the end of the year, was warned that any future misbehavior would probably lead to his deposition. Bambatha's suspicions of white intentions had been revealed in 1904 when he had questioned the motives for having the census. At the time of the promulgation of the poll tax, however, he made no open complaint to the magistrate of the division; but considerable discontent was expressed by the Zondi tribesmen, led by one of their *induna,* Nhlonhlo. The protests of people living on private lands and, like Bambatha himself, heavily in debt were, not surprisingly, the loudest. As a result of this opposition, Bambatha's people were the last to be called upon to pay the tax in the Umvoti division, and the magistrate, J. W. Cross, decided to make the magistracy itself, Greytown, the center of collection.

On 22 February, the day appointed for the collection of the tax, Bambatha, as was customary among many tribes, arranged to meet his men outside Greytown, but found at the rendezvous that some of the younger men, suspicious of the change of venue, had arrived armed with assegais and shields. Still others had failed to bring the money, or were likely to contravene borough regulations which prescribed that Africans wear European-type clothing within the municipal area. Apparently swayed by the fears of those who thought that if he went to Greytown he would be arrested, and perhaps by the thought that he could better control the wilder elements in the tribe if he remained with them, Bambatha sent on those members of the tribe who were prepared to pay the tax; about ninety-seven paid, and fifty-three were exempted on this occasion. He himself remained about two miles from Greytown with those men who had refused to lay down their arms and sent an apology of ill health to the magistrate.

According to Stuart, Bambatha's mistake at this point was in not reporting what had occurred to the magistrate, as Mveli had done under similar circumstances. From this time he became more and more closely associated with the armed section of his tribe, and it became more and more difficult for him to respond to messages from the white authorities instructing him to report to the magistrate. That Bambatha failed to have much confidence in the assurances of his local magistrate may, in part, have been related to the personality of Cross. Although Cross had been in the colony some forty years, and had by 1906 been in government employ for over thirty, he was something of an alarmist and tended to believe exaggerated stories of African unrest. It was apparently for this reason that he had been temporarily removed from a magistracy near the Pondoland border in 1897. Despite the fact that he spoke Zulu fluently, his tactless remarks to the Africans assembled to welcome him to his new post at Greytown in 1904 (he had informed them that the land was the white man's and not theirs) had even led to a private reprimand from the Natal cabinet. In the same year the Governor had expressed doubts as to the wisdom of his deposing Acting Chief Njengabantu. Like so many magistrates of his generation, Cross believed that a freer use of the lash for the punishment of infringements of beer-drinking regulations and the Masters and Servants Acts, and as a means of preventing faction fighting, would vastly improve "native" behavior in Natal. He was unlikely to have viewed with sympathy Bambatha's troubles with his people or his own past history of unruliness, whatever their economic causes.

The chief's troubles were increased by the fact that on the night of the tax collection a false rumor had spread that his tribe had surrounded Greytown and intended to attack it. All the whites spent the night in laager, and extra police were sent to the area to deal with the "emergency." At the same time the Umvoti militia were called out. Members of Bambatha's tribe now became even more determined to prevent their chief giving himself up to white authorities. The feelings of the Zondi were expressed by one of Bambatha's followers before the Greytown court-martial:

> The white people should they want the Chief must take him from our hands . . . our wish is that the Chief should not be shot as a buck [nor] as a beast or an ox driven to the slaughter house.

Bambatha's position became more difficult not only because of his own action, or inaction, and because his previous friction with the authorities had made him fear punishment, but also because, as the days passed, the nature of "punitive action" in different parts of the colony became clearer. His original reluctance to report the presence of armed men in his tribe had occurred only a week after two of Mjongo's followers had been shot for their part in the Trewirgie affray; troops were still in the Ixopo and Mid-Illovo districts hunting out the rest of that armed band and burning their crops and kraals. While Mveli had reported the defiance of this group in his tribe and had later apparently welcomed the opportunity of ridding himself of dissident elements in his location, this solution may well have appeared increasingly impossible to Bambatha as the troop movements continued and came closer to Greytown. The proceedings against Ngobizembe in neighboring Mapumulo on 5 March may also have increased Bambatha's determination to evade the clutches of the police and armed forces sent to arrest him on 9 March. Two days later he made his way into Zululand and, ultimately, to Dinuzulu's headquarters at Nongoma.

Much was made of this last fact by the government of Natal in 1907-8, when it was discovered that Bambatha had left his wife and children at Dinuzulu's headquarters for safekeeping. It was widely believed at the time of the disturbances and afterward that he had been given arms and ammunition by Dinuzulu and had been actively encouraged by him to start a rebellion in Natal, being assured of Dinuzulu's future active support. The evidence for and against such a view —which was rejected by the majority of members of the special court which tried Dinuzulu —cannot be considered here. Whatever happened at Nongoma, however, at the end of March Bambatha returned to Natal accompanied by Ngqengqengqe, one of Dinuzulu's messengers, and by Cakijana ka Gezindaka, who was believed to be one of his *induna*. Cakijana was soon to become a key figure in the rebellion as Bambatha's "right hand man."

It is difficult to know at exactly what point Bambatha made his momentous decision to oppose the white man with force. The evidence of both Ngqengqengqe and Cakijana seems to suggest that the decisive moment came when he returned to his tribe and discovered that Magwababa, his uncle, had been appointed regent in his place. At this point Ngqengqengqe, who had ostensibly been sent by Dinuzulu to find a doctor for him in the Greytown district, returned to Zululand—without the doctor—as he feared trouble. On this, his evidence is consistent and straightforward. There are, however, many variants of Cakijana's evidence. In his first deposition, before members of Dinuzulu's defense counsel, which he subsequently repudiated, he stated that on the fourth day after he had accompanied Bambatha from his father's home—also to look for Dinuzulu's doctor—he came upon Bambatha talking to some members of his tribe. At this point he was told: "Go back, we are still talking. I have found that the white people have placed some other person in my place." Only after this conversation did Bambatha appear with guns. This would suggest that it was only after he had heard of

Magwababa's appointment that he decided to take up arms—although Cakijana's later evidence, given both while he was detained at Nkandla jail after his arrest and at his own and Dinuzulu's trial, stated that he had been instructed by Dinuzulu to join Bambatha in order to start a rebellion. The difficulties of interpretation are considerable since, in both instances, Cakijana, an extraordinarily shrewd character, was giving the evidence he expected his audience to want—in the first instance he was talking to Dinuzulu's defendants, in the second to his prosecutors. (It is interesting that Cakijana's father reported to Dinuzulu's defense team that Cakijana said he had joined Bambatha when the latter was surrounded by white troops after he had attacked Magwababa and that as a result he, Cakijana, "could not escape"; this was also Cakijana's first version of his evidence.)   It is clear however that Bambatha's first openly hostile move was on the evening of 2 April, when he captured Magwababa, whose life was saved only by Cakijana's intervention.

There had long been a rift between that section of the tribe which now supported Magwababa as regent and the younger followers of Bambatha, a rift which had in fact been revealed at the time of the poll tax collection when Bambatha had identified himself with the more turbulent members of his tribe and was described by one of his followers:

> We dogs of Bambata had no quarrel with the government. Bambata's quarrel was with his father Magwababa because Bambata alleged that Magwababa was the means of getting him deposed.

Once Bambatha attacked Magwababa, a government appointee, it was inevitable that his quarrel would be with the government, a fact of which he must have been aware. His final decision to oppose the white man with force by attacking the magistrate and the police sent out to arrest him on 4 April may have been prompted further by a feeling that he might as well be hanged for a sheep as a lamb and die fighting. He followed up the capture of the regent by looting a hotel and the house of a white man in a search for arms. Two days earlier, the shooting before the assembled Africans of Richmond of twelve of Mjongo's men was an awful example of the white man's punishment, an example which would have acted as a spur to a man who felt by this time that he had nothing to lose. By 3 April Bambatha may have considered that he had no alternative to armed rebellion. The government of Natal, however, denied that there was any connection between Bambatha's taking up arms and the Richmond court-martial, maintaining that the time difference between the two events was too small. This contention fails to recognize the fact that the sentences had been announced several days earlier and had received widespread publicity as a result of the Natal cabinet's resignation when the British Secretary of State for Colonial Affairs requested further information about the Richmond executions.

At any rate, on 5 April Bambatha fled to the dense Nkandla forests on the borders of Natal and Zululand, an area which had more than once served as a royal sanctuary. From the tactical point of view, this area could hardly have been improved on for defensive warfare. After a few days in hiding Bambatha began to build up a rebel army. Here, apparently, his plan was to keep to the forest, sending messengers to chiefs to join him, and using Dinuzulu's name as his authority and maintaining that he possessed his support.

Bambatha seems to have had little intention of attacking the Europeans in the open; it was simply a matter of waiting for them to come into the bush and then taking them unawares.   Despite an attempt by Bambatha to force the Africans in the area to join him, however, he met with little success until Sigananda and his Cube tribe, one of the largest in the Nkandla district and the guardians of the royal grave of Cetshwayo, decided to throw in their lot with the Zondi. At first accompanied by only his own Zondi followers—they were reported to be about two to three hundred strong—Bambatha now quickly began to attract individuals from the Nkandla chiefdoms. For the first time since the declaration of martial law on 8 February, a resistance movement was being built up. For this reason, the disturbances as a whole are frequently referred to as the "Bambatha Rebellion."

Sigananda's tribe had already signified their opposition to the poll tax. Shortly thereafter Sigananda's heir, who was in effective control of the chiefdom, was fined for failing to provide eight men for compulsory labor for the Department of Public Works.   When Bambatha fled to this area, Sigananda, together with the other chiefs in the neighborhood, was ordered by the Commissioner of Native Affairs to arm his men and hunt out the rebels, and on 8 April Sigananda's messenger reported to the magistrate that Bambatha had entered his ward.   However, after an apparently halfhearted and brief attempt to find Bambatha, the attitude of the Cube changed. One of Sigananda's sons, who had given the information to the government that Bambatha had been seen, was victimized by the Cube people, and on 13 April Saunders began to suspect that Sigananda had joined the rebels. By 16 April Bambatha was apparently moving about freely among the Cube, who had all been "doctored" for war by Bambatha's Sotho war doctor, the whole force then consisting of twelve to fourteen companies, according to one estimate—or about 700 to 1,000 men. Sigananda sent messages to the warriors of the surrounding chiefs—Ndube, Mpumela, Makubalo, and others—and, while the chiefs did not join, members of their chief-doms began to filter toward the rebel army.

Despite statements to the contrary, poverty appears to have been among the root causes of Cube discontent. Sir Charles Saunders, who discounted the rumors that it was Dinuzulu's messages which had led Sigananda's people to rebel, also pointed out that Sigananda and his chief son and heir, Nkabaningi, were "paupers." As in the case of Bambatha, exceptional poverty was one of the clues to the above aver-age frustration felt by the Cube people and their leaders, and therefore to their low threshold of resistance in the face of an appeal to take up arms. The high correlation between low economic status and criminal-ity, both because of the higher level of frustration and because of the lesser "inhibiting influence of anticipated punishment," has frequently been noted. At the same time, people who have been ground down by poverty for generations do not usually rebel against their lot. It is the recently poor and the recently conquered who are most prone to "do something about it." It should be remembered that the Nkandla-Nqutu area of Southern Zululand had only relatively recently come under colonial rule. Unlike the Africans of Natal, the Zululanders had more re-cent memories of a "glorious past." That they should in so many cases have responded to Bambatha's call is hardly surprising. In the case of Sigananda, especially, these memories must have proved a potent spur to action.

Sigananda, a venerable old man, reputed to have been about ninety-seven years old, had been an *udibi* or mat-carrier during the last campaigns of Shaka's army. He was also said to have witnessed the killing of Retief at Dingane's kraal. Be that as it may, he had had a more recent history of loyalty to the Zulu royal family, having been closely involved in the troubles of the 1880's. It was he who had granted Cetsh-wayo sanctuary in his flight from his enemies in 1883. In the 1888 dis-turbances he had been held in Eshowe jail on a charge of treason. In a sense he was among the oldest living representatives of Zulu military pride and tradition. For such a man, it must indeed have been difficult to become reconciled to European rule. Certainly a mes-sage he is reported to have sent to Dinuzulu in reply to his instruction that he should pay the poll tax fits in with this interpretation. He is re-ported to have accused Dinuzulu of cowardice in not openly fighting against the white man—a message which Dinuzulu, a younger but per-haps wiser man, rejected with the words: "He is bodaring [talking non-sense] when he says I am afraid. Who can fight the white man? I have been sent over the seas by 'them'. I do not want my children to suffer."

On the other hand, the Natal government maintained that secret

messages from Dinuzulu to Sigananda, instructing him to look out for
Bambatha, led to his change in attitude.   While, in fact, Dinuzulu
admitted to having sent such a message, he maintained that it was sent
before the outbreak of violence—before he knew that Bambatha intended starting a rebellion—and when he thought that Bambatha was
simply looking for land on which to settle. At the court-martial of Sigananda and his sons, evidence was given which suggested that Cakijana's claims that he had been sent by Dinuzulu had made considerable
impact on the Cube.   How important this factor was in the light of
the visit of Dinuzulu's chief adviser, Mankulumana, to the Cube, in
an attempt to disillusion them, is difficult to gauge. On 23 April Mankulumana arrived at the Nkandla stronghold and, according to his version
of what happened, was given a very hostile reception by the Cube,
who refused to let him see Sigananda.   Although some considered this
visit simply a part of Dinuzulu's double-dealing and thought that he
had probably sent other more sinister messengers simultaneously,
the Commissioner for Native Affairs was sure at the time that Mankulumana's visit, while not affecting the Cube decision to rebel, materially affected the decision of other tribes in the division and that "rebels
from other tribes appear to be melting away."

Another interpretation was given to the actions of the Cube tribe
by some of its members. Thus Polomba, the *induna* of the tribe, stated
at the time of his court-martial that the tribe was only recognized to be
in open rebellion after the arrival of the troops, and that when they did
not report Bambatha's trail (which Sigananda maintained had become
imperceptible) they were treated forthwith as rebels.   Cakijana, a
highly unreliable witness but one who in every other way tended to
implicate Dinuzulu in the disturbances, maintained in May 1908 that
when Mankulumana addressed Sigananda's tribe they replied:

> We have no answer for you only that we have been armed by Matshi-
> qela [Saunders] and we are now armed for good and intend fighting
> for he fired on us while we were still looking for Bambata.

Several other defense witnesses in the Dinuzulu trial gave similar
evidence,   and at the court-martial of Sigananda and his sons even
the counsel for the prosecution maintained that their fault lay in attempting to remain neutral (instead of actively assisting the European
forces), for "of course [in war] there is no such thing as neutrality."
Although Stuart denies that the Cube were first fired upon by the white
forces, it does appear as if it were simply assumed that they were in
rebellion once they failed to hand Bambatha over, and the evidence of
some of the tribesmen that they were fired upon by the troops when

they were still looking for the rebels does have to be taken into consideration. To expect a man with Sigananda's background to relish handing Bambatha over to the white forces was probably expecting too much—or too little—especially when one considers that in the days of Mpande Sigananda had fled to Natal for fear of his life and had been succored by Jangeni, Bambatha's grandfather.

It would thus appear that at first Sigananda had tried to remain neutral; but his poverty, the tribe's opposition to the poll tax, and his own memories of past glory and the laws of hospitality, had made him reluctant to pursue Bambatha in any very enthusiastic fashion. When he and his people realized that if they did not hand Bambatha over they would be regarded as rebels, and were perhaps so regarded already, they decided to throw in their lot with the rebels, although admittedly some of the outlying sections of the tribe might not have been fully aware of the decision.

After Sigananda, the most influential chief to join Bambatha was Mehlokazulu of the Qungebe people, another man with roots deep in the Zulu past. In many ways the motives which induced him to throw in his lot with the rebels in the Nkandla forests appear to have been similar to those which had initially spurred Bambatha into action. Once again, Mehlokazulu had a long history of past conflict with the authorities, both British and colonial. He had first gained notoriety at the time of the Zulu War of 1879, when he crossed the border of Natal in order to kidnap two of the adulterous wives of Sirayo, his father, who had fled to the colony. This incident had provided Sir Bartle Frere with one of his pretexts for war against Cetshwayo in 1879. Prominent in the Zulu War and in the tussles between the Zulu royal family, both against the British and against Zibhebhu, Dinuzulu's arch-rival, Mehlokazulu's existence during the 1880's and early 1890's was turbulent and harried. He was driven from district to district as now one loyal chief, now another, accused him of offenses, such as cattle stealing, against their white neighbors. He settled for some time in the New Republic, in Faku's location, but ran into trouble there when a Boer farmer accused him of insulting his wife: He was imprisoned at Vryheid for the offense.   Finally, he returned to the Nqutu district where his father's people lived, and, in 1893 when Sir Marshal Clarke became Resident Commissioner in Zululand and British attitudes toward the Zulu royal family and their adherents became less uncompromising, he was appointed as the chief of his father's tribe. It was felt that restoring him to a position of responsibility might ensure his loyalty.

From that time Mehlokazulu does indeed appear to have led a peaceful, law-abiding life—until the time came to pay the poll tax at the beginning of 1906. On the day appointed to pay the tax, he failed to appear before the magistrate with his men, and the magistrate was disposed to take a serious view of the matter.   Nevertheless, for the first three months after the proclamation of martial law, Mehlokazulu made no openly hostile move, despite many rumors that he was planning to do so. As the armed forces drew nearer to his district, however, Mehlokazulu apparently became apprehensive about white intentions toward him. These apprehensions increased as rumors spread among the whites that he had been sending messages to Chief Kula in Umsinga division and that they were planning a joint action against the whites.   There were close ties of kinship and friendship between these two chiefs, and it is true that Mehlokazulu had sent messages both to Kula and to Dinuzulu about the poll tax.   It is not unlikely that these communications were attempts to ascertain whether joint opposition to the tax was possible. It must, therefore, have been with considerable fear and trembling that Mehlokazulu saw the arrest of his friend and neighbor by the white forces on 8 May.

Kula, one of the most important of the government-appointed chiefs in Natal, headed an amalgam of tribal fragments formed into a "new tribe" by the British administrator, Sir Theophilus Shepstone, in 1869.   Conspicuous in their loyalty to the government both in 1879 and during the Anglo-Boer War, his people had always considered themselves the "government's tribe"—a fact which tended to draw on it the enmity of its neighbors, both African and Boer. At the end of 1905 and the beginning of 1906, there were several reports by spies of pending faction fights among the many tribes of the very densely populated Umsinga district, where Kula's was by far the largest. Perhaps as a result of the arming of young men for these fights, and also because this was an area where Africans had been killing white animals from October 1905, white farmers in the area, predominantly those of German and Dutch descent, began to express their fears of being "wiped out."   At the beginning of March there was a "panic" among the white settlers in Kula's division over "nothing definite," which was followed in turn by the arming of one of the sections of Kula's tribe under the *induna,* Mabulawa, "who feared arrest."   At the same time, the magistrate of Umsinga division, with whom Kula's relationship was of the worst, sent frequent complaints about the chief's behavior to the Minister for Native Affairs, although "he furnished no specific charges." In part, the magistrate's suspicions may have been roused by his chief informant, who was a man from Sibindi's tribe, a tribe which had been involved in many boundary disputes with Kula's people.   Finally, Kula was summoned before the Minister for Native Affairs at the end of March and was warned that if he did not mend his ways his fate would be similar to that of the chiefs the government had already dealt with.

Apparently awed by this warning, Kula returned to his people and handed over Mabulawa, despite the obvious dissatisfaction of the rest of the tribe at this action. In fact at this point his uncle, Mtele, led the dissidents into open rebellion, being joined by another small tribe in the division. Though with some reluctance, Kula, however, continued to do his duty as a government servant, and on 4 May reported Mtele's rebellion. A few days later, when the local magistracy had been reinforced with militia reserves from Helpmekaar and by the Natal Mounted Rifles, Kula, with several of his leading men, once more made his way to the magistracy to tell of further developments in his tribe. On the advice of the magistrate, the officers decided to transfer him to the officer commanding the troops at Helpmekaar, where, after being questioned, Kula was detained in custody. Despite orders from the head of the defense headquarters in Pietermaritzburg to the chief leader of the reserves in Helpmekaar that Kula should be released immediately, as he had been arrested while visiting a magistrate and should have been regarded as holding a safe conduct, the leaders of the reserves at Helpmekaar telegraphed to headquarters that the release of the chief would spread the rebellion among adjoining tribes and would "cause grave condition amongst our men which we will not hold ourselves responsible for." According to the resident magistrate and neighboring magistrates, the Boers (and the surnames of the leaders of the reserves at Helpmekaar bear out his interpretation) were seeking to avenge themselves on Kula for his services to the British during the Anglo-Boer War.

In the face of this threat of mutiny from the reserves, Kula was removed to Pietermaritzburg, where he was held for the duration of the disturbances. A few days later another portion of his tribe, under his brother Manuka, joined Mtele in open rebellion. This may have been the result of resentment at the government action in removing their chief, or lack of adequate control once Kula had been detained; to the local settlers it was evidence that Kula himself had been fomenting rebellion all along. However, the government considered that there was insufficient evidence to prove this, for, although Kula was deposed and removed from his tribe at the end of the disturbances, he was not brought before either a civil or military tribunal.

Other chiefs, and Mehlokazulu in particular, were left, however, to draw their own conclusions from Kula's visit to the magistrate and his consequent arrest. Mehlokazulu's followers feared that his would be a like fate. Almost immediately after Kula's arrest, when the column of Lt. Col. D. W. Mackay (the officer in charge of the troops in the district) marched through the Nqutu district, they urged him to hide in the forests to save his life and cattle. When he was instructed by the

officer commanding to provide men to fight that portion of Kula's tribe
which had rebelled and crossed the Buffalo River, he refused and fled
with his wives, cattle, and a few followers to the bush.   The majority
of his tribe apparently took no further action on either side. The magistrate of Nqutu tried his best to keep up negotiations with Mehlokazulu
and to persuade him to return to his tribe, but, according to one witness, Mehlokazulu's reply was: "I can't go back now. I have been surrounded by troops. I do not know what harm I have done."

It was at this time that the government found it necessary to instruct the magistrates of Dundee, Ladysmith, Estcourt, Greytown, and
Krantzkop   to assure chiefs in their divisions that they need not worry
about being interfered with; in Nqutu division, however, where the
magistrate asked permission of the government to hold a meeting to
allay the fears of the chiefs, Mackay instructed the Commissioner for
Native Affairs to "discontinue any further diplomatic negotiations"
with Mehlokazulu. The conference of chiefs was apparently not held
either.   Finally, after a few days in the bush, Mehlokazulu decided
on 18 May to throw in his lot with Bambatha and made his way to the
Nkandla stronghold. (It is possible that his action was partly influenced
by the burning of Cetshwayo's grave by white troops on the previous
day.) He was joined by members of Faku's tribe under Lubudlungu,
who had been armed in accordance with the instructions of the magistrates to guard the fords when Mtele and others had crossed into Zululand. The story of the tribesmen was that after Mehlokazulu's flight
they had seen their kraals burning and, thinking that this was rebel
action, had gone to see what was happening, but were fired on by the
white troops. They therefore "ran away and . . . joined Mehlokazulu
and went to Nkandla with him, without Faku's orders."   This may, of
course, have been a convenient excuse on the part of men who had
already decided to rebel against the government; that most of the Africans of Zululand were reluctant to fight against their fellows in Natal,
despite previous tribal enmities, was an undoubted fact. Whether this
in itself constituted rebellion depends on one's point of view. Their
situation is reminiscent of that of the Boers in the Cape at the beginning
of the South African War in 1899.

The plaint of Faku's men, however, that they were fired on by the
white troops when they were in fact assisting them is to some extent
supported by a very interesting correspondence between the Commissioner for Native Affairs in Nkandla and the magistrate of Nqutu, C. F.
Hignett, in which reference is made to the white troops "trying to goad
the whole population" into rebellion and to the difficulties the magistrates had in protecting "people who one knew perfectly well were
faithful to us."   Hignett's words are strikingly supported by a long,

and, for him, unusual letter sent by Archdeacon Johnson, the Anglican missionary at St. Augustine's in the Nqutu district, to the secretary of that organization in London. He wrote:

> Many thinking people have been asking themselves "What are we going to do with this teeming native population?" Some stronghanded men have thought that the time was ripe for the solving of the great question. They knew that there was a general widespread spirit of dissatisfaction amongst the natives of Natal, Freestate and Transvaal, but especially in Natal, and they commenced the suppression of the rebellion in the fierce hope that the spirit of the rebellion might so spread throughout the land and engender a war of practical extermination. I fully believe that they were imbued with the conviction that this was the only safe way of dealing with the native question, and they are greatly disappointed that the spirit of rebelling was not strong enough to bring more than a moiety of the native peoples under the influence of the rifle. Over and over again it was said, "they are only sitting on the fence, it shall be our endeavour to push them over"; and again speaking of the big chiefs, "We must endeavour to bring him in if possible." Yes, they have been honest and outspoken enough—the wish being father to the thought, they prophesied the rebellion would spread throughout South Africa; had they been true prophets, no doubt the necessity of solving the native question would have been solved for this generation at least.

Archdeacon Johnson was a highly respected member of the Natal community. He was one of the four non-official members of the Native Affairs Council set up by the government of Natal after the disturbances. He was no wide-eyed novice or fiery philanthropist. Johnson had been in Natal since the age of seven, and justly described himself as "no negrophilist in its narrow rabid sense . . . [but] a colonist and proud of that position."

It could also be argued, however, that it was only the already disaffected and the guilty who would allow themselves to be provoked into aggressive action by the troops. The case of Chief Matshana ka Mondisa would appear to illustrate both the degree of military provocation and this latter point. Although the majority of his tribe assisted the government forces at Nkandla and the chief himself remained in touch with the authorities ever since Bambatha had fled to the district, some members of the tribe broke away under five of his sons, with whom Matshana had been having considerable difficulty for several years.   During the third week in June the tribe was fined five head of cattle per rebel. This fine was promptly paid by Matshana to Mackay, and he was given a "complete discharge." But a week later, a further column under Lt. Colonel J. R. Royston swept through Matshana's ward, gathering up "almost every beast it could find." According to the Commissioner for Native Affairs in Zululand, Royston's "handling of the matter in view of what had already happened under Mackay and Colonel George Leuchars (to whom Matshana had rendered every assistance) was, to say the least, extraordinary." The civil authorities immediately reassured Matshana and his people that their cattle would be restored to them. Although this had not been done by December 1906, no further members of the tribe joined the rebels.

In the midst of offensive operations it must have been very difficult, in any case, for the troops to distinguish between black friend and black foe, even had they been willing to make the effort. With many of the contingents, especially those of volunteers from outside the colony, there was often only one European who spoke or understood the Zulu language.

For them, it must frequently have seemed impossible to draw the distinction between "goading into rebellion" and "taking the necessary precautions." In the Nkandla-Nqutu area, where there undoubtedly was open rebellion—whatever the initial reasons for its outbreak—from the European point of view, that rebellion had to be stamped out as swiftly as possible. The terrain was extremely difficult to operate in, the Mome forests and the Nwandla mountains constituting a natural stronghold, with steep cliffs, deep gorges, and dense bush. If, in the course of the converging movements considered necessary for surrounding the rebels and hunting them out, other, more or less innocent, chiefs and tribes were dragged into the hostilities, it could be held that this was an unfortunate but unavoidable concomitant of warfare.

The Third Stage: Rebellion in the Mapumulo Division

It is, however, more difficult to accept these arguments in the case of the third stage of the disturbances—the outbreak of "rebellion" in the Mapumulo division. On 10 June McKenzie inflicted a crushing and decisive defeat on Bambatha and his followers at the battle of Mome Gorge. Most of the leaders of this phase of the disturbances, including Bambatha himself—whose head was cut off for purposes of "identification"—and Mehlokazulu, were killed. The Governor believed that this blow had brought the rebellion in Zululand to an end, and that there was "no chance whatever of the rebellion spreading into Natal." But on 18 June Africans of Mapumulo attacked Thring's Store, killing a trooper as well as destroying some wagons at Otimati River; it was reported that hundreds of tribesmen had taken up arms.

The timing of this action was the more surprising as Mapumulo, a very densely populated, almost entirely African, area, had been among the first of the districts reported to be disturbed by the poll tax. After the initial refusal on the part of the followers of Ngobizembe, Swaimana, and Meseni to pay the tax, and a subsequent meeting of the Minister for Native Affairs with chiefs in the area, a strong body of police had been sent there at the beginning of February. Following further adverse reports from the division, where tribes had had themselves "doctored" for war, a second column of the field forces had been mobilized under Leuchars especially to deal with them. At the end of February Leuchars delivered an ultimatum to Ngobizembe to hand over within six days three hundred men who had shouted war cries, danced, and brandished sticks in front of the magistrate in January.   Ngobizembe protested that, after the lapse of nearly six weeks, it would be impossible to find all the offenders in the allotted time. He handed over only twenty of the culprits, and, as a result, on 5 March Leuchars bombarded Ngobizembe's kraal with artillery fire from a distance of two hundred yards.   This was reported to have had a "splendid effect." Leuchars, who had been Secretary for Native Affairs, was congratulated by the Governor, Sir Henry McCallum, on his superb understanding of the "native mind," and all over Natal the Africans were reported to have "changed their attitude of studied insolence to one of thorough submission."   Ngobizembe immediately surrendered with a large portion of his tribe, and plans were made to send him to northern Zululand. Half his lands were confiscated and the people thereon placed under adjacent chiefs. He was further fined 1,200 head of cattle and 3,500 sheep and goats. Mounted troops "drove" the country for further "rebels" and cattle. No opposition was shown to these disciplinary actions, although Bambatha, at this time deposed from his chieftainship, was in the neighboring Umvoti bush, watching no doubt with some interest.

While Ngobizembe's was the most drastic fate in Mapumulo at this time, Leuchars also demanded that the "rebels" from Meseni's and Swaimana's chiefdoms be given up. Meseni himself had not actually been present at the time of the alleged defiance of his people over the poll tax. (He had been attending a trial at the Stranger magistracy.) Nevertheless, for not handing over more than fifty-five of the hundred men demanded by Leuchars for trial by court-martial for their participation in the defiance of the Mapumulo magistrate, he was imprisoned without trial for six weeks.   The opportunity was also taken to limit his jurisdiction to those of his people in the Mapumulo-Ndedwe divisions, ostensibly as punishment for his part in a 1905 faction fight.

In March, Ndlovu ka Timuni, another chief in the Mapumulo division, was summoned to Stranger for having failed to appear before the magistrate on two previous occasions and was, "owing to a mistake," detained for more than a month before he too was released without trial.   The arbitrary nature of these proceedings was further illustrated by the case of acting Chief Geveza of the Cele people. Arrested for failing to obey a command to report to Leuchars, who apparently wanted him to be present when Ngobizembe's deposition was read out, he was sentenced under martial law to three months' imprisonment. Geveza's tribe was, in fact, divided between the Krantzkop and Mapumulo divisions, and it would appear that the original summons to hear the deposition had gone to the *induna* of the Mapumulo section of the Cele, Geveza himself residing at Krantzkop. The Krantzkop magistrate himself thought that this was the most likely explanation for Geveza's behavior.

Although the bulk of Leuchar's column, which had been operating in the Mapumulo-Lower Tugela River area, was demobilized in the middle of March, small numbers of troops, especially the Umvoti Mounted Rifles, were retained there. These were later supplemented by a garrison of the Natal Mounted Rifles and the Durban Light Infantry, who were sent there because of the rumors of rebelliousness among the tribesmen, although nothing of a definite nature was proven at this stage. At the end of April some of Ngobizembe's men joined Bambatha in the Nkandla forests.

By the middle of April there were indications that the presence of the troops in the Mapumulo and Lower Tugela divisions was not entirely beneficial. The magistrate of the neighboring Krantzkop division wrote to the Undersecretary for Native Affairs that Chief Tshutshutshu, who had men in both divisions like Geveza, had complained that several members of his tribe had been unjustly flogged by the troops at Mapumulo and that he (the magistrate) had heard several other complaints of a similar nature.   The young men of Tshutshutshu's tribe were later described as having been "insolent and insubordinate" during the initial poll tax collection, but during the actual outbreak of violence in the division to have been "loyal and zealous" in hunting out rebels.

On being asked for an explanation of these allegations of unjust floggings, the head of the Umvoti Mounted Rifles replied to the commandant of the militia that:

> The natives in question were punished for insolent behaviour and for not showing the required respect for the King's uniform. Strong measures had to be resorted to to teach the natives who had utterly got out of hand . . . to pay their respects to the white man.

This action was fully approved by the commandant of the militia   and apparently roused no further comment at the time. Yet a few weeks later Sir James Liege Hulett, a man who had held various responsible positions in the colony—having been a member of the Natal Parliament since responsible government and Secretary for Native Affairs in 1899, as well as being one of the largest sugar farmers in the colony with considerable interests in Zululand—was to write earnestly and urgently from his sugar estates in the neighborhood of Mapumulo to the Prime Minister of the serious state of affairs there. Once again, these words cannot be dismissed as those of an attention-seeking negrophile and have to be quoted at some length:

> The native population is absolutely docile and quiet throughout the district, [though] how long they will remain so depends upon the government; if they are to be harried by irresponsible men who act as demi-Gods and who, armed with a kind of self-imposed authority, think it the correct thing to flog unoffending people . . . then the area will be drawn into the area of disaffected with the result that the [European] people [here] . . . will have to leave their homes, wives and plantations to the mercy of an outraged foe. . . . Pray let us have a level-headed man at the head of affairs at Mapumulo and put a stop to this nonsense of having every man in uniform requiring every native to conform to his idea of what salutation consists of. This [illegible] people is being driven into rebellion and it speaks volumes for [their] good sense . . . that they have not risen.

A few days later ministers heard from another source that the troops were using their leather stirrups to impress upon the natives "due respect" and to obtain information, and gave as their unanimous opinion that this "should immediately be put to a stop."

Even in peacetime, the extent to which Natal magistrates resorted to the lash was greater than in any of the other South African colonies at this time. As de Kiewiet has remarked, the temptation for a small, insecure white population to resort to rule by terror was immense. In the absence of consent, the Africans of Natal were governed by a thinly veiled use of force, even in peacetime.

In all the South African colonies except Natal, sentences involving flogging had to be reviewed by a judge of the supreme court. In 1907 in Natal, where there was no such check, one in every four hundred of the total male population was flogged, exclusive of young boys sentenced to birching;   during the disturbances, according to the *Times of Natal,*   seven hundred Africans had their backs lashed to ribbons and four thousand seven hundred sentences, including lashes, were carried out before the government itself put an end to this "judicial violence." The paper continued: "We wonder if any official record exists of the number flogged, so to say on sight, during the . . . expedition . . . in that year."

In Natal there was little of the lynching and public violence which has characterized race relations in the southern states of the United States; nevertheless, this form of legalized brutality appears to have constituted an adequate substitute and was, in many ways, probably the outcome of the same psychological factors. It is beyond the scope of this essay to explore this aspect of settler mentality; nevertheless, in finally prompting into action those Africans who had already watched their cattle confiscated and their kraals destroyed, it cannot be ignored. It would also go a long way toward explaining the "puzzling" feature of this last phase of the disturbances—why it was that after the rebellion was so clearly a hopeless and dying cause the chiefs in the Mapumulo-Lower Tugela area should suddenly have taken up arms, especially after many of them had already paid their poll taxes and had suffered for their previous recalcitrance. If the "doctoring" of tribes in January and February, regarded by Stuart as revealing the most hostile intentions to the white man, was intended as a preliminary to war, it is difficult to explain why more of the Mapumulo men did not either join the Nkandla army or rise at the same time when the bulk of the forces was engaged there.

Stuart's explanation of this very odd course of action is that messengers were sent from Dinuzulu's uncle, Siteku, to Meseni, Matshwili, and Nklovu ka Timuni, inciting them to rise only after the Battle of Mome Gorge. Yet this hardly seems a sufficient reason for their curious action, especially as the Commissioner for Native Affairs himself found these allegations "most unsatisfactory"; he had had a long interview with Meseni and Ndlovu ka Timuni when they surrendered and, despite the most careful examination on the question of whether they had been encouraged from Zululand, "they gave not the slightest hint that that was so." Many may have been induced to take up arms by the rumor that the Africans had been successful at Mome Gorge and that all the white soldiers had been killed which was apparently circulated in the Mapumulo area by survivors of Mome Gorge.

That this rumor could long have lasted in face of the overwhelming disaster inflicted on 10 June, however, seems most unlikely. A member of Chief Ngobizembe's people in this division appeared to be giving the general African view when he told the Natal Native Affairs Commission that:

Before they had an opportunity of making any reply and stating that they thought the taxes already existing were heavy enough, they were threatened with being shot. They thereupon paid, but while they were still paying hostilities broke out. It was a matter of curiosity on their side as to whether the government really wanted this tax or whether they wanted their lives.

The Mapumulo rebels were to pay dearly for their uprising: about 1,500 Africans were killed, 1,300 prisoners taken, and thousands of people rendered homeless and starving by the burning of their crops and kraals in the division.   Even after the surrender of the chief leaders of the rebellion there, and long after the government considered such action to be necessary, these "punitive measures" continued.   The Governor referred to the "sweeping actions" and "mopping up operations" in this division and neighboring Lower Tugela as "continued slaughter," and Frederick Graham, at the Colonial Office, a man not given to hyperbole, called it a "massacre."   While many atrocities had been ascribed to the troops in other areas, it could be argued that these were generally in the heat of battle. In this area, the atrocities continued long after the heat of battle had burnt out. They were eventually stopped only as a result of action by the government.

Conclusions

There were those, even in 1906, who saw the entire rebellion as deliberately contrived by the government, the white settlers, or, indeed, by that bogey of left-wing thought in the early twentieth century, the Transvaal mine owners, for the purpose of grabbing the Africans' land and forcing them to work in the goldfields. There is little evidence to support such views. Both the government and the settlers feared rebellion as much as they were determined to stamp it out completely once it occurred. Their blundering, misunderstanding, and insensitivity must, however, be counted among the factors which led to the flare-up of violence in 1906. There is more evidence, but even this perhaps in the very nature of things is not absolute, that once the military men were in the field they exacerbated the situation considerably. Although it is true that in the long run the mine owners profited from the 1906 disturbances, as the number of Africans forced onto the labor market of the mines grew from 17,900 in 1906 to 34,200 in 1910,   it was certainly not only the rebellion which caused this. Nor, of course, can one argue from this that the mine owners were in any way directly or indirectly responsible for this result, however much they had wanted to increase their labor supply. Among neither blacks nor whites is there much evidence of a conspiracy, although much of "cross purposes rampant on a sea of rumor."

Nevertheless, the official view in Natal that the campaigns were conducted with the utmost humanity and the contention that only swift action saved thousands of white women and children from being murdered by black hordes also does not bear much scrutiny. Of both extreme views it can be said "not proven." The words of the veteran Cape politician, John X. Merriman, summed up the feeling of the more liberal element in South Africa, when he wrote to Goldwin Smith in September 1906:

> We have had a horrible business in Natal with the natives. I suppose the whole truth will never be known, but enough comes out to make us see how thin the crust is that keeps our Christian civilization from the old-fashioned savagery—machine guns and modern rifles against knob-sticks and assegais are heavy odds and do not add much to the glory of the superior races.

If the rebellion had not added "much to the glory of the superior races," it had inflicted a shattering blow on the African population of Natal and Zululand. From the military point of view, the army had indeed "solved" the "native question" for their generation. Although there was some change of heart among a handful of white Natalians on the subject of their treatment of the African population, and an attempt was made to "reform" the "native policy," there was little change in the poverty-stricken and depressed conditions of African life. Among whites outside Natal the disturbances illuminated the dangers of allowing a small white community to handle a question so vital to the rest of southern Africa. The growing movement toward a unification of South Africa in order to ensure the dominance of the white man was given a considerable spur forward. But on the positive side, Africans too were increasingly realizing the need for political unity. While all over southern Africa the futility of opposing the white man by force of arms was realized once and for all, the need for education, for new political organizations, and modern political weapons was appreciated more widely than ever before. In the formation of the South African Native National Congress in 1912 (later to be renamed the African National Congress) the lessons of 1906 were writ large.

THE NYABINGI CULT OF

SOUTHWESTERN UGANDA

ELIZABETH HOPKINS

The coalescence of traditionally diverse populations in opposition to European rule has been a recurrent feature of the colonial process. In the Mfumbiro region between Lake Kivu and Lake Edward there was, however, an unusual, if not unique variant, for the polarization of anti-European sentiment into active and co-ordinated resistance occurred before the local implementation of administrative control. The immediacy of the response, the degree of regional and tribal coordination and, above all, the effectiveness and duration of resistance, distinguish the Nyabingi cult from similar movements of protest.

The matrix for protest was familiar: an initial claim to superior supernatural powers, later used to validate claims to a monopoly of secular control. The idiom for political opposition—an indigenous possession cult—is again not without historical parallel in Africa. What is striking is that, despite a strong parochialism of method and purpose, the Nyabingi cult succeeded in immobilizing the administrative efforts of three colonial powers for nearly two decades, until its final suppression in 1928. That a traditional possession cult, without significant ideological modification, could remain such a tenacious and effective vehicle for opposition to alien rule ensures the Nyabingi cult a distinctive position in the history of colonial Africa.

The Cult of Nyabingi

The cult of Nyabingi was one of a number of possession cults found throughout the western interlacustrine area which celebrated legendary heroes called *emandwa*. While in a number of cults the *emandwa* could be summoned by any initiated member, in the Nyabingi cult access to the spirit was limited to the *bagirwa,* or specialists, each of whom claimed to have been selected by Nyabingi as her medium and therefore to have the exclusive power to invoke her presence and to interpret her will. In consequence, there were no initiation rites or communal rituals to provide a more egalitarian focus for cult activity.

As in other *emandwa* cults, the presence of the spirit was marked by possession, but the diagnostic behavior, to confirm the claim of privileged access to the spirit, was more elaborate and demanded greater skill. Among the techniques associated with possession by Nyabingi were the assumption of a stylized trembling movement, ventriloquism, and the ability to hold a "dialogue" with the spirit in an esoteric language and in falsetto. Other eccentricities of behavior reinforced these attributes of possession. Emin Pasha, describing similar specialists in the court of Bunyoro, observed that they were "most striking figures" who "vie with one another in eccentricities." One "grunted every minute," another "spoke in the highest falsetto," while a third "sat down beside one of [Emin's] company, and wanted her shoulders rubbed and her head bent." This erratic behavior, intensified by its supernatural associations, could easily be parlayed by a skilled practitioner into more pervasive claims of influence. Muhumusa, one of the more forceful and feared of the Nyabingi leaders, was acknowledged by colonial officers to be "an extraordinary character":

> By dint of years of training, she has acquired a high falsetto voice and professes inability to walk normally, her method of position being on tip-toe in a crouching position with the aid of two sticks. . . . The chiefs with scarcely an exception trembled whenever her look was directed toward them. She also made most noticeable efforts to exercise some form of hypnotism over me.

Basic to the demonstration and revalidation of the claimed power of the *bagirwa* was the ability to evoke supernatural forces to punish those who angered or ignored the spirit or who failed to accede to Nyabingi's demands for offerings. Once their power to curse had been demonstrated by a few strategic acts of misfortune, the mere threat of such action was sufficient to ensure that further demands for grain, livestock, or beer would be met. So strong was local belief in the ability of an offended *mugirwa* (specialist) to inflict violent physical illness that any sudden acute pain was called *nabingi amuunbe* or "Nyabingi has cursed me." Evidence given during the trial of a cult leader in 1938 confirms the critical role of the curse in establishing the reputation of a *mugirwa*:

The Acc. used to ask people forcibly to offer to him cows in the way of frightening them. There was also a Munyarwanda man called Ka-bundami who refused to give the Acc. a cow but afterwards this man was killed by a lion because the Acc. used to say that as the man had refused to offer him a cow he would not live long. Therefore this was a surprise to other people and immediately they began to fear Acc. very much.

While the threat of acute illness served as the major technique for intimidation, an aura of supernatural power was also cultivated to reinforce the claims of the *bagirwa* to curative and malevolent powers. As J. E. T. Philipps reported, "Every attempt is made to surround the simplest action with supernatural significance."¹ The studied eccentricities of behavior also provided a major psychological barrier between the *bagirwa* and ordinary Africans.

The influence of the *bagirwa* was further strengthened by secular conventions which marked their social distance as important political leaders. All relied on restricting the access of outsiders to specific cult channels by remaining in seclusion in their encampment and by receiving suppliants within the sacred hut. Some were never seen by their adherents, while others only appeared publicly on litters—a prerogative of royalty in the interlacustrine area—shrouded in bark cloth or with their faces veiled. This public posture unquestionably created social distance by manipulating the traditional symbols of royalty. It also reinforced the claims of the *bagirwa* to unique supernatural powers through depersonalization and, for the male cult leader, through the affectation of a female pattern of dress.

Finally, physical violence or the threat of physical violence was also used to consolidate the authority of the *bagirwa* both within the cult and among non-adherents. Philipps states that force was "frequently" used against those who showed evidence of disloyalty. Non-adherents who resisted the movement and its demands for allegiance and gifts were also subject to punitive raids in which their property was destroyed or confiscated. While the claims of a *mugirwa* to supernatural power were in themselves a major incentive for compliance, they were unquestionably reinforced by the presence of a sizable armed following in his personal entourage. Testimony elicited during the trial of Ndungutsi in 1938 indicated that he was accompanied by some sixty men who conspicuously displayed the traditional weapons —the bow and arrow and shield—long after they had been eliminated by political conditions and by the administrative pressures of *pax Brittanica*.

As the reputation of a *mugirwa* increased, his ability to exact offerings from the local population also grew. This in turn meant an enlargement of his personal entourage, for the tribute permitted the elaboration of a redistributive network based on personal patronage. The allocation of cattle, in particular, provided an effective way of attracting supporters. One witness stated:

> I know that my cattle died of 1936 rinderpest and when I was in sorrows then there came to me a munyarwanda man and told me that I should not cry because of my cattle died as there was a new king at a village called Kibeho . . . that he is saving people by giving them cattle as presents. On receiving this information I went and joined Acc. . . . where he gave me a heifer Kahogo as present, which was offered to him by one called Mazosio.

Thus the entry of a *mugirwa* into a new territory was marked not merely by his acquisition of goods but by the promise of the distribution of beer and cattle. As in the secular system of authority, economic action was used to support political claims.

The ascendancy of Nyabingi over other *emandwa* cults in the Mfumbiro area was based in large part on the distinctive hierarchical pattern of the cult structure. By restricting access to the spirit to the *bagirwa*, the cult provided considerable leverage for the economic, political, and psychological manipulation of followers and for the extension of control over those who did not voluntarily seek the protection of Nyabingi. The continuity of the movement was further facilitated by the belief that were a leader killed or removed from an area, the spirit of Nyabingi would select another host. Thus the death or disappearance of any given leader did not threaten the cult itself. This ideology of a shifting locus of supernatural power was unquestionably central to the rapid acceptance of the Nyabingi in areas which had successfully resisted secular control by adjacent kingdoms.

Origins of the Cult

The origins of the Nyabingi cult are obscure but two persisting traditions serve to illuminate the character of the cult during the colonial period. In one version, the cult was introduced into Rwanda during the last half of the nineteenth century by two Rwanda cattle traders returning from Uzinza, a kingdom to the southeast. When misfortune befell those refusing to acknowledge Nyabingi, the reputation of the cult and the recruitment of adherents rapidly accelerated. The response eventually became so widespread that the "enormous flow" of gifts and fees seriously disrupted not only the traditional Rwanda cults but the collection of royal tribute as well.

The movement entered a more activist phase when local cult leaders, protesting the defection of so many of their adherents, appealed to the Rwanda chiefs for support. The *bagirwa* countered by urging the Hutu of the area to rebel against the privileged position of the Tutsi. As the cult continued to grow and to encourage such openly seditious sentiments, it became of direct concern to the *mwami*, the ruler of Rwanda. In response to appeals of the local chiefs, he sent an expedition against the Nyabingi. Although the cult leader and many of his entourage were killed and their livestock confiscated, unrest continued for the spirit of Nyabingi was reported to have "moved on." Soon a *mugirwa* claiming the powers of Nyabingi and effecting dramatic cures appeared in another area. Again, as the cult gained members, it became more explicitly political in character, stressing its protective role toward the Hutu and the iniquities of the Tutsi superstructure. As before, local chiefs soon complained to the *mwami* of their weakening authority but it was only when labor and tribute were no longer given in the dissident area that the *mwami* again marched against the cult. The leader and his adherents were killed and the countryside in the rebellious area destroyed, but once again a girl from the subjugated area was rumored to have received the spirit of Nyabingi and the influence of the cult moved northward. This pattern of extortion, disruption of existing channels of labor and tribute, and subversion against the Tutsi, followed by retaliatory expeditions and the execution of the cult leaders, continued as a cyclical phenomenon in northern Rwanda throughout the final years of the precolonial period.

The second tradition of origin places the focus for cult development and activity north of Rwanda in Mpororo. In this version, Nyabingi was a historical figure who ruled Ndorwa-Kajara before the formation of Mpororo. In the dynastic accounts of the Hororo, Kamurari, the founder of Mpororo, found the region ruled by an "Amazon Queen," Kitami. By procuring the royal drum from Kitami, Kamurari obtained control over the heartland of Mpororo. According to this version, Kitami was only later apotheosized as the spirit Nyabingi. J. M. Gray, in contrast, feels that the name Nyabingi, "she who possesses many things," was an alternative title to Kitami. He also suggests that the usurpation of her authority by the invading Hororo provided the key to the recurrently seditious character of the Nyabingi cult:

> After her death she became immortal and continued to issue her decrees through the mouths of her Bagirwa (lit. "those who initiate"), who were almost invariably women. The doctrines preached by these Bagirwa were those of the old regime. It is therefore not surprising to

find that the latter-day rulers of the land regarded them as enemies and made war upon them. It is also not surprising to learn that upon occasion devotees of the cult rose in rebellion and killed leaders of the invading races.

Rwanda sources, in contrast, assert that Nyabingi was either a royal princess of Ndorwa or—perhaps a later ideological expediency —a Hutu attached as a servant to the Ndorwa court. In either event, as in the Abashambo legends, she never married and, under varying circumstances, met a sudden and violent death. Marcel Pauwels, who provides certain linguistic evidence in support of the northern origin of the cult, asserts that before 1865 and the accession of Rwabugiri as *mwami* in Rwanda, the Nyabingi rarely carried their activities south into Rwanda.

In the origins as perceived in this version, we also find a key to the politically volatile role which the cult played in Rwanda during the latter half of the nineteenth century: "Il est également à noter que les Batutsi du Ruanda ne montrent aucun enthousiasme pour ce culte de Nyabingi; mais cela n'est pas étonnant puis qu'il est censé honorer une princesse étrangère dont la famille fut fréquemment en guerre avec les rois du Ruanda." Although it is not clear under what circumstances Philipps acquired his version of the Nyabingi legend, the corroborative evidence of the presence of the cult in Mpororo would seem to point to a northern rather than southern origin. Here the only puzzling discrepancy is May M. Edel's statement that the movement reached the Kiga, who are territorially contiguous to Mpororo and in an area designated today as Ndorwa, from Rwanda. Her informants in 1933 seemed in accord that the movement had been recently introduced into their area by Rwanda moving in from the south. Yet the claims of the *bagirwa* to the Ndorwa tradition could only encourage Kiga identification with the cult. The royal idiom of the Ndorwa tradition also provided a more effective validation of both the political pretensions and the patterns of centralization which the cult imposed without hesitation in the more acephalous areas.

Early Political Techniques of the Nyabingi Cult

The earliest European reference to Nyabingi confirms the presence of the cult in Mpororo during the final years of the nineteenth century. Although Stanley had alluded to reports in Karagwe of an "Empress of Ruanda," it was only during his expedition of 1889 that reports were first heard of the "Wanyanvingi." It is apparent that during his second expedition Stanley retained the impression that Rwanda was "Unyavingi." To judge from his location of the territory, however, he was actually describing Mpororo: "a large, compact country, lying between the Alexandra Nile [the Kagera River] and the Congo watershed to the west, and reaching to within one day's long march to the Albert Edward." The confusion is compounded by his observation that "the late Queen has been succeeded by her son, Kigeri," for at no time was the Rwanda throne under the control of a woman.

The final journey of Emin Pasha north in 1891 provided important information on the position of the cult in Mpororo:

> The Queen of Mpororo . . . said to be a woman named Njavingi . . . has never been seen by anyone, not even her own subjects. All that they ever get to know of her is a voice heard behind a curtain of bark cloth. Such theatrical practices have gained for her, throughout Karagwe, Nkole etc., the reputation of a great sorceress, capable of bewitching people and also of benefiting them.

Her authority over the chieftaincies of Mpororo was, however, far from monolithic. Emin Pasha observed, "[she] appears to be acknowledged by part of her subjects only." As for her ability effectively to control those areas of Mpororo which she claimed, Emin noted:

> The whole of Mpororo has fallen into a complete state of lawlessness, owing to the circumstances that the Queen has no authority whatever, and there is no protection whatever for the subjects.

Yet his diaries indicate that those chiefs who did acknowledge her suzerainty were fearful and anxious to avoid her anger.

A partial explanation for these discontinuities in control lies in the political state of Mpororo at that period and in the *modus operandi* used by the *bagirwa* to gain the obedience of the existing Mpororo chieftaincies. In consequence of raiding from the adjacent and more centralized kingdoms of Rwanda, Nkore, and Buganda, Mpororo had become depopulated, a "no man's land." The ascendancy of the Nyabingi cult in this area appears to have been in large part a response to the severe dislocations caused by these external political pressures. Exploiting the existing instability, the leaders of the cult were able to assert an uncontested if nominal claim to sovereignty over Mpororo, though their actual control over the Hororo chieftaincies was at best erratic. This failure of the cult to provide a viable focus for political unification despite the external stimulus for consolidation is of particular interest, given the later role of the cult in the more acephalous areas of Kigezi to the west.

It is also apparent from Emin's account that the incumbent Nyabingi was well aware of the tenuous character of her claim to power. Nevertheless, she was clearly determined to impose control over the entire Mpororo area. In fact, she hoped to manipulate Emin to this end. Exploiting the vulnerability of Emin's caravan and its need for guides, porters, and fresh supplies, she urged Emin to remain in Mpororo "to set the country in order, so that Njavingi might rule again." As an inducement for such services, Emin was told to "pillage wherever I liked, seize people and confiscate cattle."

If Emin's information is correct, control over the fragmented chieftaincies of Mpororo required secular techniques which he himself had observed:

> Queen Njavingi has repeatedly called in the aid of her more powerful neighbour, King Ntali of Nkole, to punish her rebellious chiefs, and on such occasions he pillages their respective districts. Something of the kind happened here three months ago, the northern part of Makovoli's district being laid waste; he therefore hastens now to make his peace, quite neglecting us in his anxiety.

Thus it is clear that the effective domination of the Hororo demanded not merely the familiar cult techniques of secular intimidation or threatened supernatural vengeance but the manipulation of a larger intertribal context. By exploiting the raiding patterns of adjacent, more powerful kingdoms, the *bagirwa* acquired a far more efficient executive machinery than could have been generated internally, given the competing claims of an hereditary chiefly structure. The basis for cult power thus rested both on the threat of supernatural retaliation and on the enlistment of a more powerful polity (in this case, Nkore) as an ally in the exploitation of this unstable and vulnerable area.

The pattern of cult expansion into Mpororo reflects the structural limitations of such a movement. Unable to compete for control of the core areas of Rwanda or Nkore, and presumably unmotivated to exploit the acephalous, predominantly agricultural Kiga, the cult was restricted in the precontact period to marginal but centralized areas on the periphery of the larger pastoral states. As such, the motives for intimidation were there, as well as the mechanisms for the accumulation of goods through existing redistributive networks. To utilize these networks, however, it was essential either to displace the Hororo chiefs or to obtain their tacit co-operation. Whereas to the south, in Rwanda, the cult stood in active opposition to the existing chiefly structure, in the Mpororo area the strategy for control emphasized the incorporation of the indigenous chiefs into the larger cult structure as local representatives of Nyabingi.

Despite continuing intertribal unrest and the expansion of European colonial activity, Mpororo remained under the nominal control of the Nyabingi cult throughout the final decades of the nineteenth century. The earliest colonial references to the cult come from the adjacent territory of Ankole, which was established as an administrative district at the end of 1898. In the political reports for 1901, reference is made to the "disturbed state of a place east of Buchika under a chief named Muhumuzi." Perhaps even more illuminating is a report that cattle captured by German patrols after a punitive expedition against a local chief "are now with Navingi, chieftainess of Omupundi."

Thus, by 1901, the cult had moved within the orbit of the German administration and appeared to be manipulating the Germans to consolidate its position against the secular chiefly structure. Two years later the Germans were openly drawn into the political network of the cult when two *bagirwa* near the border sought the support of Lieutenant Weiss of the Anglo-Belgian Boundary Commission. One, on the German side, was concerned with suppressing local dissidence; the other, in British territory, saw the presence of the Boundary Commission as an opportunity to overthrow her weaker rival to the south. Weiss refused to help either one and urged the latter to return to her own country. Also south of the border at that time was the *mugirwa,* Muhumusa, who within a few years would achieve notoriety in both British and German territories. In 1903, however, she was fully cooperative with the survey party. From Weiss's account it is clear that even at that time she exercised considerable authority over her followers.

The open co-operation of the cult leaders with these alien intruders reflects the political focus of the cult at the time of contact. Whether intent upon consolidating the small, weak chieftaincies of the Mpororo area or upon subverting the central authorities of the larger kingdom of Rwanda to the south, the cult represented throughout the region the major vehicle for opposition to the established authority structure of each tribe. The initial response of the *bagirwa* to the European betrayed no re-alignment of cult interests which would place the cult in opposition to colonial rule. Their action reflects, on the contrary, a consolidation of existing political contests to accommodate this new political perimeter. Cult intent was, however, to be rapidly redefined during the initial years of colonial overrule. With this realignment, the parochial concerns of the indigenous period were cast aside to permit a co-ordinated intertribal action which openly and simultaneously challenged the suzerain claims of three colonial powers. Yet it is in the traditional expectations of the cult leaders and in the tactical and ideological resilience of its indigenous history that we must seek an explanation for the character of cult activity during the colonial period.

Muhumusa

At the beginning of the twentieth century, northern Rwanda was controlled by a series of refractory chiefs who refused to acknowledge the
suzerain claims of the incumbent *mwami*, Musinga. Foremost among
them was the *mugirwa*, Muhumusa, whose position in the traditional
Rwanda structure had unquestionably facilitated her rapid ascension
to unchallenged regional prominence among the *bagirwa* of the Nyabingi cult. A widow of the late *mwami*, Rwabugiri, Muhumusa was,
according to M. J. Bessell, also the mother of the designated heir,
Bulegeya, who had been an infant at the time of Rwabugiri's death
in 1894. Bulegeya's selection was, however, successfully challenged
by Musinga, and Muhumusa was forced to flee northward, at last
finding a safe refuge in Ndorwa, the mountainous area of southeastern
Kigezi. There, by the borders of Ruanda, she was removed from any
further harassment by the new *mwami*.

Undeterred by her defeat, Muhumusa decided to use Ndorwa as
a base of operations from which to reassert a claim to the throne. To
secure her position there, as an intruder, it was necessary to acquire
local political influence, for the Kiga were fragmented into isolated,
hostile hamlets by internecine feuds. Unless her reputation could
transcend the xenophobic predispositions of the Kiga, it would have
been impossible for Muhumusa to maintain her organizational network
or to contact her supporters in Rwanda.

It was in order to achieve such authority that Muhumusa turned
somewhat ironically to a cult which had proven in Rwanda an effective
vehicle against her late husband and against the Tutsi chiefly structure. In the Ndorwa area, on the periphery of Mpororo, however, the
cult represented a viable agency for unification, not sedition.

Although Muhumusa's activities were not initially anti-European,
her considerable influence with local chiefs in German Ruanda
marked her as a potential political threat to the newly imposed colonial administration. Moreover, increasing German control in Ruanda
and German recognition of the legitimacy of Musinga made the movement by implication hostile to German authority as an extension of the
existing chiefly structure.

In 1907 the German Resident capitulated to Musinga's demand
that Muhumusa be driven from northern Ruanda, for he recognized
the importance of consolidating the authority of the Rwanda throne.

It was not until the following year, however, that Muhumusa, while in German Mpororo, was arrested by the Germans and detained in Bukoba for two years. Although the official charge was that she had conspired against Kisiribombo, the chief in whose territory she was apprehended, Bessell refers to Kisiribombo as an "influential adherent" and ascribes her visit to German Mpororo as an effort to enlist military support for her claim to the Rwanda throne.

Upon her release in 1910, Muhumusa returned to British Ndorwa where she strengthened her forces by recruiting two notorious Rwanda outlaws. Although they were attracted to her services by motives of personal gain, not political commitment, her choice revealed considerable tactical acumen, for one was a Hutu and the other a Twa. By selecting as her lieutenants men who represented non-Tutsi strata of Rwanda society, she maximized allegiance within her following and muted the issue of royal factional interests in favor of a more generalized image of liberation. It was at this time also that Muhumusa again proclaimed her son Bulegeya to be the rightful *mwami* and, with considerable popular support, began a peaceful advance on the capital. The Germans, by now quite sensitive to her political potential and presumably concerned by her rapid resumption of cult activity, quickly intercepted her and forced her final retreat to Ndorwa.

The Occupation of Kigezi

During the three years of quasi-civilian British occupation which preceded the appointment of a District Commissioner in 1913, the administration of Kigezi was assumed by a Special Mission under the charge of a single European officer. Handicapped both by his small military force and by the tenuous international status of the mission, the Political Officer was assigned to Kigezi primarily to validate the British claim to effective occupation of the area, not to supervise the population or to impose any fiscal or administrative requirements. However, his relationship to the local population, his response to openly defiant acts, and the decision, perhaps inevitable, to employ Ganda as government agents, were all critical in defining the character of subsequent civilian administrative patterns in Kigezi.

The problem of effective administration was further exacerbated by the geopolitical character of the district. At the time when the British assumed control of Kigezi, northern Ruanda and the adjacent British areas of Bufumbiro and Rukiga were areas of political marginality, territorial and ethnic ambiguity, and physical inaccessibility. They had, in consequence, become a refuge for fugitives from both

British and German authorities and from the pressures of the indigenous political system.

Efforts at control were further complicated by the arbitrary character of the international boundaries which defined both the southern
and western margins of Kigezi district. Although the international
boundary to the east was later revised to conform to the natural and
indigenously recognized barrier of the Kagera River, Kigezi's borders
remained subject to the original international agreement, which had
placed political concessions and compromise above the ethnic or political realities of the region. In consequence, the international boundaries
arbitrarily transected two of the three major tribes of the district, the
Kiga and Rwanda, creating an artificial political barrier in the existing
networks of communication within ethnically homogeneous areas. Only
the Hororo, who occupied northeastern Kigezi, retained their traditional political integrity during the colonial period.

The ethnic heterogeneity of the district further exacerbated the
task of early administrative control. While two of the three tribes spoke
mutually intelligible languages, all were culturally and politically distinct: the Hororo of Ruzumbura formed the westernmost extension of
Mpororo, an ethnically homogeneous region of small autonomous chieftaincies; the Kiga represented a mountain enclave of acephalous peoples
within the interlacustrine area; and the Rwanda, the northernmost extension of the kingdom of Rwanda, whose capital now lay well to the
south, in German territory. Moreover, all three tribes brought with them
the legacy of Rwanda's efforts to expand northward into areas occupied
by the Kiga and the Hororo. Although these invasions had been successfully resisted, they had created the conditions for mutual distrust
during the colonial period and for the priority of tribal identification
to district affiliation.

The lag in time between the final clarification in Europe of the
international boundaries of the Mfumbiro area and their actual demarcation in East Africa also led to local political tensions. During the
years in which the boundaries were surveyed and marked, the disputed
territory along the Congo and Ruanda borders was avoided by each
colonial power. With the delineation of these borders, previously un-
disturbed patterns of raiding were suddenly recast as acts of international hostility, to be avenged by the aggrieved colonial power in
order to validate its claim to effective authority. Intervention during
this period was, however, arbitrary, occurring only in response to
protests initiated by local administrators. Such protests, in turn, were
only elicited by the more spectacular acts of indigenous aggression,
such as raids which involved not merely the confiscation of cattle but
the murder or abduction of women.

While such sporadic regulative action might have had some effect, for the most part the traditional political networks continued to operate without interruption, both because of the limited visibility of events from the British post at Kumba and because control of these networks was not at the time considered a responsibility of British claims to suzerainty. In August of 1911, however, a series of events occurred which could not discreetly be circumvented by the officer at Kumba, for they represented a direct challenge to his authority.

Muhumusa 1911

In retreating to Ndorwa after her unsuccessful march upon the Rwanda capital, Muhumusa had been forced to redefine both her political goals and her strategy. The alignment of German forces in support of Musinga had signaled the futility of any further action with regard to the Rwanda throne. Furthermore, this shifting balance of power in German Ruanda had been complemented by the British occupation of Kigezi during the years of Muhumusa's detention in Bukoba. Returning to Ndorwa after an absence of two years, Muhumusa was confronted both by a loss of influence among the Kiga and by the British political post at Kumba. In addition, although earlier military routes had avoided Ndorwa, the Anglo-German Boundary Commission in 1911 crossed the center of her putative territory, erecting boundary pillars.

The conjunction of the failure of the Rwanda offensive, Muhumusa's deteriorating position among the Kiga, and the threatened encroachment of the British into Ndorwa transformed the Nyabingi cult under Muhumusa into a militant and explicitly anti-European movement. Proclaiming herself Queen of Ndorwa, liberator from European domination, Muhumusa, in August and September of 1911, began a series of raids against the Kiga who refused to give her cattle or resisted her claims to authority. Although ostensibly her intention was to drive all Europeans from the area, her efforts during this initial campaign were directed only against the Kiga. The testimony of one Ganda chief does suggest, however, that the ideological focus for punitive action was the degree of local co-operation with the British:

> When she came in August . . . she had many Ruanda people with her and also Ruhiga people. She gave out that she had much power and that if anyone would follow her, she would drive out the Europeans. . . . She did no harm to those people over there until she

reached the country of those who were willing to be under the Europeans.

Directly confronting this conflicting claim to sovereignty, Muhumusa demanded cattle from local loyalist chiefs as a symbol of their renunciation of British affiliation. Any ambivalence about continuing contact with European agents was met with a series of ruthless and punitive raids in which villages were burned and pillaged. All those who resisted were killed or driven to seek refuge elsewhere.

Her *modus operandi,* and the pattern of her advance into central Kigezi from the Ndorwa area, are most effectively revealed in the following affidavit by the Agent:

> I first heard of her in last August of this year. In that month a Chief . . . came and told me that Muhumusa was stopping him from coming to me; that she, Muhumusa, said that he and other Chiefs belonged to her and not to me. I sent for Ruagalla, the big Chief to confirm this, which he did.
> . . . When Ruagalla came to me he complained to me that Muhumusa had sent word to him and others to take cattle to her. Ruagalla asked me, as they were hitherto under British Protection, whether this was right.

When Ruagalla and other chiefs refused to change their allegiances, Muhumusa began a series of attacks which laid waste to the district and forced their displacement northward to areas adjacent to the British post at Kumba.

Her success in intimidating the Kiga soon led Muhumusa to be more audacious and less oblique in her efforts to eliminate the British threat to her suzerain claim. The bitterness generated by the failure of the British post to take action, despite local appeals for protection, unquestionably accelerated support for the movement. The Political Officer was handicapped, however, not merely by the size of his forces and his isolation but by the indeterminate status of the area occupied by Muhumusa—then designated "Eastern Rukiga"—and by the international range of her operations.

By the end of September, however, Muhumusa had attained a position of "complete ascendancy" over the Kiga. As a mark of her confidence, she moved her fortified headquarters well within British territory. Her encampment now represented a direct challenge to colonial control for it was located within a few miles of the Kumba post. From there, Muhumusa openly confronted the British by threatening to burn down the post which had, by that time, become swollen with refugees and their livestock.

Faced with such an unambiguous act of insolence, E. H. Reid, the Political Officer, found it necessary "in the interests of British Prestige" to take military action against her. On 28 September, a combined force of the King's African Rifles, the Uganda police, and local loyalist levies quietly encircled her encampment and attacked without warning. The confrontation was both brief and successful. The decisive factor appears, however, to have been the expectations and morale of Nyabingi's adherents, not the efficiency of the British forces.

Critical to the rapid routing of the encampment was "the particular legend which obtained the greatest credence among the local Bakiga . . . that the bullets of the Wazungu [Europeans] would turn to water against her." When the ammunition of the British forces proved clearly superior to Muhumusa's claims of immunity, resistance broke and her followers fled. Muhumusa herself was wounded in the foot and captured.

The arrest of Muhumusa created further political complications, for the area in which she was captured—although internationally recognized as British territory—had not yet been officially incorporated into the Uganda Protectorate. In consequence, the Principal Judge in Entebbe ruled that the Political Officer had no jurisdiction to prosecute Muhumusa through the courts of the Protectorate.

After the arrest of Muhumusa, nominal peace returned to the district and chiefs previously ambivalent or aligned with Muhumusa once again came to the British post to acknowledge their subordinate position within the British superstructure. The detention of Muhumusa in the Kigezi area continued, however, to generate unrest. Kikeri, a Tutsi chief, refused to submit to British authority, protesting "his deity says he will die if he should go into Kumba to see the White Man." More indirectly, rumors reached the British officer that Kikeri was organizing a plot to rescue Muhumusa which involved the importation of "numbers of Ba-ruanda" and the "murder of loyalist chiefs." Again, however, the Political Officer was handicapped by the jurisdictional limitations to his authority:

> As Kikeri is at present in territory still nominally German I am disposed to leave him for the present in the hopes that either [his followers will] disperse quietly, or, should he raid the local natives, that they may settle him by themselves.

Responding to a warning from the Resident of Ruanda, Reid did prepare for a possible invasion by strengthening the installations at Kumba and by deploying patrols of Ganda agents and "local natives" along the road to German Ruanda. These patrols, it was felt, would

ensure "ample warning of any attempt at rescue en route." Once
Kikeri had advanced into British territory, Reid would then seek his
arrest. Beyond this, Reid could do little but affirm that should Kikeri
continue to maintain his "uncompromising attitude," punitive action
would be initiated once the new frontier had been established and the
ceded territory formally transferred to Great Britain.

To remove the most immediate catalyst for continuing political
unrest, the Chief Secretary suggested that executive action be taken
against Muhumusa to permit her transfer to Mbarara, in the adjacent
district of Ankole, where she would be confined "until the District
Commissioner is sure of her reformation." The Governor concurred,
but ordered rather that she be transferred to Kampala, for Mbarara
"is too near her own country." The Political Officer, observing that
Muhumusa, "having been always served by a number of attendants,
is quite incapable of doing anything for herself and cannot, in fact,
walk more than a few hundred yards," sent with her a small retinue
of four personal servants and "a few head of cattle." Upon her departure, Reid observed to the Chief Secretary that it was "most un-
desirable in the interests of future peace that she should ever be permitted to return to the country where her influence [had] caused such
loss of life and destruction." Muhumusa remained near the court of
the Kabaka of Buganda until her death in 1945.

The advisability of permitting Muhumusa to return to Kigezi was
periodically reviewed by the central administration. Each time, however, the action was rejected by both the local chiefs and British officials for it was feared that her continuing reputation could easily
polarize further political unrest. In reviewing the tenacity of her reputation nine years after her removal from Kigezi, the Provincial Commissioner observed:

> So far as I know, no limit has been fixed to the detention of Muhu-
> musa. It would, in my opinion, be a grave mistake to allow her ever to
> return to Kigezi for I am confident she would, in a very short time, be
> the cause of serious trouble. The cost of building another hut for her
> [in Kampala] would be trifling . . . the cost of suppressing a native
> outbreak in Rukiga, which Muhumusa would be quite capable of
> causing about the middle of the next beer drinking season might be
> very considerable, not only in money but in lives.

German Ruanda

While the Nyabingi movement in Kigezi presented a unitary threat to
British control, the German Residency in Ruanda faced a series of

open rebellions by dissident Hutu and Twa in the more independent northern areas of their territory. The successful rout of Muhumusa in 1910 was only the first of a number of such encounters. It was followed in 1912 by renewed opposition to the Rwanda chiefly structure led by fugitive cult leaders who, after the arrest and deportation of Muhumusa, fled south to resurrect and manipulate earlier anti-Musinga sentiment among the northern Hutu.

The role of Ndungutsi, while pivotal, is somewhat ambiguous. Ugandan sources regard him to be no more than an influential lieutenant of Muhumusa. Rwanda sources, however, view him as one of Muhumusa's sons, by Mibambwe IV, Rwabugiri's successor, who had been killed within a year of his succession. In supporting Muhumusa's claim to the throne for her son, Bulegeya, mentioned earlier, Ndungutsi had thus been reinforcing the political aspirations of his mother and half-brother. It is suggested that upon his retreat to Ruanda his commitment to the interests of his half-brother became increasingly attenuated as he vacillated between claiming the title for Bulegeya and for himself.

By manipulating Tutsi clans on the succession issue and by promising to emancipate the Hutu from their position as servants to the Tutsi, Ndungutsi soon acquired popular support throughout German Ruanda, the "open or passive support of many important chiefs," and "enormous popularity" among the Hutu of northern Ruanda. As his influence increased, he gained sufficient strength to initiate the characteristic raiding pattern of the *bagirwa* of the Nyabingi cult. Now, however, the axis of expansion was reversed and raiders moved south from Rukiga.

Although the increasing influence of Ndungutsi was the source of considerable anxiety for Musinga, it did not actively engage the German authorities until rumors reached Gudovius, the German Resident, that Ndungutsi claimed that the Germans "were harmless" and that under his protection only water would come from their guns. The similarity of this claim to those of the Maji Maji rebellion of 1905 could only impress upon the Germans the need for prompt repressive action. Therefore, on 5 February 1912 a German police officer and fifteen troops were sent to form "emergency posts" in the area immediately south of the "troubled region." In this manner Gudovius hoped both to discourage further expansion of the raiders to the south and to create an intelligence network in the threatened area. Northern Ruanda remained, however, under the control of the cult.

On 8 April, guided by two Tutsi "spies," Gudovius moved a detachment of thirty men into the rebel area. In order to surprise Ndungutsi and to prevent his retreat into British territory, they moved by secret

forced night march from Kigali. The body of the force encircled the
encampment while Gudovius, with a small escort, attacked directly.
Most of the persons within the encampment, including, it was reported,
Ndungutsi, were slaughtered. At the same time, forces which had been
left to the south under the command of a German officer began to
move through the rebellious area, destroying villages and killing those
who resisted.

The stated intent of the expedition had been the "punishment" of
the insubordinate populations by imposing "the greatest possible damage until complete submission." Once subdued, the region was to be
placed under the administration of loyalist chiefs from central Ruanda.
The attack on Ndungutsi and against the dissident areas to the south
was so ferocious, however, that organized resistance rapidly collapsed.
As a punitive rather than political measure, the Germans continued to
lay waste to the area although Gudovius later reported that "less
violence" was required because the population was, by then, "thor-
oughly intimidated and 'obedient'." By 20 May martial law was lifted.
Sporadic acts of violence continued against patrols and caravans but
they were isolated occurrences and betrayed no organized or ideologically incited resistance to German rule. Control of northern Ruanda
remained tenuous, however, for the limited German staff could only
govern through Musinga's representative, and his influence in these
outlying areas traditionally had little reality beyond the annual tribute
acknowledging his suzerainty.

Ndungutsi

During the period between the arrest of Muhumusa in 1911 and the
outbreak of World War I, sporadic resistance to European rule continued in the Kigezi area. The major impetus for unrest was the continuing presence of an individual claiming to be Ndungutsi. Whether
he was in fact Ndungutsi is uncertain as the Germans claimed he had
been killed in the action of 1912. What is significant is that a Tutsi
identified' as Ndungutsi, the son of Muhumusa and the rightful heir
to the Rwanda throne, re-entered Kigezi from the south, proclaimed
himself "King of Rukiga," and was apparently accepted as such by at
least "several minor chiefs."

Hostility toward European overrule initially was expressed by the
refusal of cult-influenced chiefs to carry out governmental orders and
by a general recalcitrance toward Agents and loyalist chiefs. By
December, however, protest had become both more organized and
more overtly anti-European: after threatening to burn Kabale, two

chiefs began a series of open attacks upon loyalist chiefs. Acting on the appeal of one of the chiefs so harassed, the District Commissioner was drawn once again into direct confrontation with the forces of Nyabingi. His efforts to send an expedition against Bukola, an ally of Ndungutsi, were defeated by the tactical retreat of the dissident chief. Upon his return to Kabale station, the district officer made an effort to appease Bukola by sending him a message affirming his desire for peace and stating that "he should come and meet me and tell me his grievances." Bukola replied that "he did not want any dealing with the English, that he was Ndungutsi's man." His subsequent attack on "friendly natives" engaged in road construction convinced the district officer of the need for more forceful measures.

The actual confrontation was far from decisive, however, for the rebel chiefs, having by now reached a more realistic measure of the power of Nyabingi, retreated at the approach of British troops. As the district officer's military force was small, he contented himself with firing the abandoned kraals and confiscating thirty-one head of cattle. Before leaving, he reassured the fugitive chief that "if he would come in I would forgive him and return his stock." This limited and seemingly ineffectual action was later to have considerable effect, however, for the rebel chiefs subsequently submitted to British authority in Kabale. Fully as relevant in breaking the force of the resistance was the arrest in January 1913 of "Ndungutsi" in the adjacent district of Ankole. In response to local administrative pressure, Ndungutsi was promptly removed from Mbarara to Busoga, in eastern Uganda.   With Ndungutsi in detention, the residual power derived from Muhumusa was effectively extinguished. The open confrontation of the District Commissioner with Ndungutsi's leading chiefs, compounded by the arrest and removal of Ndungutsi himself, suggested to other less powerful chiefs the expediency of "offering their submission" to this new and superior power.

Protectorate Reforms

At the end of 1912 Kigezi was formally incorporated into the Uganda Protectorate and political responsibility for the area transferred from the temporary supervision of the Special Mission to a more formal district administrative structure. At this time, as well, a number of innovations were introduced in order to standardize the local administrative operation and to bring it into greater conformity with other areas of Uganda. Foremost among these was the appointment of six chiefs "selected by the natives themselves" to serve as governmental representatives in the acephalous areas. "Native Agents" from Buganda were then assigned to reside nearby and instruct them in their duties. In contrast, in the centralized areas of Bufumbiro and Ruzumbura, the authority of the traditional chiefs was recognized in the expectation that their hierarchies could be readily absorbed into the larger district structure. In these areas as well, however, Agents from Buganda were placed in supervisory positions.

Although the fiscal and political demands of the British in Kigezi were initially minimal, the response of the population to the extension of the administrative network was unpredictable and often quite volatile. This was perhaps inevitable, for the decision to assume control of the region had been unilateral, the expectations of the inhabitants were thought irrelevant, and the burden of effecting the incorporation was left largely to individuals whose interests were firmly aligned with their European masters.

As intruders, the Ganda Agents derived their legitimacy solely from the colonial superstructure. As F. G. Burke noted in another context, "his powers in fact were limited only by his accountability to the District Commissioner." In this unnatural skewing of channels of responsibility and validation lay the primary dangers of the Agent system. By presenting an alien and often extortionate barrier between the European staff and the indigenous population, the Agents exacerbated local mistrust of British motives.

These dangers seem to have been well understood by the British. Thus the Governor in 1910 urged that very great care be taken to select "suitable and reliable" men as Agents; other administrators warned of the need to regulate the size and character of the personal entourage permitted the Agent, for "cases of extortion and petty annoyance to natives are in most cases traced to the Buganda followers of those Agents." Despite local resistance the Ganda had, by the end of 1913, imposed an effective system of private extortion.

In response, the powers of the Agents were "defined and restricted." The actual reforms adopted reflected both a concern with extortion and political intimidation and with the dangers of alienation and resentment inherent in the institution of the Agent itself. The District Commissioner urged 1) the reduction of personal retainers (apart from officially assigned armed followers) to three, and 2) the introduction of judicial responsibilities into the local councils. By expanding the local chiefly functions to include the official adjudication of minor criminal offenses, it was felt that the newly imposed system of political centralization could be more effectively validated. The Agent system itself was not questioned, however, by the British for they felt that the Kiga would not be able to govern themselves "for many years" and that the removal of the Ganda would only lead to political chaos.

The increasing regularization of relations between the British authorities and the indigenous chiefs was reflected in the growing confidence of the British. The successful action against Ndungutsi at the end of 1912, and the voluntary capitulation of his local representatives in Kigezi after his arrest unquestionably encouraged the British to use similar techniques to extinguish further acts of political unrest. The deployment of military expeditions into recalcitrant areas and the confiscation of abandoned livestock led to the submission of other unruly chiefs. The firm disciplinary action taken against Nyindo, a major Tutsi chief, for his role in the abduction and revenge murder of a Tutsi from German Ruanda, was also strategic in reaffirming the dominant political position of the British in Kigezi. It was assumed by the British that the severity of their action would suggest to local populations the wisdom of modifying traditional patterns of raiding and retaliation and of seeking recourse to the court system of the Protectorate. In reality, however, it led merely to the development of displaced patterns of aggression and to techniques for evading British detection of continuing acts of personal vengeance.

In 1913 the first major effort was also made to extend disciplinary practices to the acephalous populations of Rukiga. However, their resistance to any formal judicial inquiry into their notorious predisposition to homicide, and their unerring retreat into swamps or across the border into German East Africa upon the appearance of any British patrol, led to the application of the Collective Punishment Ordinance of 1909 to justify the seizure of any livestock left behind in their sudden flight. The imposition of collective fines of this character when communities proved un-co-operative in the location and indictment of criminals became so common a practice that a separate ordinance, the Kigezi Prevention of Crime Ordinance, was promulgated in 1914.

The War and Anti-European Activity

For the British officer in Kigezi, 1914 was a year of crisis and ultimate desperation, for, with the inclusion of Kigezi in the East African theater of operations, the gradually emerging district structure was abruptly dislocated, then abandoned. The first months of 1914 had been characterized by an absence of political unrest and increasing support for the British judicial structure. By mid-year the district officer was encouraged to introduce a more odious aspect of colonial administration: the collection of taxes. At the end of 1914, 10,000 taxpayers had been enrolled, the majority of whom were Kiga. As no pressure was applied in outlying areas, it was only the Kiga, by virtue of their geographic centrality, who were vulnerable to such unwanted administrative reforms.

In July of 1914, the Tutsi chiefs of southern Kigezi once again began to defy British authority. During that month, an Agent was attacked "near the German border" and one of his followers killed. In addition, Nyindo, the leading Tutsi chief, had refused to come to Kabale where several cases had been lodged against him. The final provocation, however, was an unambiguous affront to British authority: the release "by armed force" by several southern chiefs of a prisoner being sent to Kabale. These "fits of foolishness," each perhaps a minor irritant in itself, marked the onset of wide-scale unrest which was to prove totally disruptive to civilian administration in Kigezi.

The outbreak of World War I on 4 August 1914 marked a second resurgence of anti-European activity, for the political discontent which had characterized the initial years of British rule was exacerbated by the position of Kigezi within the East African theater of operations. Local military action in this area was probably unavoidable, for controversy over the region north of Lake Kivu had resulted in a comparatively heavy concentration of Belgian and German military forces which were still intact at the outbreak of the war. The immediate consequence of the war was the rapid polarization of local British and Belgian personnel against the German officers in Ruanda. This in itself did much to aggravate local unrest for the European no longer presented a monolithic image of suzerain power or of common political purpose.

The perceptions of the European in Kigezi, a border area, had never been confined to the administration which claimed direct jurisdiction but encompassed as well the politics and actions of colonial personnel in adjacent territories. This international orientation, characteristic perhaps of any border area, was further encouraged by the long-standing controversy over the demarcation of both the Congo and German borders and by the ethnically arbitrary character of the boundaries once established. Continuing ties of tribal identification and of marriage, kinship, and friendship eroded the reality of these political distinctions.

The additional dislocations of World War I, particularly the offensive movement of German troops against installations in Kigezi and the Belgian military occupation of the district in 1915, gave the tribes in this area a unique opportunity to observe the concurrent operation of three colonial powers in the area. Rather than illuminating the relative strength of any given power, the fluctuation in personnel served mainly to weaken the legitimacy of all foreign claims to territorial control. In this respect Kigezi was particularly vulnerable for

Belgian forces had been granted immunity from British supervision. As the District Commissioner noted at the end of 1915:

> The district is still under military control, and up to a recent date has been entirely occupied by the Belgians, which has at times been a source of considerable embarrassment to the local Administrator. Offenses committed by Belgian troops against British natives are not punishable by British Courts. . . . It is not surprising that the natives have begun to wonder to whom the country now belongs.

The conjunction of these conflicting images of colonial power did much, once again, to generate an increasing sense of the vulnerability of the British position, and with it the belief that liberation from British overrule could successfully be effected.

The immediacy of the East African campaign was particularly serious in Kigezi for, at the onset of the war, the district had only been subject to civilian administration for two years. Rather than consolidating the district against a common external threat, as in Ankole, the threat of open conflict brought these initial exploratory efforts at civilian control to a "standstill." Far more serious than the threat of outside attack were the internal disruptions which both led to and were made possible by the deterioration of the civilian structure. Politically, the most serious consequence of the war was the alignment of the Tutsi chiefs in the southern sector of Kigezi with Musinga of Ruanda, and, by extension, with the German authorities. This shift in allegiance led to a resurgence of anti-European, and, more specifically, of anti-British sentiment throughout the southern and central portions of the district, culminating in a series of attacks on local patrols, Ganda Agents, and even, in one dramatic instance, on the Anglo-Belgian installation at Chahifi. Nyabingi again provided the idiom for protest.

While the seemingly random incidents of July 1914 could be dismissed as eccentricities of Tutsi temperament, the events of August left little ambiguity as to the underlying pattern of dissent. Foremost as an index of growing disaffection was the exodus of numbers of Tutsi from southern Kigezi. While some migrated to Belgian territory, the majority crossed into German East Africa to reaffirm their allegiance to Musinga. Most significantly, Nyindo, the Tutsi chief, was among the defectors. While the Provincial Commissioner professed no alarm or surprise at the loss of this ranking British chief, the action could only have further eroded the slipping prestige of the British in southern Kigezi. The events of August betrayed an increasing arrogance toward the British. As was the case in July, a prisoner being sent to Kabale under escort was released "by armed force" by one of the Tutsi chiefs. Similarly, efforts on the part of the District Commissioner to apprehend fugitive criminals in the southern sector of the district were met with open and irreverent evasion. In one instance, a night march of ten hours was made to ensure a surprise arrest, but the chief "and all his people and cattle had already fled into Belgian territory." The increasing recalcitrance of both the Kiga and Rwanda in border areas, provoked initially by the thrust for more effective fiscal and political supervision during the prewar months of 1914, was sharply exacerbated by the political dislocations of World War I.

Resistance, evolving spontaneously as a response to the instability of the period, initially employed the major indigenous technique for political defiance in both the centralized and non-centralized areas: physical evasion. The pattern of retreat and concealment had unquestionably proved an effective tactic for the Kiga in dealing with Rwanda's political expansion. Similarly, the characteristic interlacustrine idiom for political insubordination was essentially passive: to remove oneself, one's followers, and one's cattle from the offending patron or chief. In using the international boundary as a means of political evasion, the border populations were merely absorbing into their traditional repertory a new but highly effective constraint on the movements of a suzerain power. The political dynamics behind the fastidiousness of the colonial powers were probably not understood, for intertribal relations were traditionally predicated on the assumption of political expansion and the constant flux of borders. What was appreciated, however, was the predictability of such fastidiousness.

The political uncertainties and increasing local unrest occasioned by the onset of the war were to have an additional ramification: the reappearance of the Nyabingi cult, dormant since the arrest of Ndungutsi in January of 1913. The resurgence of cult activity in central Kigezi appears to have received its initial impetus from Ruanda, most probably from dissident Tutsi who, in addition to actively participating in German military raids into British territory, continued to urge the Hutu in southern Kigezi to rebel against British authority. In choosing the idiom of Nyabingi to generate dissent among the local Hutu, the cult leaders were, of course, exploiting a political technique which had proved highly successful in the pre-colonial period. The weakness of British control was reflected in the rapidity with which the possibility of liberation from British overrule was accepted, not merely by border Hutu, but by the Kiga of central Kigezi.

Thus, in August 1914, rumors originating in German Ruanda reached Kabale that Muhumusa had escaped from Kampala and that she and the Germans would soon appear to drive out the British. The imminence of her arrival seemed confirmed by the appearance of several "female 'witches' of the Mamusa type" who claimed that their powers were superior to those of the British. With these developments, the district officer at last acknowledged the necessity for action and resolved to repress the movement before it could further "inflame the natives with anti-European ideas."

The arrest of Changandusi, a prominent *mugirwa,* near Kabale at the end of August and the failure of either Muhumusa or the Germans to appear broke the force of the resurgent movement in central Kigezi and did much to discourage correlative but independently organized acts of civil disobedience against the British. The position of Changandusi within both the traditional and modern colonial structure revealed, however, both the vulnerability of British authority and their defective access to popular sentiment, for she was the mother of Katuleggi, a Tutsi chief near Kabale.

With the arrest of Changandusi and the deterioration of cult influence in central Rukiga, the focus of unrest shifted once again southward to the Ruandan border. Although the idiom of protest remained secular in this region, anti-British activity was now undertaken not by local residents but by raiding parties of Tutsi based in German East Africa and organized under German direction. At the beginning of October, the district officer was attacked by "three hundred Batusi"; then on the following day, a "raiding party of some 1500" destroyed several villages before being driven once again into German territory.

At the center of this paramilitary activity was Nyindo. Although their military sophistication was limited, the threats of these raiders kept the people of southern Kigezi in a state of anxiety and terror.

The final months of 1914 witnessed the deterioration of any pretence at administrative control in the Kigezi district. Nevertheless, the region north of the border area remained relatively quiet throughout the critical years of World War I. Pressures from disaffected Tutsi chiefs in German East Africa did, however, continue to threaten the political stability of the entire district, not merely that of the border populations.

Other difficulties also arose from the needs of the war. Although normal judicial and fiscal expectations had long since been abandoned, the war did bring comparable demands on local resources: food for troops stationed in the area and labor, particularly as porterage. In much of the region the response to British military requirements was apathy or evasion. In the border areas, however, which had remained under the influence of fugitive Tutsi chiefs, virulent anti-British sentiment soon manifested itself in open resistance. The persistent refusal of these populations to work or to bring in food was supplanted in December of 1914 by open rebellion in the Kyoga Valley. Marked initially by the murder of a chief sent to claim a quota of porters, subsequent messengers sent by the district officer to investigate the murder were "driven back and had arrows fired on them." Not content with a defensive strategy, men from Kyoga Valley also made two attacks "in large numbers" on the headquarters of the local Agent. Although the District Commissioner conceded that passive hostility might be "somewhat overlooked," such open contempt for British authority required punitive action. The arrival of British troops led to a massive and rapid depopulation of the valley toward the frontier. "Between 400 and 500 armed Bahororo" remained behind to harass the patrol. In the confrontation which followed, 38 Hororo were killed. The livestock captured were later converted retroactively into a political fine.

The violence at Kyoga and the regular implementation of a system of collective fines against recalcitrant communities led to a prompt decrease in overt demonstrations of hostility to British rule. While the threat of British action unquestionably served to deter any further obstruction of British authority, the hostility remained. When it again erupted, the degree of co-ordination and local support accorded the rebels throughout Kigezi attested to the intensity and pervasiveness of anti-colonial sentiment.

In the early months of 1915 considerable political instability was generated in the interior of Kigezi by Katuleggi, the son of Changandusi, who had followed Nyindo into Ruanda after the arrest of his mother. From German territory he organized a series of raids which thrust deep into Rukiga. Although there is no evidence of his continuing alliance with the cult, his anti-British sentiments were openly expressed in the harassment of official runners and messengers.

The British response to Katuleggi reflected a new and more realistic measure of their political handicap under such marginal adminstrative conditions. Rather than insist that he be apprehended and brought to trial, it was now felt that he had been "dealt with" when he had been driven back into German Ruanda. The elimination of political agitators by forcing them across international boundaries became increasingly favored as a technique for political action.

In July of 1915 central Kigezi was again subject to the influence of Nyabingi with the appearance of a female *mugirwa* who proclaimed that she had "driven out the English." Anticipating that her presence would "doubtless produce the customary foolishness amongst the savages," the British resolved to deal with her "as soon as her whereabouts are definitely known." There is no record of her apprehension; however, reference is made in the annual provincial report to the "prompt and firm" suppression of several *bagirwa* by military action. Philipps implied in 1919, however, that the presence of the cult in Kigezi had been uninterrupted since the arrest of Muhumusa in 1911, for "on the death or deportation of each apostle or local personification, another representation is possessed by the spirit." By July 1916, although the activities of the Tutsi chiefs, Katuleggi and Nyindo, had been contained, new opposition to British control arose in the Congo to the west of the Kigezi district. With this shift in the locus of resistance from Ruanda to the acephalous areas of the eastern Congo, the Nyabingi cult once again assumed ascendancy.

Resurgence of the Cult in 1916-17

The resurgence of the cult as the dominant idiom for political protest represented a major ideological shift in anti-colonial activity. Earlier resistance had come primarily from disaffected Tutsi chiefs who, under pressure from Musinga, saw in the divisive international oppositions of the war an opportunity to shift the regional balance of power and, in so doing, both to reaffirm their identification with central Rwanda and to exploit the greater degree of autonomy from colonial supervision permitted under German rule. Although these Tutsi had manipulated the colonial context for their personal ends, they did not challenge the validity of colonial control itself. In addition, their claim to authority rested firmly within the matrix of both the indigenous and colonial political structures. They were not intruders or rebels, intent upon seizing power where no legitimate claim lay. Finally, their actions against the British and their appeals to their followers were totally secular in character. In contrast, the authority of the leaders of the Nyabingi cult was predicated on supernatural power and lacked support from the indigenous power base. Having no legitimacy within the traditional secular hierarchy and therefore no claim to possible recognition within the colonial system, the cult could emerge in full opposition to colonial rule.

The recrudescence of the Nyabingi movement as a serious threat to the political stability of Kigezi occurred early in 1916, with the appearance of Ndochibiri on the southern borders of the district. Unlike the earlier leaders who had entered Kigezi from the south as Tutsi aristocrats, Ndochibiri [lit. "two fingers"] was Congolese in origin, of the Hunde tribe, and reputedly an epileptic. His activity as a *mugirwa* had begun after the onset of World War I and the deterioration of the Belgian administration in the eastern Congo. There, in the name of Nyabingi, he had attacked both the local Belgian installations and the German posts in adjacent Ruanda.

In January 1916 Ndochibiri began his operations in British territory with a strategic attack on the Anglo-Belgian installation at

Chahifi; this was the fort which had provoked the sole German offensive action in the western theater a year before. Presumably, if Chahifi could be taken, Ndochibiri's superiority to both the German and the Anglo-Belgian forces would be simultaneously demonstrated. Supported by "over two thousand fanatics" and the sacred emblem of the cult, a white sheep, Ndochibiri and his followers besieged the fortification for five hours under heavy machine gun fire, retreating only after capturing three rifles and some ammunition. Certainly the most auspicious aspect of the attack was the remarked ability of the sacred white sheep "to defeat all attempts at marksmanship at comparatively close quarters." In describing the assault on Chahifi, the Provincial Commissioner reported the "prophet" as "severely wounded," adding that "one may hope [this] will keep him quiet for a time."

Although no mention is made of further harassments by Ndochibiri, his continuing presence in British territory was defined as provocative by the British government. In February an unsuccessful punitive expedition was organized to effect his capture. In addition, to enhance the colonial image, all those who had been forced to contribute cattle to the cult, presumably under pressure of supernatural punishment or physical coercion, were compensated. Through this measure, an effort was made both to gain the goodwill and gratitude of the loyalists and to encourage others to oppose Ndochibiri. The seizure of livestock, in itself a well understood sanction within the traditional systems of the pastoral interlacustrine area, was thus manipulated to secure political allegiance to the colonial superstructure. To this end, the image of the extortionate cult leader, ruthless, self-serving, punitive, was balanced against that of the intrusive yet benevolent, concerned administration. Both represented unwanted encroachments into economic autonomy; but the British at least carried the promise of political protection and of liability should that protection fail.

Ndochibiri's sphere of operations was centered on the southwestern borders of Kigezi. In January 1916, however, evidence of the existence of the Nyabingi cult was discovered considerably to the north of the area of Ndochibiri's activities, in areas which had been virtually abandoned by the British since the outbreak of the war. The base of operations for this second *mugirwa*, an unidentified female, was also the Congo. Her intent, however, was not to challenge British authority but, by evading British detection, to pass through the tenuously administered areas of northern Kigezi to Ruzumbura. Ruzumbura, openly neglected by British authorities, offered a perfect locale for cult activity unmolested by colonial intervention. There is no reason, therefore, to attribute to this *mugirwa* any conspicuous anti-British motive.

Rather, she appears to have been manipulating the cult for personal aggrandizement. Regrettably for this particular entrepreneur, she and her "large following" chose to traverse Kigezi near the Kumba post. She was discovered and detained and her following was forced back into the Congo. To discourage further local interest in the cult and to compensate those who had been victims of extortion several "temples" were burnt and "a large number of cattle that were recently stolen [were] recovered and returned to their owners."

In April, raiding again erupted in southern Kigezi with renewed incursions by rebel Tutsi chiefs and with the resumption of "looting" under Ndochibiri's leadership. Both received "military attention," but in both instances the raiders evaded the British patrols. The operational pattern of Ndochibiri had changed significantly in the months following his initial assault on Chahifi, for his activities were no longer directed at British installations themselves but rather at Kiga who resisted the material demands of the cult. To what degree anti-European sentiment determined his raiding pattern is not clear. His most serious attack, in April, in which he "ravaged the country" within a few miles of a border post, suggests that his aggression was directed against loyalist Kiga and that it was an oblique but unambiguous challenge to British authority.

After Ndochibiri's raid, an effort was made to counter his increasing influence and to deter his return to Kigezi. While British forces had failed to capture Ndochibiri, it was at least hoped that a border post would "force him to confine his attentions to the Congo." Although discovered and driven briefly back across the Congo border in July and October of 1916, Ndochibiri had gained sufficient support to move freely through Kigezi.

In November, efforts to apprehend Ndochibiri became more concerted and for the first time involved a co-ordinated strategy on the part of British and Belgian authorities. The maneuver failed, however, for Ndochibiri was by then sensitive to the limitations of the European forces and skilled in anticipating their action against him. It was this tactical acumen which enabled him to evade, for over four years, the intensive efforts of the British and Belgians to capture him.

At the end of 1916 Ndochibiri remained at large, a continuing threat to the political stability of the district. The year had seen, however, the effective removal of most of the dissident Tutsi chiefs who had returned to British territory with the advance of Belgian forces into German East Africa. In May of 1916 Nyindo surrendered and was removed to Mbarara and then to northern Uganda. With his capitulation, other dissident Tutsi chiefs also placed themselves under British jurisdiction. With the exception of Ndochibiri, other *bagirwa* were similarly contained by being driven back into their forest refuges or into the Congo.

The Nyakishenyi Rebellion, 1917

With the displacement of the rebel Tutsi chiefs from southern Kigezi, the cult of Nyabingi became the dominant modality for protest against British rule. This shift in personnel and motive also heralded a major shift in sphere of operations. Whereas the earlier impetus for protest had come from Rwanda to the south, the Congolese origins of the new *bagirwa* and their reliance upon the Kayonza forest as a refuge from both British and Belgian patrols increased the political prominence of the areas to the north of Kabale, particularly that of Kinkizi to the northwest. By February 1917 political activity had been virtually eliminated south of Kabale. Only one rebel chief, Buego, remained uncaptured but his arrest was regarded as "only a matter of time."

British efforts to alienate the people of Kigezi from the movement failed, however, as did efforts to arrest Ndochibiri. His success in resisting capture was based both on his tactical skill in avoiding British patrols and on the tacit co-operation of the Kiga. Their sympathy permitted him to assume control of an elaborate communications network which, despite the acephalous and even xenophobic character of the area, had existed in the pre-colonial period. Thus, each move of the British and Belgian patrols was reported to him, enabling him when pressed to retreat with his entourage into the mountainous rain forest which defined the Congo-Uganda border. As Philipps observed:

> The difficulties are such as to almost negative any military proposition. A vicious circle of spies surrounds the slightest movement of any military force. The element of fanaticism in Nyabingi adherents and terrorism of those who are not, renders every local native at least unreliable and provides a refuge for members of the cult.

The effectiveness of the network also inhibited the flow of information to the British. Ganda Agents were "grossly" and, Philipps implies, deliberately misinformed, while local Kiga could not be coerced into revealing the movements of Ndochibiri. Only through "endless tact and secrecy" was Philipps able to obtain any reliable information concerning Ndochibiri.

No activity directly ascribed to Ndochibiri was reported in 1917, but events revealed not merely the degree of general disaffection which the cult had generated in northeastern Rukiga, but an organizational skill which betrayed the presence of this leading *mugirwa*. Sporadic and small-scale raiding, initiated at the border, erupted periodically throughout 1917. In April, a Kiga chief from the border areas attacked a village in central Rukiga, surrendered to the Agent, then escaped. The arrest of other raiders in July pointed more directly to a Congolese origin for this activity.

These raids, however, did little to prepare the British officer or his agents for what was to be the most serious and concerted operation of the cult during the colonial period. On Sunday, 12 August 1917 at 6:30 A.M., the headquarters of Agent Abdulla at Nyakishenyi was attacked by what was initially identified as "a horde of Bakiga and Bahororo from the adjacent country." The force, estimated at 1400 men, represented the followers of seventeen Kiga and Hororo chiefs. Not since Ndochibiri's initial attack on Chahifi in 1916 had indigenous anti-European sentiment been able to generate a co-ordinated force of that magnitude.

The attack, although employing traditional techniques for dealing with local recalcitrants, was unprecedented in its savagery; in addition to looting and burning the residences of the inhabitants, the raiders murdered and mutilated sixty-three members of the community while only fifteen were injured. The ferocity of this action, which involved the indiscriminate slaughter of unarmed men, women, and children, may have in part represented an extension of the raiding patterns of the western Congolese tribes. Also relevant, however, given the local recruitment of the raiders, was the tribal identity of the victims. Although some of those massacred were Kiga, the majority were Ganda and Nkore: direct appendages of the alien and much resented Agent system. The explicitly anti-European character of the attack was reflected in the symbolic destruction of the courthouse, the Anglican church, and the mosque. In addition, five poll tax registers, the case books of the native court, and five books of poll tax tickets were destroyed. Also the day chosen for the attack, Sunday, was probably not fortuitous. Curiously, the European rest house, although situated near other buildings which were razed, remained untouched.

Initially the District Commissioner claimed that "the cause of the massacre is obscure [although] there is every reason to believe that the affair was engineered by a 'Nabingi' or witch doctor named Kaigirwa,"¹ who was reputed to be the "sister" of Ndochibiri. The incontestable solidarity of local participation could thus be rationalized in the following manner:

> As might be expected among unsophisticated savages the powers of superstition are enormous. This explains the influence of the local witchdoctors, who suitably combine their claims to supernatural powers with promises of liberation of the natives from European rule and restoration to their former condition of a) absence of obligations and

b) freedom to plunder and loot their neighbours, a pastime much favoured by sections of the Bakiga.

Although no evidence of Ndochibiri's direct participation in the raid was contained in the political reports of 1917, the *modus operandi* and size of the attack suggested his organizational skills. In 1919 Philipps did obtain information which confirmed Ndochibiri's role in the massacre. According to these sources, after his rout from Kigezi in 1916, Ndochibiri had retreated to Kisali on the Congo frontier. There, to secure his position locally, he had contracted an alliance with the frontier chief. From this base, with the aid of the "chief's daughter," Kaigirwa, and her Kiga husband, Luhemba, he organized the attack on Nyakishenyi.   Although the initial impetus for the massacre may be attributed to these *bagirwa*, the size and intertribal composition of the attacking force clearly betrayed the extent of local support which the cult commanded. Certainly one of the most striking features of the raid was the secrecy which shrouded its organization, particularly when the scale of the operation is considered. As Philipps noted, "Not a suspicion of the plot leaked out beforehand despite the fact that the British native political Agent and his [Ganda] followers had Bakiga wives and boys."

Of the hundreds participating in the raid, only twenty-two were arrested. Rebel casualties were estimated at about one hundred, but attempts to apprehend other participants met with little success.   British action with regard to the leaders was, however, somewhat more efficient. Of the seventeen local chiefs who had led the attack, three were killed and seven arrested, with only seven remaining "at large." The other fifteen chiefs who were apprehended only confirmed the degree of local solidarity both in the attack and in resisting subsequent action by the British. Three were women "believed to have aided and abetted a witch doctor in engineering the rebellion"; as members of the *mugirwa's* personal entourage they were more obvious during the attack and, presumably, more defiant in its aftermath. The remaining twelve chiefs were rather lamely rounded up after "stolen property" was found in their houses.

In the weeks following the attack, additional information on the raid was obtained from raiders who were "becoming tired of hiding in the swamps . . . and are not adverse to giving other people away." Yet by the end of August only three hundred of the local rebels had returned to their villages. The others, the District Commissioner assumed, had "betaken themselves to other parts where they doubtless hope to escape arrest for complicity in the rebellion, and to avoid taking their share in the rebuilding of dwelling houses, etc. destroyed

by them." From those who did surrender, however, the popular motives for the massacre emerged:

> The rebellion was an attempt by a section of the residents of Naki-
> shenyi to free themselves from European rule, and to restore former
> conditions of independence; and absence of obligations in the shape of
> Poll Tax and Labour.

Nor was the choice of Agent Abdulla a matter of pure chance.
Agent Abdulla was the most active of the Ganda in the suppression of
local unrest and in the pursuit of the intrusive *bagirwa* and Tutsi rebels. Short of an attack on the British posts themselves, his destruction
would most effectively have symbolized the ascendancy of the cult
over the intrusive colonial structure. Although his elimination had a decided tactical advantage for the *bagirwa*, Abdulla's zealousness in dealing with political irregularities must also have been displayed by his
local administration. The population under his jurisdiction would thus
have been subject to inordinate administrative demands. Efficiency in
such political contexts breeds vulnerability: communities initially com-
pliant were being increasingly exploited by a staff reluctant to test its
strength in more recalcitrant or distant areas. The exploitation of the
Nyakishenyi area by Abdulla made the population particularly responsive to promises of emancipation by the Congolese *bagirwa*.

To judge from the political reports, support for the cult was initially elicited from the lowest echelon of chiefs. These men, selected
by the British, were by virtue of their local origins and position in the
colonial hierarchy both more closely identified with the people of the
area and more vulnerable to the hostility evoked by British demands
for food and labor. The strength of the Nyakishenyi revolt lay with
these men. Once they had pledged support to the *bagirwa*, their organizational framework, although the creation of the British, provided
the necessary matrix for effective protest.

To convince the general population of the merits of driving the
Europeans from the area required little effort. The following affidavit,
submitted to the District Commissioner, was regarded by him to be
"typical of many":

> Our chiefs told us "we see you are tired of work, we have made a plan
> to kill the Baganda and the Europeans, so that they may leave the
> country and we shall be independent as we were before. You will pay
> no more tax and we will serve Nabingi who used to rule over us
> before." When we heard what the chiefs said, we agreed, as we did
> not want to do any work.

The appeal of this ideology of protest is striking, for it was based on a series of premises whose distortions and inaccuracies must have been evident to those whose support was being sought. The Nyakishenyi area had not fallen within the indigenous thrust of the cult in Mpororo to the east nor would it have been subject to the later advance of Muhumusa into Ndorwa from the south. The Kiga of this area therefore had no model for the operation of the cult and, in addition, no reason to appreciate the merits of supplanting one centralized system of tribute with another. We must assume, therefore, that they in turn regarded the cult instrumentally, as a mechanism for ridding the area of the hated and burdensome colonial structure. To drive out the British was not to achieve independence, but rather to face another series of tributary demands from the *bagirwa*. The dubious merits of such a shift in masters must have been balanced by the belief that the requirements under Nyabingi would be either lighter, more palatable, or more easily evaded.

Receptivity to the cult, it is true, was enhanced by the familiarity of its reputation in the central areas of Rwanda and Mpororo. Moreover, the *emandwa* cult was within the tradition of the Kiga, although the autochthonous *emandwa,* as might be expected in an acephalous society, had failed to transmute their religious influence into claims of political ascendancy. The political focus of the Nyabingi cult, derived from the model of the interlacustrine chieftaincies, was thus foreign to the Kiga. The cult also represented for the Kiga an intrusion of personnel; their xenophobic predisposition, in itself, would militate against their acceptance of Congolese *bagirwa* as their masters.

What then was the perceived advantage of the cult over British rule? Here the British records are of little value for it was in their political interest to project as unfavorable and unsympathetic a view of the movement as possible.

There is *no* evidence in the political reports of *any* cult activity in the Nyakishenyi area before the attack on 12 August. From this conspicuous silence one can assume that the characteristic earlier Nyabingi pattern of harassment and intimidation or of punitive raids had not been applied in this area. To the contrary, Ndochibiri appears to have used northern Rukiga as a tactical extension of his forest base. The co-operation of the population in this region, both in communicating the presence of patrols and in protecting his movements, was more important to him than their potential material wealth. Ironically, in accelerating their attempts to apprehend him, the British had unquestionably reinforced this redefinition of the *mugirwa's* relationship to his adherents. Far from being an intrusive religious figure claiming

political domination over the existing structure, and prepared to enforce his claims with threats of supernatural and physical punishment,
the *mugirwa* needed the support of the local population to evade yet
another series of political pressures. In order to achieve their goals,
bagirwa now turned to the political channels erected by the British
themselves, and sought the aid of local, British-appointed chiefs. The
structure created by the British system was thus used to unite the Kiga
against British rule.

The motives of the Congolese *bagirwa* need little amplification.
What is curious is the degree of solidarity exhibited by the local Kiga
and Hororo populations, not merely during the raid but in the period
of preparation and the subsequent period of investigation. Traditionally, in both Mpororo and southern Kigezi the people had feared the
extortionate and punitive tactics of the Nyabingi. With the tactical shift
of Ndochibiri, the *bagirwa* emerged in contrast as sympathetic leaders.
By confining their activity to a direct confrontation of British rule
rather than turning against dissident or uncooperative Africans, as
did Muhumusa, the local population became, in effect, spectators to an
open contest between the British and the cult leaders.

As Ndochibiri proved himself capable of evading even the most
concerted efforts of the British and Belgian forces, his popular appeal
could only increase. Moreover, he became a vicarious symbol of defiance for the docile yet politically restless Kiga who chafed under the
requirements of British administration. Thus, when the call came to co-
operate with Ndochibiri in a raid upon the most efficient and therefore
most threatening of the Ganda Agents, it was reinforced by his reputation and by his proven skill in avoiding apprehension for a year and
a half. Under such circumstances, even the direct subordinates of Abdulla were induced to join him.

The solidarity exhibited during the period of secret preparation,
involving as it did the forces of seventeen local chiefs and the complicity of the Kiga in Abdulla's entourage, is a striking testimony to
the degree to which the raid had engaged the imagination of the entire
population of the area. Such unanimity of support could never have
been borne, as the British implied, of intimidation.

After the devastating loss of prestige suffered at Nyakishenyi, the
British attempted to salvage their reputation and to re-enlist the support of the local Kiga by awarding compensation for lost livestock, by
rebuilding damaged property, and by taking punitive action against
those who had participated in the revolt. Also, in October, five Kiga
chiefs were tried during a special session of the High Court at Kabale
on the technical charge of "unlawful assembly." Four of the accused
were sentenced to ten years rigorous imprisonment and the fifth to

five years. Additional efforts were made to apprehend two elusive Kiga chiefs who continued to harass the Ganda in Nyakishenyi. To provide an additional incentive for information leading to their arrest, a reward of ten head of cattle was offered. "Run to earth" in Ruzumbura in November 1917 on the basis of information furnished by "a native of Nakishenyi," they were publicly executed in Kabale in February 1918. In addition, an effort was made to penalize "the peasantry" who had participated in the raid by assigning additional disciplinary duties, preferably in "rebuilding the habitations they destroyed."

Compensatory and punitive tactics failed, however, to gain public support for the suppression of the movement. Intelligence reports from the Belgian post at Rutshuru indicated that Kaigirwa had in November moved from her Congo base into Kigezi. A reward of twenty head of cattle was offered for information leading to her arrest, yet no reports were forthcoming. The refusal of the Kiga to be tempted by such a reward lay as much in their active sympathy as in any fear of retaliation. Given prevailing support for the movement and the solidarity of anti-European sentiment, the notoriety and wealth of the reward would bring little pleasure, considerable danger, and certain disgrace.

The revolt at Nyakishenyi had repercussions considerably beyond northern Rukiga. The southern and southeastern sections of Kigezi, quiescent since the arrest of the leading Tutsi chiefs, now began to show "signs of active sympathy" with the rebels against the British. Within a few days, while on tour the Agent at Butale was challenged by a border village which refused to let him pass. Although this was interpreted as "merely an isolated expression of ill will by the inhabitants of a small village," the District Commissioner proceeded promptly to Butale with twenty police. The inhabitants of the village fled into the swamps "at the first signs of our approach" but sixty goats and three head of cattle were captured. The action of the village was initially perceived to be idiosyncratic and without political provocation for "tax is not being in any way pressed in these parts, and the calls for labour [are] few." By the end of the year, however, it was apparent that Nyabingi was providing an increasing focus for resistance.

The Reassertion of British Control

The ferocity of the Nyabingi resurgence in 1917 and its organizational elaboration provoked a number of administrative adjustments designed both to contain the cult's influence and to discourage any further overt expression of anti-European hostility. Primary among these was the application of the 1912 Witchcraft Ordinance to cult practitioners.

Whereas previous *bagirwa* had been dealt with extrajudicially as political prisoners, in 1917 those that were apprehended were charged with the exercise of witchcraft.

By avoiding any attempt to designate a specific series of actions as witchcraft, the ordinance provided a flexibility of interpretation which could include a wide variety of actions as potentially indictable. In addition, by defining the charge in terms of "professing," "pretends to be," or "holds himself to be," the ordinance circumvented any need to consider either the phenomenological reality of witchcraft or the causality of the actions in which the accused engaged in an attempt to control supernatural forces. Such phrasing eliminated any need to document the consequences of the actions of the accused. The *intent* of the accused, whether elicited verbally or inferred from behavior or from the objects which the defendant was alleged to have manipulated, became the basis for conviction. Given the supernatural matrix of the Nyabingi cult, both as the idiom for leadership and in the patterns of intimidation used to secure adherents, the movement, while secular in intent, could be readily proved to manipulate "supernatural powers" and so to be subject to prosecution under the Witchcraft Ordinance.

The degree to which the administration consciously planned to influence local sentiment by defining cult activity as an act of witchcraft is not clear. Given their simple rubrics in dealing with traditional supernatural categories, the British officials may well have failed to appreciate the cult's position within the indigenous religious structure. The *bagirwa* were preeminently curers, powerful if specialized mediaries, but not, in any technical sense, witches. The conditions for their anger or pleasure were well understood and openly declared, their role being confined to the satisfaction of cult interests. Theirs was not a general skill to be applied, for a fee, to the personal grievances of any applicant. Until revised in 1957, the ordinance failed to distinguish between black and white magic and designated all attempts to manipulate supernatural power as potentially indictable. By avoiding any statutory designation of the attributes which were to characterize an act of witchcraft or enchantment, the ordinance retained a flexibility of interpretation which enhanced its value as an administrative tactic.

The British use of "witchcraft" as an instrument for more effective political control in Kigezi would seem to have been directly correlated with a growing administrative awareness that cult support had not been extorted under threats of punishment or death but that it represented a general and quite voluntary response to perceived political grievances. As suppressive political measures had proved ineffective, the redefinition of cult protest as an act of witchcraft provided new leverage for British authorities in dealing with political resistance in

Kigezi. Well aware of the futility of applying political or military measures to problems of civil disobedience and alarmed by the increasing
alienation which such measures provoked, the British chose to transmute a political contest into a juridical frame of reference.

The application of the Witchcraft Ordinance to the Nyabingi cult,
although patently a political decision, provided a jural idiom which
minimized British intervention and opposition to local leadership and
local political values. Psychologically it was far preferable to the alternate charge of "unlawful assembly" which emphasized the polarity of
local and British interest and did little to foster a climate of local co-
operation. By moving from a political action to a jural act reasserting
public order, a homogeneity of value and purpose could be claimed
which could subsequently be invoked to alienate the population from
further acts of political rebellion. Moreover, the association of the cult
with witchcraft—a traditional crime of high emotional valence—once
accepted, would secure a common identification with the maintenance
of the public order and with further British action against cult activity.

At issue, really, was the relative strength of local identification with
the definition of the cult as a criminal or anti-social activity or, conversely, with the legitimacy of the claim of the cult leaders. Prosecution
under the Witchcraft Ordinance was thus a conscious tactic—a tactic as
much of indoctrination as of political control. However, in 1917 its
effectiveness remained to be established.

During that year three men and three women were convicted under
the Witchcraft Ordinance. The application of the ordinance immediately led to certain penal complications for it became necessary to
construct additional accommodations for female prisoners. An additional problem, intrinsic to the ordinance itself, was the difficulty of
obtaining adequate evidence for conviction. Liability, inasmuch as it
required evidence of intent not of action, rested exclusively on the
testimony of witnesses. Yet belief in the power of the practitioners and
fear of reprisal were such that few were willing to testify. Prosecution
under the Witchcraft Ordinance thus often served only to aggravate
the political situation for, when released on grounds of insufficient evidence, the *mugirwa* could return in triumph, proclaiming the superiority of the forces of Nyabingi over those of the Europeans.

The restricted powers to sentence under the Witchcraft Ordinance
also created serious political problems, for the *bagirwa*, even if convicted, could not be detained for more than a year. By 1918 the implications of this restriction were well appreciated for certain *bagirwa*
convicted in 1917 were due to be released. Recognizing that "these
fanatical women are a curse to the country" and that the movement

could only be controlled by their removal, the British developed the convention of extending the period of detention extrajudicially by requesting deportation at the expiration of sentence.

For similar reasons, the repatriation of the *bagirwa* deported earlier as political prisoners to other areas of Uganda was strongly resisted by local British administrators. For example, in 1917 the Governor urged the return of Ndungutsi as a clement act. In informing the District Commissioner of this request, the Provincial Commissioner revealed both his concern with the tenacity of cult influence and his continuing fear of the volatile nature of Kigezi district:

> Unless you can assure me that you consider Ndungutzi's former power has gone and that he will be without influence on his return and that there will be no risk of his causing trouble again, I can not take the responsibility of recommending his return. These fanatical witch doctors, with their sacred sheep, are a menace not to be despised and even an upstart like Ndochibiri whose influence compared with Muhumusa and her offspring was trifling, caused very serious trouble for a lengthy period. Please give the question your very careful consideration with due regard to the safety and welfare of the natives of the district under your administration.

Similarly, the District Commissioner, on sentencing a *mugirwa* for witchcraft, stressed that it was "essential for the peace and good order" that she be detained 250 miles from the district for "at least" three years "to prevent her from exercising her evil influence on the said District."

By the end of 1917 the political viability of the Nyabingi cult was conceded to be an issue of public sentiment. In contrast to the initial encroachment of Muhumusa into a fearful and reluctant Rukiga, the cult was now openly embraced as an alternative to British occupation. The increasing absorption of the cult into the local political matrix required as well the revision of British strategy. Whereas the earlier phase of the movement was contained by direct military assaults on cult leaders, control now required the conversion of the population at large. It was for this reason, above all, that the District Commissioner emphasized the expansion of formal educational facilities to combat "the influence of witchdoctors." Although such efforts to undermine indigenous religious practices seem strikingly displaced given the virulence of the movement at the time, it was recognized that only by prolonged, systematic, and early indoctrination could the sentiments supporting resistance by the cult be changed. Only when they had been effectively undermined would the *emandwa* cults cease to be a potential political danger.

The 1919 Rebellion

The political memoranda of 1918 little suggest the character of the events to come. Only one incident offered even oblique evidence that the passivity which had followed the Nyakishenyi rebellion might be a superficial and temporary adaptation. This occurred when the efforts of the District Commissioner to introduce a formal educational system into southern Kigezi were countered by the Tutsi chiefs who, in a formal resolution, stated that although they "realized the value of their children being literate [they] were opposed to obtaining the advantage at the price of Christianity." The political importance of this conservatism as an index both of increasing resistance to further assimilation and of the continuing strength of traditional religious practices seems to have been unappreciated by the District Commissioner. Nor was the gradual deterioration of relations between the colonial government and the people of Kigezi perceived by the local administration, which proceeded to consolidate the reforms instituted after the war with little understanding of the tensions they might create. It was these tensions and the insensitivity of the European officers to the increasing abuses perpetrated by the Ganda Agents which underlay the resurgence of cult activity in 1919.

No overt activity occurred against the British until April 1919, yet, in the preceding months, several signs of growing alienation betrayed an increasing antipathy toward European rule and the possibility of violence. By early 1919, the station at Kabale "was avoided by Bakiga wherever possible" while court activity also sharply declined during this period. One major source of rising anti-European sentiment was natural, not political: the sudden concurrence of severe epidemics of influenza and cerebrospinal meningitis, a conjunction of events which readily received a magico-political interpretation. "The extreme suddenness of death [in both instances] led numbers to attribute the scourges to alien influence."

Far more critical, however, in explaining the increasing antipathy toward European rule was the introduction of several administrative innovations which severely dislocated the already strained relationship between the indigenous population and the Ganda Agents. Foremost among these was the introduction of Luganda as the official language of Kigezi, presumably in the interests of administrative efficiency. In retrospect the innovation was recognized by the District Commissioner to be "a distinct political error": "The local population has been submerged, incoherent and voiceless. Their attitudes, needs and aspirations have only reached the Government indirectly coloured by Baganda intermediaries [who constitute a] small but noisy oligarchy."

In addition to the control exercised by the Ganda as interpreters, the activities of the Agent and his petty chiefs were becoming increasingly corrupt and overbearing as their power grew. At the end of 1918 a number of changes were made in the *gombolola* (subcounty) system which further increased the power of the Ganda in administrative positions. These were implemented by the incumbent district officer without the approval of the Provincial Commissioner, who had strongly opposed early efforts to "Buganda-ise" the district.

The resentment of the local population over the introduction of these alien practices was inevitable for they brought with them "innumerable cases of abuse and oppression." In addition to extortions of tribute and labor claimed as a prerogative of office and the establishment of elaborate nepotic networks, the Ganda also manipulated their judicial powers in an arbitrary and abusive manner. That the local populace was less than docile in the face of such abuses is suggested by the District Commissioner's observation: "The Mwalimu bears nineteen spear wounds since August 1919, but appears not to have learnt wisdom therefrom." It was these abuses, both judicial and administrative, which formed the political context for the events of 1919.

The first evidence of the recrudescence of cult activity, dormant since 1917, occurred on 10 April 1919 when an unidentified "Ruanda Nabingi" established himself on the northern slope of Muhavura mountain. From this base he organized three hundred followers in an attack on government-employed road laborers near Chahifi, the scene of the initial assault by Ndochibiri at the beginning of 1916. The attack proved unsuccessful, and the government forces, now alerted to the rebel's presence, captured him three days later. He was promptly convicted under the Witchcraft Ordinance and sentenced to the maximum punishment of one year.

However, by early June reports reached Kabale that Ndochibiri had been joined at Buitwa, his Congo refuge, by four other *bagirwa*, including Luhemba and Kaigirwa. The conjunction of so many leaders and the report that twenty-five rifles had been seen at that time convinced the District Commissioner of the seriousness of this latest cult activity. Similarly ominous was the sudden deterioration of British intelligence contacts; after the meeting in Buitwa further information about the *bagirwa*'s movements suddenly became most "difficult to obtain." Alerting the Belgian Resident at Kivu to the immediate danger of some action by the *bagirwa*, the District Commissioner urged that "even should no disturbances occur, these rebels should be hunted mercilessly in our respective districts [for] their death or capture will alone ensure peace."

In contrast to the earlier apathy exhibited by the Belgian administrators, the Ruzizi-Kivu officer now promptly agreed to co-operate. The logistics of locating and apprehending Ndochibiri were fully appreciated by the Belgians for they had also, "on many occasions," made unsuccessful efforts to capture him. In Belgian territory, as in British, his tactical skill depended both on the effectiveness of his communications' network and upon the measures which he took to evade detection. There, as in Uganda, it would appear that he was "always informed of our slightest movements." Again, as in Uganda, the implicit solidarity of local support was not acknowledged by the authorities. Rather, the failure of information to reach Belgian officials was attributed to Ndochibiri's malevolent reputation: "He is held in terror by the native population . . . and no one dares to denounce his gathering from the additional fear of reprisals."

To overcome both the efficiency of Ndochibiri's network and the inability of patrols and loyalist chiefs to determine his movements, the District Commissioner in June resorted to rather extraordinary political measures: the deployment of local Africans "in plain clothes" to obtain information leading to Ndochibiri's arrest. To increase their incentive for efficiency, a "large reward in cash or stock" was offered. Such inducements proved perhaps sufficiently tempting for, with the murder of one intelligence agent who had been keeping them under observation "not wisely but too well," Ndochibiri and his followers retreated once again into the refuge of the Kayonza forest.

Convinced that the reputation of both colonial administrations and the stability of the area depended upon the prompt arrest of Ndochibiri, the District Commissioner "after a careful study of the methods of the rebel . . . throughout his murderous career" devised an elaborate strategy which anticipated the major features of Ndochibiri's *modus operandi*. To achieve this, the British and Belgians organized a joint operation which would entice him from his forest base and effectively manipulate his intelligence network for their own purposes.

> The measures adopted were to surround the forest with patrols leaving one attractive bait which might give an opportunity of engaging his force in the open and cutting off his retreat. . . . It appeared probable from his past tactics that his opening raid would have an objective in which success would be both certain and easy, to instill confidence into his followers for future operations. It was . . . unlikely that he would at first risk collision with any armed force.

On the night of 19 June 1919, a British intelligence agent reported that a Nyabingi "priestess," presumably Kaigirwa, had crossed into British territory with a force of six hundred recruited from "border nationalities." Ndochibiri had by that time secretly entered the Kigezi area and was at Ruagara Hill opposite the Kabale station, where, with Luhemba, the husband of Kaigirwa, he was engaged in consolidating his support for a large-scale attack against the British through ceremonies of blood brotherhood with "leading Bakiga."

As in the earlier Nyakishenyi rebellion, the co-ordination of the Kiga in the Kabale area was essential to the *bagirwa's* plan of attack, for the first and most strategic phase of the operation required the seizure of the district station at Kabale. This was then to be the signal for "a general rising all over the District." The preparatory tactics of Ndochibiri—his undetected entry into the station area and his consolidation of control through blood brotherhood with influential Kiga—suggest the mechanisms and scale of organization which underlay the earlier massacre at Nyakishenyi.

The British, however, now more alert to the possibility of an impending attack than in 1917, succeeded in intercepting a messenger returning to Kayonza forest. From the information obtained from this hostage and by noting fires in the uninhabited forests near Kumba, the British were able to locate the encampment of Ndochibiri on 23 June. Attacking without warning, British troops surprised and killed both Ndochibiri and Luhemba. Philipps reports that before the *bagirwa* died, they deliberately broke their rifles, crying "we will not look upon a white man, he shall not have our [iron] but a curse."

The decision of the British to publicize their success by the display of both bodies for one day at Kabale station   was an index of their prolonged frustration and their fear at renewed unrest following the death of these leaders. Their concern was well placed for Kaigirwa with the major body of followers, by dispersing and moving only at night, successfully evaded both the British troops and a detachment of Belgian police which was sent to the border to cut off their retreat. Although the District Commissioner attributed his failure to elicit local co-operation once again to "terrorism," the ability of such a large group to infiltrate a heavily patrolled area without detection by loyalist chiefs or military patrols would rather suggest a high degree of local support and sympathy.

To further impress upon the Kiga populations the supremacy of their power, the British captured the sacred white sheep and transported it alive to Kabale where it was publicly burnt on 2 July as a "precautionary measure." To witness the event, the Provincial Commissioner convened a *baraza* of "leading chiefs"; before disposing of the sheep he "gave [the chiefs] a lengthy anti-Nyabingi lecture . . . and begged them not to listen to Kaigirwa who will only lead them to trouble." Considerable care was taken that all the skin, flesh, and bone of the animal be consumed by the fire to ensure that its potency had been fully neutralized.

Somewhat ominously, the property of the District Commissioner was subsequently subject to a series of mysterious accidents: On the night of 12 July a portion of his house fell in, between 15 July and 20 July his small flock of sheep sickened and died although other sheep in the area were not affected, and on 29 July a smoldering ridge pole was discovered in his house at dawn. Philipps does not reveal, however, what effect these incidents had on the morale of either the Kiga or the District Commissioner who was, it should be remembered, the sole European officer in Kigezi.

Sensitive to the continuing anger of Kaigirwa, whose hatred of Europeans was now compounded by her personal loss and by the need to validate her new ascendancy to the position of "leading Nyabingi," the British officers attempted to undermine the appeal of her anticipated return by rewarding those who had actively participated in the apprehension of Ndochibiri.

On 8 July, Kaigirwa made one final attempt to mobilize the population of Kigezi against the Europeans. Her commitment to the success of the operation must have been high for her own reputation as a *mugirwa* was at stake and the prestige of the cult itself was threatened. In addition, of course, her own motives for revenge would on this occasion have been particularly intense. Despite these pressures, the retaliation of Kaigirwa was brief and abortive. A chance encounter with an isolated police patrol proved a sufficient deterrent: Kaigirwa and her party hastily retreated, announcing as they departed that they "would wait for vengeance until the government relaxed their precautions and forgot their presence."   No further reference to Kaigirwa occurs in the political memoranda, although Bessell reports that she was "eventually rounded up during the same year and . . . killed resisting capture."   Sporadic unrest by raiders from the Congo continued throughout July. On 23 July, seven Hunde appeared on the southeastern edge of the Kayonza forest where they "tried to make trouble with the local Wanya-ruanda." They were "suitably dealt with at once." The scale of the organization is evinced by the simultaneous appearance on that day at Itenbero of "Nabingi malcontents with twenty-eight rifles."

The response of the colonial administration to this continuing unrest in western Kigezi was to arrange a joint withdrawal from the international border.

On communicating with the Commissaire de District Kivu-Ruzizi he caused Kisalu to be burnt out and the inhabitants removed further from our frontier. Following this arrangement our natives in Kinkizi-Kayonza have been simultaneously moved back from this storm center. While one cannot hope for any permanent result from this action, it has nevertheless had a salutary effect.

Further unrest was anticipated with the receipt of a dispatch from Mulera in Ruanda reporting that a successor to Ndochibiri had been "ordained" at Kiante. In an effort to rally the cult adherents after the death of Ndochibiri, this *mugirwa* now claimed to be able to protect his followers against bullets by merely holding out his hand.   He did not, however, appear in British territory.

Although the focus for cult activity in 1919 was the southwestern sector of Kigezi, in July a "priestess" did penetrate as far as northeastern Ruzumbura. This was the first time a *mugirwa* was observed in Ruzumbura, and government action was swift: "She has been at once apprehended and imprisoned, and will be deported."   On the night of 31 July a Tutsi chief who had been a valuable source of information for the British was murdered by two of his servants who, after burning the house over his body, fled into the Congo. The action was "announced" by the cult as "one of vengeance on an 'informer.' "   No further evidence of cult activity was reported until 9 September when a *mugirwa* was said to be "five hours south of Lake Bunyonyi with a large following of malcontents." To discourage any action in Kigezi, the District Commissioner wired requesting twenty police from Mbarara "at once."

Despite these instances of continuing cult action, with the death of Ndochibiri and the rout of Kaigirwa, the major organizational focus of the movement had been broken. Whether in response to the increasingly prompt action of colonial authorities or as a result of the absence of the charismatic leadership and tactical skill of Ndochibiri, the attacks of the *bagirwa*, although widely distributed, grew increasingly desultory and uncoordinated. In contrast to the dramatic and district-wide confrontations planned by Ndochibiri, the *modus operandi* of the surviving cult leaders deteriorated into a series of short forays from foreign bases. In addition to reflecting the absence of the organizational talents of Ndochibiri, this new pattern of raiding increasingly betrayed motives of personal gain. Rather than providing a framework for the expression of local opposition to British rule, the *bagirwa* now reverted to a pattern of extortion and intimidation. This tactical shift unquestionably exacerbated the growing disenchantment of the Kigezi populations with the movement. At the same time, the disillusionment itself probably set the conditions for the resumption of these exploitative techniques.

Neither the District nor Provincial Commissioners harbored any illusions as to the strength of Ndochibiri's support or of the imminence, at the time of his death, of an organized and district-wide rebellion. The District Commissioner observed: "I am of the honest conviction that a very serious general rising . . . had been most narrowly averted," and the Provincial Commissioner stressed: "I realize that, at Entebbe, it is not possible for you to form any idea of the very serious nature of this Nabingi propaganda nor of the narrow escape we have had from a serious native outbreak. . . . I am deeply grateful the worse did not befall us."   One European officer and a police establishment of thirty-five men, both realized, could offer little resistance to any widespread rebellion.

Recognizing that the focus for most of the local anti-British senti-ment was not the demands of the British government itself but against the Agents and that real grievances did exist with regard to the ex-ploitation of their prerogatives of office, the British in 1919 undertook a serious reform of the Agent system. Prominent among these re-forms were the immediate withdrawal of the prerogative of labor tribute and the dismissal of Agents implicated in serious abuses. By the end of the year the District Commissioner had effectively dis-associated himself from any responsibility for having created condi-tions for revolt: "Their [the Agents'] overbearing and domineering attitude to the local populations had without doubt been the direct cause of more than 90 per cent of the so-called local 'rebellions' in a country where [the] European Government has never been personally unpopular."

Years of Accommodation and Alienation: 1920-27

Despite the measures taken in 1919 to stabilize administration along the borders and to control the abuses of the Agents, in September 1920 political unrest erupted once again in southwestern Kigezi. Again, the impetus for revolt was the Nyabingi cult with its base of organization in Belgian territory. The locus of the movement had once again shifted, however, for whereas Ndochibiri had moved from the Congo into the heart of central Rukiga, the new cult activity emanated from Ruanda, southwest of Lake Bunyonyi. The analogous character of the terrain was readily appreciated by both the cultists and their British adver-saries: "These are wild mountain frontier areas which are practically unadministerable. Neither the Germans, the Belgians nor ourselves have ever succeeded in obtaining tax or labour from these people owing to the nature of the country."

Although no leader emerged during this period of instability to challenge the skill or reputation of the Congolese *bagirwa*, the climate of opinion was such that even the most trivial incident could "trigger" the highly volatile and embittered population. The mere rumor of the impending arrival of a "Nabingi emissary" was, for example, sufficient in many areas to precipitate open resistance, and any efforts by the district administrator to enforce intrusive regulations only widened the chasm between local interests and colonial intent.

When in October disturbances once again began to assume "alarming proportions," the District Commissioner, recognizing the general alienation which such unrest betrayed, chose to focus on relieving the underlying conditions which had generated such widespread discontent. Whereas 1919 had been spent in "breaking rebellious organizations," now rehabilitation, not further military action, was emphasized. It was even suggested by Philipps that the effect of Nyabingi might be neutralized by the encouragement of other, "more innocuous" cults within the traditional magico-religious system: "Since purely military measures have proved useless against the Nabingi it would appear that a considerable influence might be enlisted for European administrations by more sympathetic handling of the conservative Rwanda *kubandwa* cult and the powerful but innocuous local fortune telling, rainmaking institutions which enter so deeply into the life of these people. So might Greek meet Greek and the Devil take the hindmost."

While the basic premise for cult unrest remained that of "all native politics," that is, that the "alien Government is only temporary," a number of more specific grievances and issues were also exploited by the new Nyabingi leaders: the enforcement of township regulations, the capture of fugitive criminals, and the continuing anxiety over labor and taxes. A recurrence of an epidemic of cerebrospinal meningitis was again readily manipulated by the Nyabingi so as to increase local alienation from British rule: "There is a belief current among the native population that the germs of this disease are buried in the ground by European and alien agents as a punishment." Under such politically volatile circumstances, the District Commissioner conceded that "a certain amount of political uneasiness" had to be anticipated. In the absence of any overt aggression against either the British or their representatives, however, no offensive action to suppress the cult was taken in 1920.

Although both the provincial and local officers now displayed considerable sensitivity to the signs of continuing alienation, difference of opinion among the British officials continued, both as to the nature of the unrest and the most effective ways of neutralizing it. The Provincial Commissioner affirmed the need for "drastic measures" in the event of any resurgence of overt hostility. To avert any local participation in activities planned by *bagirwa* in Ruanda, he therefore convened the "leading people" of Bufumbiro and Rukiga while on tour in Kigezi:

> In full Baraza today I . . . spoke to them on the matter and warned them that this was the second year in succession that trouble and unrest had arisen in the country from the "Nabingi" movement and that if they again participated in the movement or did not take steps to prevent dangerous people from crossing the border and stirring up trouble here, the Government would next time take severe punitive measures in the confiscation of stock and imprisonment of offenders. I pointed out to them that this annual unrest and trouble would not be tolerated and that gave them a clear warning on this matter.

Given the pervasiveness of unrest and a population said to be in "an electric and inflammable state of mind," such an ultimatum required a considerable degree of bravado. However conscientious or disciplined the military or police forces might be, they were ultimately defenseless against a population of several hundred thousand distributed over several thousand square miles.

In contrast, the District Commissioner argued that "the best remedies and safeguards against future trouble" would be to combine more regular systemic changes with a continuing tolerance for local unrest and an acknowledged capitulation to certain long-standing grievances. He advocated five measures:

1) The gradual civilization of the district;
2) The levelling up of administrations on both sides of the two international frontiers;
3) Abstention from the pressure of tax or labour in frontier areas;
4) Increasing toleration of the Rwanda *imandwa* [an anti-Nyabingi institution];
5) Employment of Tutsi, the hereditary rulers, whenever possible.

Clearly, the suggested deferment of fundamental administrative requirements and the wide-scale social reforms implicit in this list represented a major departure from earlier administrative policy. Token deference was made to the external impetus for political unrest; but his conditions suggested that the District Commissioner was fully aware that such resistance was neither superficial nor intrusive and that it in fact represented a pervasive antagonism which could only be weakened by a gradual attitudinal reform. This in turn would require certain prompt concessions in the most volatile areas, considerable tact and patience where resistance was met, and a gradual standardization of administrative practices, particularly in the immediate border areas.

The five major points of reform were rather perfunctorily conceded by the Provincial Commissioner. Immediate efforts were made to substitute "where possible indigenes for aliens in the control of local affairs." The replacement of the Agent in Bufumbiro was recognized to be both a political imperative and most feasible for this area which, in spite of a history of political turbulence, was regarded in 1920 as "by far the most progressive County in Kigezi." Only two qualifications were now regarded as essential for the office of Agent: that the candidate be a Tutsi, that is, "anti-Nyabingi," and that he be of the royal family. As a final stipulation, it was also suggested that "if possible, he be acquainted with Ugandan fiscal and judicial methods and have a knowledge of Kiswahili."

Tutsi affiliation was specified in an attempt to gain the support of that segment of the Rwanda population which had little enthusiasm for the Nyabingi movement. By appointing a member of the royal clan, traditional lines of political identification would be reinforced, not disrupted, and existing Tutsi sentiments toward the cult, already congruent with British interests, could be manipulated in the event of further cult activity. However, the appointment of a Tutsi as chief, although politically strategic in one respect, represented considerable political risk for, by reinforcing the traditional lines of privilege within the Rwanda hierarchy, the British rendered themselves vulnerable to identification with the hated aristocracy and to further alienation on the part of the Hutu majority.

During 1921, no political disturbances occurred in Kigezi. Although it is not clear whether the period of quiet reflected concerted British efforts to introduce a number of preventive and deterrent measures or, alternately, an internal shift in the dynamics of local political relations, the activities of the *bagirwa,* when they did occur, were strikingly apolitical in nature. It is possible that the reinforcement of the district police establishment with twenty men from Ankole and the co-ordinated patrol of the southwestern frontier by British and Belgian detachments provided a sufficient display of force to deter any open cult activity.

A major reform of the 1912 Witchcraft Ordinance also occurred in 1921 which facilitated its application in Kigezi. Although prosecution under the Witchcraft Ordinance had proved the most effective political instrument for inhibiting the activities of the cult leaders, the British conceded in this year that the penalty provided in the Witchcraft Ordinance was "no longer adequate as a deterrent." The maximum sentence was increased from one to five years, thus empowering the courts to remove any potentially disruptive leader for long enough to undermine both his authority over his adherents and the residual structure of cult organization. In addition, although the ordinance carefully avoided classifying witchcraft as either a felony or a misdemeanor—it is referred to only as an "offense"—the severity of the increased sentence brought the application of the ordinance well within the range of felony. The enhanced sentence further provided a technical basis for claiming exclusive jurisdiction over all witchcraft cases, for the maximum sentence in itself would warrant the removal of such cases from the local African courts.

The 1921 amendment further secured the probability of conviction by making "possession of witchcraft articles" a punishable offense. Absent in the principal ordinance, the addition of this clause unquestionably increased the efficiency of prosecution for, provided such tangible evidence could be recovered, the onus of proof of innocence was now on the defendant. Moreover, the admission of such evidence eliminated the need to rely upon reluctant or intimidated witnesses. The revision provided, however, for a maximum penalty of only six months. This, as one Provincial Commissioner noted in the 1950's, "renders it virtually useless as a protection to the community in which the pretended witch is living."

As 1922 remained a year of political tranquility, the few practitioners of Nyabingi apprehended were dismissed as "of the witchcraft variety and without any political significance." In evaluating the continuing quiescence of the movement, the district officer stressed the relevance of the gradual incorporation of the area into a larger attitudinal framework, and urged an even lighter sentence for those convicted under the Witchcraft Ordinance. This laxity of the British in the prosecution of the less dangerous *bagirwa* had, however, repercussions, for it was rapidly exploited by the cult leaders. Ever concerned with the size of their following, the *bagirwa* claimed that the relaxation of British control represented a capitulation to their superior power. In particular, when they did not receive maximum sentences, the *bagirwa* used their early release to enhance their reputations and to demonstrate the potency of Nyabingi over the Europeans.

Although no political activism was reported in the political memoranda of 1922, a *mugirwa* moved into the Kigezi area from Ruanda at the end of the year urging others "to go out and kill the white man and drive him from the country." With her arrival, the first syncretistic elements appeared in the ideology of the movement, for she commanded "on threat of immediate death" that the "old Nyabingi custom" of no cultivation or cooking on Monday be restored. Her influence was such that over a year later the District Commissioner observed: "The fear of the power of the 'Nabingi' is so great that with very few exceptions the people keep strictly to this command." Many attempts were made to apprehend this *mugirwa* once her anti-European focus and power became apparent, but by the time systematic action was taken against her "the sect [was] too well guarded to allow of it."

In 1923, Kigezi district remained politically quiet. The few arrests made were of a "non-political" nature, leading the District Commissioner to interpret the absence of the more virulent forms of cultism as "encouraging proof of the advancement of the District." His confidence, however, was premature. During a tour of Bufumbiro at the end of December 1923, the local strength of the movement at last reached the attention of the British authorities. In response, the District Commissioner warned both the chiefs and the populace against participation in the movement, emphasizing that any further activity would be met with prompt repressive measures and heavy punishments for those implicated. Despite British precautions, even the chiefs were found to be involved. No measures were taken against them, but they were warned that "in future" any evidence of association with the movement would result in their dismissal.

The year 1924 witnessed a subtle but significant deterioration in the local administration of Kigezi, as a consequence of both the growing disaffection of incumbent chiefs and the increasing encroachments of the larger protectorate network. Disaffection was marked among the parish chiefs by a growing alienation from the *saza* (county) and *gombolola* chiefs themselves as well as from the British superstructure. The District Commissioner noted: "in each Saza I visited there were numerous complaints by the Chiefs about their Bkungu, these cases were tried by me and in almost every case were proved and exemplary punishments meted out 'on the spot.' "

The discipline and education of chiefs remained a continuing concern for the British administration. Even more serious, however, was the evidence of increasing unrest on the part of the population at large. One significant index of this growing alienation was renewed difficulty in the collection of the poll tax; in Bufumbiro, for example, the people of one area proved so recalcitrant that an *askari* (soldier) was stationed there "to help matters." In Ruzumbura, to the north, the District Commissioner reported in October "approximately 3,330" tax defaulters of whom "over 2,000" had gone to Buganda.

Within this socio-political context, the cult of Nyabingi quietly but discernibly began to regain its strength in 1924. In April 1924 the District Commissioner observed that "minor," i.e., non-political, cases of Nyabingi were becoming increasingly common. Attributing the increase in cult activity "to the fact that too lenient sentences have been inflicted in the past," the British tried to suppress the movement by exemplary sentences in the "several serious" cases that were brought to their attention.   In addition, by defining cult activity as "an evil practice," government propaganda attempted to appeal to the incipient Christianity of the district. Both directly and indirectly efforts were made to establish a climate of opinion which, it was hoped, would alienate the "agriculturists" from the movement.

Although by 1925 cult activity was regarded as politically inconsequential, it remained a continuing problem in Kigezi. It was assumed, however, that cult support would "doubtless disappear with the spread of education." The District Commissioner acknowledged the "large amount of witchcraft being practiced" but affirmed that a new and intensive campaign against practitioners and the increasing prosecution of those found in possession of ritual articles had had "good results" leading to a "noticeable diminution of this danger."

However, in 1927, eighteen cases charging possession of witchcraft articles were tried in the District Court. The tribal distribution of the defendants revealed that "Ruzumbura country is probably the worst in this respect followed closely by Bufumbiro, the Bahororo and Banyaruanda being the two tribes most versed in their practice."   Although administrative hostility to local magico-religious practices was presumably stimulated by the recognition of the potentially volatile role of such specialists, no mention was made in the reports of 1927 of the political genesis of such activity, or more specifically, of the continuing strength of the Nyabingi cult. From their indifference, one can only assume that the British staff was totally unprepared for the events of 1928.

The 1928 Rebellion

While cult activity had remained a peripheral administrative consideration during the decade following the death of Ndochibiri in 1919, suddenly, in 1928, the cult of Nyabingi erupted once again as the organizational focus for open and widespread anti-European resistance. The extent of its appeal, the suddenness of its recrudescence, and the degree of organization which it manifested must be viewed both as responses to then current administrative practices and as consequences of the growing alienation of local chiefs from the district administrative structure.

The earliest evidence of renewed cult activity was reported from Kinkizi county in northwestern Kigezi, where the Ganda Agent had been rebuked in the preceding year for losing control of his district. The extent to which this had in fact occurred is evidenced in the arrogant centrality of the cult operation. As with Chandugusi, the leading *mugirwa* was revealed to be the mother of the *gombolola* chief at Kayonsa. The District Commissioner, upon learning that the cult had been operating "right under the nose of Agent Sulimani," moved quickly to apprehend the *mugirwa*. "Unfortunately, as so very frequently happens, suspicion had been aroused of the intention of my search with the result that a particular chair used in these seances, a drum, and a special iron wand were made away with before they could be seized with the remaining things." Despite the absence of these key ritual objects, the woman was arrested and convicted after being charged with the possession of witchcraft articles. The *gombolola* chief himself, it was tersely noted, "has been recommended for dismissal."

At the same time, the District Commissioner reported "an insidious recrudescence" of the cult to the south in Rukiga. Although initially the district officer was unable to obtain sufficient information from the Kiga to locate or arrest this southern *mugirwa*, he was aware of the virulence and potential danger of this new leader who openly proclaimed the superior power of Nyabingi and his intention to drive Europeans from the land. Pressing both the symbolic claims of the 1922–23 resistance and a more secular exhortation to resist British demands for tax and labor, the *mugirwa* called for immediate action against British rule. "One of the curious decrees is that no work (i.e., in shambas [gardens]) may be done on a Monday or Tuesday—these two days being set apart for 'Nyabingi' of course—and it is amazing how very generally this is observed by the Rukiga natives." The prominence of this proscription in the ideology of protest was attributed by the Provincial Commissioner to "the action in the past of certain C.M.S. evangelists who some years ago tried to prohibit the pagan Bakiga from working in their gardens 'on the Lord's Day' and is in the nature of a reprisal."

In addition, a curious and presumably intrusive motif found in other African rebellions, notably in the Maji Maji of Tanganyika and the Allah-water of the Dinka of the Sudan, was incorporated into the ideology of this new *mugirwa*, for he claimed that the bullets of the Europeans, when confronted with the powers of Nyabingi, would be "rendered harmless." The degree of influence which he exercised over the local population was reflected in the inability of the British to elicit any information as to his location from even the more loyalist or assimilated Kiga.

Despite an auspicious beginning, the 1928 movement was destined to be brief for, although a co-ordinated action against the British was planned by the *bagirwa*, they exhibited little of the tactical sophistication of their predecessors. Nevertheless, their initial advance into the Kabale area was ingenious. Bessell reports that "for some days beforehand the Nyabingi war-anthem, 'the Queen has come to her country' was continually sung by a man from the top of the hill facing the station." This, it may be imagined, served not merely to encourage the Kiga of the area but to erode the morale of the sole European officer.

The injudicious decision of the *bagirwa* in February to convenc three hundred followers for an "armed witchcraft dance" in the hills a few miles from Kabale led to a prompt and ill-fated confrontation with the forces of the District Commissioner. Although Bitura, the most influential of the leaders, escaped and fled south into Ruanda, his two sons were arrested and sentenced to the maximum punishment of five years. One of the most striking indices of the extent of the influence of these *bagirwa* was a large water pot confiscated at the time of their arrest. Used as an urn for votive offerings, it contained 305 shillings, almost entirely in cents. The degree of their power was also evidenced during the trial of Kamunda: "In order to get [the witnesses] to speak it was found necessary to place the accused in such a position that the witness would neither be facing him or could see him." His position as a "great" *mugirwa* was also established during the trial, for those present at his unsuccessful flight from British authorities testified that he had been carried by "large numbers" of his followers. This, the assessors noted, "would not be done if he were a witchdoctor of minor importance."

Later intelligence reports confirmed that the intent of the cult leaders in moving into the Kabale area had been to co-ordinate a direct attack on the British station and mission headquarters at Kabale. Their planning had in fact gone so far as to allocate, on paper, the houses and contents of both the station and mission to various favored members of the immediate entourage. We are dealing then, in this final phase of the movement, with men who had clearly spent sufficient time in the colonial educational system to acquire the skill of literacy and the mannerisms of European bureaucracy.

The confiscated plans also revealed that the local *gombolola* was to be the initial focus for attack, to be followed by the capture of the mission headquarters, then the district station. Presumably this order of advance was selected with a concern for the relative vulnerability of each installation and a concomitant likelihood of success. It did, however, reveal a curious myopia as to the presumed response of the district officer when alerted to the presence of "large excited and armed gatherings" in the adjacent hills. In confirmation of this priority, Bessell reports that the cultists, before their dispersal, succeeded in killing three minor loyalist chiefs.

With the arrest or escape of the Kigezi *bagirwa*, the seat of the Nyabingi movement shifted into Ruanda. There, in March of 1929, a series of attacks were made upon Belgian chiefs in border areas only fifteen miles from Kabale. During this action, which was regarded by the District Commissioner as "undoubtedly coordinated" with the abortive rising in Kigezi, six Belgian chiefs were murdered and the region along the frontier burned and looted. The leader directing these operations was reported to be Ndungutsi. However, as he was "carried from place to place with his face veiled," the District Commissioner conceded that "proof of identity may be difficult."

Although the activities of the cult in northern Ruanda remained a potential political threat to the Kigezi administration, the district was quiet after the initial arrest of the leaders in February 1928. However, British officers continued to co-operate in the location of cult leaders who remained at large.

It was further recognized that active measures would have to be taken to impress upon the population that the administration "will not tolerate these Nyabingi outbursts." The Provincial Commissioner therefore suggested in April that a collective fine of seventy-five head of cattle be levied against those resident in the area where the "secret dances" had been held. There is no indication, however, that this punishment was implemented. However, despite British efforts, the cult continued to receive the tacit support of both local populations and chiefs. When two "priestesses" entered Kigezi in August, for example, their presence was not reported by the local chiefs.

By now sensitive to the futility of any precipitous or categorical handling of popular sentiment, the British consoled themselves with an interpretation of the cult which both justified their ineffectiveness and offered a promise of its eventual dissipation:

> The leaders are fanatics aided by elementary, but locally terrifying, stock in trade developed from the natural phenomena of hypnotism, ventriloquism and mental suggestion. The followers are principally the terrorised, also the aggrieved. It must be emphasized that every local grievance, whether real or imaginary, and every misapprehension, is greedily exploited, hence the need of going slow, of constant personal contact, with the peasantry, and seeing under the surface in Kigezi.

Even so, the District Commissioner could not foresee the final suppression of cult influence as long as the "present generation" of cult adherents survived.

The inability of the Belgians to control cult activity in northern Ruanda presented a continuing political threat to Kigezi. In anticipation of further unrest a police superintendent was transferred to Kabale to provide a second European officer. The police establishment remained, however, far below the figure regarded as adequate during the earlier periods of resistance. Further political instability was created by fugitives driven north by the raiders in Ruanda, who continued to seek refuge in Kigezi. The disturbances themselves, however, did not at any point break across the frontiers into British territory, presumably because of local disaffection with the cult rather than any fastidiousness on the part of the Rwanda *bagirwa* themselves. Although the British attributed this welcome immunity to their increasing accommodation to local grievances, of far greater relevance was the persisting inability of the *bagirwa* to effect their claims to superior power. Their failure, in 1928, to attack Kabale, compounded by their subsequent arrest by or flight from the British, unquestionably did much to undermine the force of the movement, however congruent with existing local sentiment.

One index of this growing disillusionment with cult efforts to challenge British authority was the dramatic increase in the number of converts to Christianity in the months following the suppression of the Nyabingi movement. As was later disclosed, this new enthusiasm for Christianity was motivated far more by political expediency than by the demonstrable merits of Christianity:

> A recent roundup of those terrorized into tribute to Nyabingi "priests" is alleged to have caused a mass-production of Christians. It was due principally to action indiscriminately taken against both credulous pagans [as well as] avaricious malcontents [and] the real organizers of the Society. . . . The pagan therefore feels the need of some protection. Baptism and a Hebrew name seem to him to offer a kind of alibi.

A further impetus for conversion appears to have come from the "boys in charge of Protestant bush churches, ambitious to gain merit with their employers by a fat convert-roll," who readily recognized the exploitative potentialities of pagan anxiety. To impress upon the uninitiated the advantages of Christianity, they circulated rumors that the government had warned that "those who did not become Christians [within six months] would be considered as sympathisers with the Nyabingi and thrown into prison."   Lest the pagans in confusion stray into Catholicism, the rumors further stipulated that such protection lay in seeking "the Government religion," i.e., Protestantism.

Although no further political unrest occurred in Kigezi after the initial eruption in February, investigations revealed the scale of the planned revolt, its anticipated co-ordination with other regions and the degree of popular sympathy which it had elicited in each area.

The movement [was] not only both synchronized and widespread, but also [showed] signs of a quite cunning, if elementary organization. Manifestations of differing importance, but [using] the same tactics, varied only to take advantage of local weaknesses, occurred in the same period in Uganda, Belgian East Africa and even in Tanganyika Territory.

The seriousness and scale of this latest manifestation of cult activity prompted the British abruptly to institute a number of major administrative reforms in an effort to eliminate certain long-standing local grievances. By such action, it was felt, the impetus for further rebellion would be effectively undermined, for the key to cult popularity was believed to lie in the articulation and manipulation of these grievances.

Of foremost importance was the removal of the Ganda Agents who were reluctantly recognized to be "chauvinists to a man," indifferent to local expectations and local customs and intent upon "Gandaising" the district rather than developing it within a more familiar and sympathetic frame of reference.   Acknowledging the tensions which their arrogance and abuses had engendered, the Provincial Commissioner resolved to replace them in Rukiga and Ruzumbura by the end of 1929.

In a second major thrust to correct local political tensions, Swahili was once again instituted as the official language of the district. Local resentment toward the earlier adoption of Luganda, both as a symbol of alien domination and as a barrier to communication between the local population and the District Commissioner, was, of course, intimately drawn into the constellation of hostilities associated with the Agents themselves. Facilities for instruction in Swahili were "somewhat vaguely if not reluctantly" provided by the missions in August.

Meanwhile, the dislocations caused by the continuing unrest in Belgian Ruanda were exacerbated by conditions of famine in Belgian territory and by the completion of the Kabale-Rutshuru road into the Congo. By October the southwestern portion of the district was subject to a heavy influx of immigrants from both Ruanda and the Congo. With their arrival, the political stability of the area deteriorated, and this led to an increase in the incidence of frontier raids for women and food as well as cattle. An effort to control the situation was undertaken in October with the prohibition of any further settlement in the frontier areas. By forcing immigrants to move farther into the district, the impetus for local raiding and counter-raiding was, it was felt, "considerably reduced."

The Redefinition of Cult Intent

With the containment of the *bagirwa* raiders beyond the southern borders of Kigezi, the threat of the Nyabingi movement as a locus for organized opposition to British dominance was permanently eliminated. Whether in consequence of the failure of a new leader of sufficient stature to emerge; as a direct response to the increasing accessiblity of colonial political and religious values; or, as claimed by the British, because of "the removal of a number of grievances, petty enough to the European [but] actual and infuriating to the African, and easily exploitable by the Nya-bingi," the cult lost its political dimension after 1928.

This shift in focus was evident as early as June 1929 when two of the more prominent participants in the 1928 rebellion escaped from the Belgian prison at Kigali. Previously detained without trial for a year at Mbarara, they were reported upon their escape to have moved northward into the mountainous border country, swearing to "do their worst to make things unpleasant" for the British. The populations of the border area were, at that time, particularly vulnerable to such agitation for "owing to drought, [they had] neither contentment arising from a full stomach, nor [were they] actively engaged in agricultural pursuits which, in most parts of Africa are shown to be one of the simplest and most effective antidotes against privy conspiracy and rebellion." Yet despite the appeals of the escaped leaders for vengeance, no overt opposition to the British ensued.

With the loss of its traditional role as a vehicle for political protest against the established authority structure, Nyabingi assumed new importance as a curative cult. As such it retained a position of prominence among the *emandwa*. By virtue of this adjustment the cult remained, at least for the ruthless and avaricious, an effective vehicle for personal intimidation and extortion.

That it has considerable influence is apparent from the large number of alleged "witchcraft" cases submitted by Native Courts. On inquiry, it is generally found that they are not genuine cases of witchcraft, but mere charlatanism on the part of imposters who are well aware of the fear inspired in the credulous, and who play upon their fears for their own personal gain.

Traditional cult sanctions were now parlayed into a more naked appeal for personal power. That the threat of the wrath of Nyabingi continued to inspire such fear is in itself significant, for the appeal of the cult in the 1930's must be measured against the promptness of government action in the detection and prosecution of *bagirwa*, the extension of missionary influence, and the direct appeal of various British administrative reforms. The persistence of the powers of the cult is reflected, as in so many other instances of witchcraft, both in the reticence of those so exploited to report the oppressive activities of the *bagirwa* and in their reluctance to testify as witnesses for fear of punitive action either to themselves or to their families or property. As the police noted, "Only when demands of witchdoctors become so exhorbitant that [it is] utterly impossible to appease them are reports of malpractices made." The number of cases prosecuted thus provides little insight into the scale of cult activity.

In an attempt to eradicate the cult itself, efforts were made to suppress local support through a policy of "ridicule, stripes and small sympathy with the duped." The effectiveness of this new tactic was reflected in the "considerable" reduction of cases of extortion by practitioners of Nyabingi. Where arrests were made, they seemed to involve those practitioners whose avariciousness had led them to accumulate either a conspicuous flock of sheep or a notoriously large sum of money, both pursuits which would eventually attract the attention of the local chiefs. To these *bagirwa* "scorn and imprisonment [were] meted out, in the hope that they would take themselves less seriously on release."

By 1934 the movement had, at least by all overt indices, been effectively suppressed. The decreasing incidence of Nyabingi cases from 1930 to 1933 and their total elimination by 1934 did not reflect a decline in cult activity, however, but rather an increasing sensitivity on the part of the practitioners to the tactical importance of evasion. By becoming both more circumspect in their operation and increasingly apolitical in focus, the *bagirwa* discouraged detection or intervention by local chiefs. These major shifts in operational tactics may therefore represent no more than an accommodation to increasing bureaucratic control on the district level.

Early in 1935 rumors originating in the Rukiga and Ndorwa *sazas* revealed that Ndungutsi was once again active along the eastern borders of the district. It was the opinion of the District Commissioner, however, that Ndungutsi was "at present merely a name": "I have been told by middle aged chiefs that they have heard of Ndungutsi all their lives and that if he still exists he must be a very old man." Although both the district officer and the Provincial Commissioner stressed the diminished influence of the movement in consequence of "the spread of education and the realization of European power," Ndungutsi remained at large throughout the year. To do so, the tacit support of the local populations was essential.

By virtue of his reputation and the co-operation which it encouraged, Ndungutsi successfully evaded the British authorities until the end of 1938. The District Commissioner of Ankole, by then fully sensitive to the uncertainties of prosecution under the Witchcraft Ordinance, ingeniously arranged his detention, by force of arms, on an irrefutable and easily substantiated charge: failure to pay poll tax.

Thus, despite British claims to increased administrative efficiency and to the ameliorative effects of Christianity and education, the detection of such cult leaders during the mid-1930's remained contingent upon the alignment of local sentiment. Where the *mugirwa* succeeded in demonstrating the efficacy of his power, the fear of his wrath far outweighed the discomforts of his extortionate demands. The official position, emphasizing as it did the "progress of Christianity and education" and the political implications of an increasingly efficient communications system, placed a premature confidence in the ability of the local chiefs to apprehend *bagirwa* "before their influence [became] great enough to cause serious trouble." Although local authorities stressed the inevitability of cult decline with "the advance of civilization," the central police more realistically assessed such assertions as little more than an acknowledgment by the civilian officials of their basic helplessness in instituting any controls which would seriously influence local attitudes toward "the problem."

Although the activity of the Nyabingi leaders remained confined to instances of personal extortion after 1928, their influence in Kigezi remained viable into the early 1950's despite decades of prompt, punitive action, a campaign of public ridicule, and a series of administrative and judicial restrictions designed both to deter the practitioners themselves and those who might seek their power. The tenacity of the cult, especially in the 1930's, impressed upon the authorities both the irrelevance of repressive methods and the critical roles of education and, by implication, of shifting values in the ultimate erosion of such beliefs. It was the missions, ironically, which were to provide the subsequent matrix for political unrest with the emergence of a virulent, evangelical sect of the Anglican church, the *balokole* or "Twice Born." This sect, which encouraged both a defiance of local administrative directives and an open confrontation with local chiefs, was designated "subversive" and made subject to prosecution in the district courts. Although under close surveillance after 1939, the leading adherents succeeded in provoking open disturbances in 1942 and 1946.

Conclusion

The transformation of the Nyabingi cult into a vehicle for colonial opposition may be viewed as a response to a series of shifting political contexts: 1) its initial position in the indigenous political network of the Mfumbiro region, 2) the conditions which defined both the impetus for and the nature of its expansion into the acephalous areas of Kigezi, 3) the degree and nature of support encountered in this region, and 4) the factors underlying its decline and redefinition as a curative cult manipulated primarily for personal, not political, gain.

Although similar to other possession cults throughout the interlacustrine area, the cult of Nyabingi had by virtue of its ideological equation of supernatural power with material gain always contained the seed of secular disruption. In Rwanda this was manifested by direct competition with the chiefly structure for the existing tributary channels; in Mpororo, by an attempt to incorporate the established chieftaincies and their networks of labor and tribute into a larger suzerain relationship. In both areas the secular dimension of cult activity was thus already well established in the precolonial period.

While the initial activity of the *bagirwa* in Rwanda was directed toward establishing personal influence through the flow of gifts, once this intrusion was challenged by the *mwami* and his local representatives, the cult became an explicit instrument for regional resistance, cleverly manipulating the existing antagonisms of the Hutu to consolidate local support against the secular chiefly structure.

In Mpororo, in contrast, instead of dividing or disrupting the existing political system, the cult sought control by establishing a higher level of political organization—one which would co-ordinate the fragmented and politically autonomous chieftaincies of the area. Here cult ascendancy was envisioned as an act of political centralization, that is, the absorption of these independent chieftaincies into a political unit coterminous with their existing ethnic identification as Hororo.

As the accounts of Emin Pasha indicate, this effort proved unsuccessful for the cult leaders who, despite their considerable influence, failed to realize more than nominal control over the Mpororo area. Although unable to override the existing political loyalties of the Hororo, the cult did provide a precedent for unification during the pre-colonial period.

The failure of the *bagirwa* to consolidate the Mpororo area was in large part due to the absence of any polarity of political identification beyond these local hereditary chieftaincies. Nyabingi itself provided the only model for unification but, as such, lacked the opposition of interests which had proven such an effective part of cult support in Rwanda. The rapidity with which the cult was later embraced by the acephalous Kiga in turn rested on the introduction of the colonial frame of reference. A condition for the political viability of the cult would thus seem to be an opposition to a larger, competing set of political demands.

Although the colonial context introduced an opponent of unprecedented scale and technological superiority, the modality for resistance was derived from cult activity during the precontact period, for it reflected both the legacy of subversion in Rwanda and the manipulation of larger political networks in Mpororo. In addition, the Mpororo pattern of incorporating the raiders of Nkore as an executive organ of the cult provided both the vocabulary and the precedent for further efforts to breach traditional ethno-political alignments in the name of Nyabingi.

The distribution of the cult in the precontact period was conspicuously restricted, due both to the systemic limitations of the cult operation and the material interests of the *bagirwa*. Until the colonial period, no effort was made to penetrate the mountainous, acephalous areas of Kigezi or to challenge directly the core areas of the larger kingdoms. Rather, cult activity ranged through areas politically peripheral and territorially marginal to these kingdoms: in the northern and loosely administered provinces of Rwanda and in Mpororo, a buffer zone between the kingdoms of Nkore and Karagwe. Both regions were, however, centralized. Both were joined as well to these more powerful kingdoms in an attenuated tributary or garrison relationship. It may in fact be argued that the political discontent and anxiety of these areas, their fear of greater incorporation, and their resentment of their position of marginal exploitation made them particularly vulnerable to the attentions of the *bagirwa*. In addition, of course, their centralized networks for the collection of tax and labor and their predominantly pastoral focus provided strong economic incentives for cult activity in these areas. The acephalous and agricultural Kiga, in contrast, afforded little economic interest or organizational potential for the traditional *bagirwa*. Only with the political pressures of the expanding colonial frontier and with the introduction of patterns of centralization by the colonial power could the cult turn with success to this previously inhospitable area.

The extension of the Nyabingi cult into Kigezi under Muhumusa was primarily a defensive action, first against the forces of Musinga, then against the actions of the German officials. Whereas the expansion of the cult in earlier contexts had been motivated by a desire to enlarge the tributary structure which the *bagirwa* commanded, the concern of

Muhumusa was not with the richness or vulnerability of the area but rather with seeking refuge from further political harassment. In her retreat northward she was forced into a region which not only lacked the exploitative potential of Rwanda and Mpororo, but also had no tradition of political subordination under either secular or supernatural leadership.

The absence of a model for political centralization, although it inhibited the rapid absorption of the Ndorwa area into the cult orbit, did prove structurally advantageous in one respect, for it eliminated the need to contest an existing political base whose leaders would view the activities of the *bagirwa* as a direct threat to their control of privileged interests. The virulence of the cult in Rwanda and Mpororo thus had no analogue in the Kiga area where conflicting allegiances to indigenous political institutions were absent. In Rukiga, rather, the issue was autonomy, the maintenance of local enclaves of agnatic kinsmen against the incursions of other Kiga, or the encroaching boundaries of Rwanda. One would assume in such a situation that any effort to superimpose a centralized structure would be resisted, let alone the predations of a fugitive and politically disabled cult leader from Rwanda.

In assessing the response of the Kiga to Muhumusa, the role of the cult in northern Rwanda would appear critical. The commitment of the Hutu to the cult as a mechanism for liberation from Tutsi domination, inasmuch as it created a barrier to Rwanda expansion, may have provided a major impetus for the passive acceptance of Muhumusa in Kiga areas.

Although there is sufficient evidence of the intimidatory tactics of Muhumusa and of her ruthlessness toward non-adherents, she clearly was able rapidly to absorb southeastern Kigezi into her tributary network. Whether this should be viewed as open and voluntary support is, however, another matter. More likely, the motive for nominal adherence was fear of her reputed supernatural or secular powers. Equally compelling were the activities of her entourage. Presumably also the rewards of cult allegiance—absorption into the patronage system—tempered the resentment of many Kiga toward her tributary demands.

The acceptance of the Nyabingi cult by the Kiga was also encouraged by certain structural and contextual factors. Foremost among these was the existence of similar *emandwa* cults within the magico-religious system of the Kiga. The cult, although intrusive, could thus be easily incorporated into an existing system. The political dimension of cult activity, although without parallel among the Kiga *emandwa*, was also implicit in the incipient ranking by reputation and territorial range which characterized the *emandwa* systems of the region. This existing hierarchy, though relevant only to reputation, again prepared the Kiga to accept the claims of Muhumusa to political ascendancy.

Additional leverage for pressing political claims came from the very nature of cult power. Secular attempts to incorporate the Kiga had met with fierce resistance, but, as religious specialists, the *bagirwa* could activate the one role which in the egalitarian Kiga society had the greatest potential for prestige and influence. Moreover, the existing reputation of the cult and its known importance in the adjacent areas of Mpororo and northern Rwanda must also have disposed the Kiga to accept the claims of Muhumusa.

The internal structure of the cult in itself provided an important model for political centralization. With access to Nyabingi confined to the individual claiming to be the personification of the spirit, cult participation was in itself hierarchical, for all others were dependent on the *bagirwa* to intercede in contacting the spirit. This systemic advantage was unquestionably compounded by the personal attributes of the early *bagirwa* who were not only supernaturally powerful but royal Tutsi. As such they entered Kigezi with a domestic entourage and life style commensurate with their secular origins. These accoutrements of royal status could not fail to impress the simple Kiga and to reinforce the validity of the *bagirwa's* political claims or the privileged inaccessibility of such power. In addition, the Mpororo legend which placed the origin of the cult in the royal court of Ndorwa unquestionably strengthened both this parameter of cult power and the legitimacy of Muhumusa's claim to southern Kigezi.

Other factors, by virtue of their discontinuity from traditional political expectations or existing social alignments, decreased the perceived dislocations of existing institutions by the cult, and, by implication, the resistance of the Kiga to its advance.

The general eccentricities of behavior displayed by the *bagirwa,* which served to validate the exclusivity of their claims, unquestionably provided a psychological obstacle of considerable proportions, for they were without precedent in the traditional political or religious roles of the Kiga. The tenacity of Muhumusa's reputation for over three decades after her arrest reveals the full impact of these mannerisms on the Kiga.

Additional mechanisms for displacement, highly effective although inadvertent, were 1) the high proportion of female *bagirwa,* a factor which directly undercut the traditional patrilineal authority structure of the Kiga, and 2) the external origins of the major cult leaders. As Rwanda or Congolese they avoided any factional indentification with either local territorial segments or local clans, affiliations which could readily have undermined their claims to universal allegiance.

The rapid transformation of the Nyabingi cult in Kigezi into a vehicle for anti-European protest occurred largely in response to the motives of the leading *mugirwa*, Muhumusa. Embittered by her treatment by the Germans in northern Ruanda and threatened by British encroachment into Ndorwa, she set aside the earlier issue of the Rwanda throne to marshal her energies against these new intruders. The anti-European focus of the movement, so striking in its rapid growth, was thus no more than a deflection of the existing political dynamics of the region. The comparability of grievances and aims and the success of traditional operational tactics in dealing with both the local Kiga and with the British may in part explain the conservative character of the cult after contact and the delay in the intrusion of syncretistic elements until the second decade of resistance. Certainly the ideology of protest which supported cult activity in Rwanda could be applied to the colonial situation virtually without modification.

The personal hostility of Muhumusa to Europeans does not, however, provide an adequate basis for co-ordinated regional protest. The increasing degree of popular support for the movement, beyond the personal entourage of the *bagirwa*, attests to an increasing degree of general resentment at the presence of the British.

Because of the attenuated character of initial colonial occupation, sensitivity to Europeans and discontent with their demands were generated by a limited series of incidents and issues. Spared any intrusion of mining or settler populations, the economic issue was not land, but rather the early attempts of the British to obtain taxes and labor from the people of the district. Although efforts to collect taxes or recruit labor were unsystematic and irregular, particularly during the war years, the tendency of the administration to counter early recalcitrance with "rigorous police operations" created a degree of hostility which bore little relation to the amounts actually collected. By 1917 the administrative structure in central Kigezi had stabilized sufficiently to permit a more effective and regular exploitation of the adjacent populations. The degree of resentment which these demands elicited is amply verified by the scale and unanimity of the Nyakishenyi rebellion.

The second major source of political tension was the presence of the Ganda Agents. The tendency of these men to maximize their personal gain through bribery, administrative abuses, and extortion; their lack of identification as aliens with Kiga interests; and their manipulation of their intercalary position between the British and the Kiga generated an atmosphere of frustration, anger, and fear on the part of the Kiga. This in turn increased their vulnerability to the counterclaims of the *bagirwa*, who promised to drive not merely the inaccessible British from the area, but also their hated representatives. Given the hostility

of the Kiga toward these alien chiefs and the tangibility of their grievances, it is not surprising that the major focus for acts of organized violence was the Agent, not the European administrator. Their role in providing the major impetus for open resistance is further confirmed by the
geographical distribution of cult-incited violence; it was concentrated
in central and northern Rukiga, areas which lacked a traditional chiefly
structure which could provide either a buffer between the Agent and
the people or a direct channel of access to the British officer. Here the
presence of the Agent under such circumstances was oppressive and
vulnerable to abuse.

If the activity of the early *bagirwa* was motivated more by personal
aggrandizement than by ideology, the response of the Kiga was also
instrumental. Although aware that the demands of cult allegiance represented in one respect yet another erosion of their traditional autonomy,
the Kiga clearly assumed that in aligning themselves with the *bagirwa*
conditions under the suzerainty of the cult would be improved: either
less oppressive, less threatening to their life style, or, alternately, more
easily evaded. Support of the cult thus became a conscious strategy
by which the Kiga sought to reinstate at least a measure of their
independence.

The modality of local resistance throughout most of the period of
cult activism confirms this interpretation for, with the exception of the
isolated, large-scale operations of 1916, 1919, and 1928, open harassment
of loyalist chiefs, Agents, or British personnel was undertaken only
by the immediate entourage of the *bagirwa* and then most frequently
in brief forays from bases in other territories. The role of the population
at large, although clearly sympathetic to the cult, was passive, devoted
either to providing the essential intelligence network to protect cult
movements or to evading by non-compliance or physical withdrawal the
demands of the British superstructure and its local representatives. On
those occasions where activism occurred, it was either a regional attempt to co-ordinate local anti-British sentiment or independently expressed as isolated and spontaneous acts of resistance to demands for tax
or labor. Similarly, cult allegiance was manifested by local chiefs for the
most part in inefficiency, evasion, and failure to perform orders, not in
an open challenge of British authority or overt noncompliance.

However instrumental the motives for local support of the Nyabingi cult, the sympathy and co-operation which the cult elicited were
crucial to its success: to its effectiveness in confronting any given British
tactic, to its evasion of detection, and to its tenacity over time. Not only
did this network of co-operation ensure that information about European movements and plans would be conveyed to the *bagirwa*, but it
constricted and distorted the flow of information to the British. The

scale of support also proved a major constraint on anyone who might oppose the *bagirwa* or serve as an informant, for opposition to the cult brought the threat of disgrace and even death.

The solidarity of support evidenced in this communications' network was not, however, a simple response to the political expediencies of the Kiga. The tenacity of the movement, despite periodic defeats of often devastating proportions, attests to the resilience of the cult itself. In addition to an internally generated predisposition on the part of the Kiga to align themselves with cult interests, there were a number of systemic and situational factors which also contributed to the enduring reputation of the cult.

Although the cult was graced with an ideological resiliency in the potency of the spirit after the death, defeat, or flight of any given *mugirwa,* the success of the major *bagirwa* and their sustained skill in evading British capture unquestionably generated considerable enthusiasm and support for the cult and a high degree of vicarious identification with the *mugirwa* in question, who became, for the more passive, a symbol of defiance to colonial rule.

The actions of Ndochibiri, who clearly attained the status of a folk hero before his capture and death in 1919, played a major role in the tenacity of cult influence during the colonial period for they confirmed the legendary power of the Nyabingi. Moreover, his abandonment of the exploitative tactics of the early *bagirwa* marked a major shift in the focus of cult activity since his concern was not with consolidating tributary networks, but rather with enlisting local support in opposition to colonial rule. The economic motives of the earlier *bagirwa* were supplanted by an ideology of political emancipation. Ndochibiri's shift from an emphasis on submission to one of local co-operation, symbolized by his egalitarian consolidation of support through blood brotherhood with local chiefs, may have been a response to the absence of an indigenous model for centralization in Rukiga. Such considerations had not deterred the more imperious Muhumusa, however, who had subdued the southern Kiga before the introduction of the British superstructure which Ndochibiri so cleverly manipulated. Far more relevant in defining Ndochibiri's egalitarian approach were his acephalous Congolese origins, the new conditions for opposition created by the tightening of British control, and their more systematic harassment of the *bagirwa*. Unlike Muhumusa, who could move freely on the periphery of British influence, Ndochibiri faced a co-ordinated interterritorial political network which imposed artificial restrictions on his movements. The intimidation and fear upon which the earlier *bagirwa* had based their influence had little place in such a world. Success could no longer be defined in terms of a reluctant capitulation to tributary demands; it required a real measure of support, an active and voluntary co-operation with the cult organization, and a willingness to protect the more activist members from British detection. As a measure of cult identification was unquestionably higher and less intimidatory under Ndochibiri, the tenacity of Muhumusa's reputation and the selection of Ndungutsi, not Ndochibiri, as the symbol of cult immortality, appear even more curious. One can only assume that the activities and the origins of these *bagirwa,* although less palatable, provided a higher degree of congruence with the traditional cult image.

Although the actions and expectations of the *bagirwa* and the displacement of cult power from any specific carrier, both intrinsic cult features, unquestionably contributed to the tenacity of the cult in the colonial period, other more fortuitous factors also proved critical to the enduring strength and periodic resurgence of the Nyabingi cult.

The character of colonial administration in the area also, if inadvertently, facilitated the success of the movement. Most critically, the European image was not monolithic. As the Mfumbiro area fell under the jurisdiction of three colonial powers with different languages, different administrative policies, and different images of their role in this area, the implicit political heterogeneity of the situation was invested with administrative reality. Moreover, the administration of each territory was not a self-contained operation. Each political power openly competed for the region as an extension of its existing colonial interests. The factionalism which this competition generated, and its eruption into open conflict during the early boundary disputes and World War I, could only erode the impression of inevitability and immutability which attends unchallenged colonial expansion.

The political position of the Mfumbiro region also proved a fortuitous, yet significant, feature of cult tenacity. For each colonial power, the Mfumbiro region represented an economic and political hinterland. This marginality to both the interests of the colonial powers and to the capital of each territory resulted in an attenuated pattern of administrative supervision within which intervention in local affairs was sporadic and often arbitrary, creating not merely an acknowledged situation of weakness, but limited access to popular sentiment or discontent.

The geographical delineation of southwestern Uganda to accommodate British claims south of the first degree parallel resulted in an administratively vulnerable definition of Kigezi district. In addition to isolating the district from other administrative centers within the protectorate, it increased its exposure to three other territories. Thus the geographic position of Kigezi, combined with the defective supervision which characterized the entire region, lent itself readily to the manipulation of international boundaries as vehicles of evasion. Given the weak administrative structure, the defective channels of communication, and the administrative encumbrances of "international" appeals for co-operation, the borders themselves provided an effective constraint on colonial action against the movement. The region itself, an area of rugged volcanic mountains, impenetrable forests, and lava caves also provided a natural refuge for the cult and a formidable barrier against effective colonial supervision. These natural advantages, again fortuitous, played a critical role in the protracted evasion of the British officials.

Although all these factors serve to clarify the tenacity of the cult in Kigezi, the degree of regional co-ordination exhibited during certain phases of the movement requires further amplification. To accept the cult as the most promising vehicle for local protest is one thing. To submerge traditional or intertribal suspicion and hostility in a common effort to eliminate Europeans is another. This new level of political identification—one which aligned the indigenous population in common opposition to the colonial intruders and which overrode traditional barriers of language and tribe—was, in a very real sense, a creation of the colonial powers themselves.

The intrusion of a colonial power, disruptive under any circumstances, was exacerbated in this instance by the assignment of homogenous populations to three separate administrative systems: Uganda, German East Africa, and the Belgian Congo. This fragmentation of traditionally autonomous groupings, in addition to creating centrifugal pressures to reaffirm the traditional unit at the expense of the international boundaries, succeeded in severely dislocating the existing political networks and the traditional dynamics of intertribal opposition. In such circumstances, it is not surprising that traditional hostilities or even predispositions to intertribal xenophobia were submerged to create a new level of political identification.

Given this pressure for more inclusive identification, the Nyabingi cult provided several organizational advantages: 1) the leader was not of the local tribe, thereby avoiding the dangers of factional identification with any local territorial segment or kin group, 2) the leaders were often women, undercutting the patrilineal authority structure which characterized the region, and 3) the cult, by projecting the source of power onto a supernatural level, both manipulated the existing pantribal institution of the *emandwa* cult as a framework for unification and removed cult allegiance from competition with existing secular political affiliations.

Although intertribal co-ordination of the movement was essential to its sustained opposition to three colonial powers, the irregular distribution of the cult suggests that the local political context was as critical in defining its more virulent manifestations as any inherent feature in the cult itself. The appearance of the cult as a vehicle for anti-European resistance was confined to the egalitarian populations of central and northern Kigezi and to the Hutu-dominated areas of northern Ruanda and southern Kigezi. The ethnic alignments of both these populations support the position of analysts who feel that an acephalous tribe under the pressure of colonial rule is particularly susceptible to such movements.

Perhaps fully as critical, however, was the degree of local identification with the lower level of the colonial administrative hierarchy. In the acephalous areas of Kigezi the British relied on the introduction of men from another tribe. Therefore, no intertribal political tensions between local chiefs and rebel leaders were created. The opposition of indigenous to colonial interests was in consequence much more salient.

These dynamics of opposition would, in turn, explain the immunity of the Hororo and the Tutsi to cult allegiance. Ruzumbura, in spite of the high degree of cult activity at the end of the nineteenth century, remained indifferent to colonial opposition and to the activities of the *bagirwa* in adjacent areas. Here, however, the chiefly structure was not merely recruited locally but had, from the earliest period, managed to maintain a considerable degree of autonomy. With the virtual abandonment of British supervision during the war, the Hororo had little occasion to protest either the presence of the British or the character of local control.

Similarly the Tutsi, long the object of cult activity in Rwanda, had little incentive for identifying with Nyabingi regardless of their resentment of the European. Sustained resistance, as we have noted, did occur among the Tutsi in British areas, but it was secular in nature and primarily an affirmation of their identification with Musinga in German East Africa. In defying the international boundaries which had severed the kingdom of Rwanda, the hostility of the Tutsi to the colonial political situation was explicitly anti-British with pro-German sentiment serving as a vehicle for reasserting their ethnic identity with core Rwanda. Also inhibiting cult activity in Tutsi areas was the character of the local chiefly structure. As in Ruzumbura, southern Kigezi had maintained both a greater degree of autonomy from British supervision than central Kigezi and a basic continuity between indigenous and colonial chieftaincies. The cult therefore remained, as traditionally defined, a vehicle for protest against the chiefly system. The major factor behind differential response to the cult therefore appears to be more immediately a consequence of the continuity and degree of representativeness of local chiefly personnel, not the degree of centralization. By implication, however, one would expect a higher degree of congruence between these variables in centralized areas.

The force of the Nyabingi cult may be put in one final perspective by examining the factors contributing to its sudden displacement in 1928 as a vehicle for anti-European sentiment. Although the redefinition of the cult at that time was rapid and final, its loss of political focus was a response to a complex series of pressures, some of which had been initiated a full decade before.

With the death of Ndochibiri, British policy toward the cult underwent a striking tactical change. Suppressive military measures, which had only aggravated the polarity of colonial and local interests, were replaced in 1919 by a strategy of positive indoctrination designed to undermine the reputation of the cult and to correct the conditions which had generated political unrest. In addition to a greater accommodation with regard to tax and labor demands, the local administrative structure was itself subject to major reforms: Agents who were known to have abused their positions were immediately removed, and additional measures were taken in preparation for the eventual replacement of the entire Agent system by locally recruited chiefs.

These positive reforms represented one aspect of British action against the cult; efforts were also made at this time directly to challenge cult activity and the existing reputation of the cult leaders. Although popular sentiment continued to identify with the *bagirwa* throughout the 1920's, the increasing efficiency of the district administration, greater efforts at interdistrict and international co-ordination, and the tightening of the communications' network within the district created more effective conditions for the detection and capture of cult practitioners. In addition, with a more systematic application of the Witchcraft Ordinance and the deportation of the more important *bagirwa*, a jural context was established which directly and forcefully challenged the claims of the cult leaders to greater power. Finally efforts were made to engage local support through the return of extorted cattle, the depreciation of cult powers, the confiscation of cult objects, and public exhortations to renounce cult affiliation. Although in isolation such propaganda would have been without value, the increasing control demonstrated by other political and judicial measures and the evidence of benign intent implicit in the various administrative reforms all served to undermine the reputation of the *bagirwa* and to support British claims to political ascendancy. Moreover, the affirmation of British strength through administrative reforms offered a positive alternative to cult affiliation. Identification with the encroaching world of the Europeans became a matter of political expediency if not of conviction.

The failure of cult leaders to command a position of political prominence after the 1928 rebellion was not only a consequence of British action per se but also reflected the increasing disillusionment of the

Kigezi populations with the disparities between the claimed goals and actual achievements of the cult in resisting the encroaching colonial powers. The inability of later *bagirwa* to generate anti-British sentiment in Kigezi reflects the degree to which this apathy was already entrenched among the acephalous populations. Although the intensification of repressive colonial measures after the death of Ndochibiri had in large part set the conditions for an eventual rejection of the movement, their efficacy required the alienation of local populations from the movement itself. The swift and decisive action of the British in suppressing the 1928 rebellion provided the critical catalyst for accelerating this growing disaffection. The dispatch with which they routed such a highly organized operation dramatically confirmed for the Kiga the futility of further resistance. It was this disillusionment alone which contained the continuing activism of *bagirwa* beyond the borders of Kigezi.

The reputation of the Nyabingi cult was unquestionably compromised by the repeated failure of the *bagirwa* effectively to challenge the British occupation, but other factors also contributed to the decline of the cult in the late 1920's. Foremost among these was the increasing incorporation of local Africans into the colonial administrative structure and into the local mission hierarchies. Through recruitment into these organizations, Africans were also absorbed into the underlying incentive system of the colonial power. This process was of particular significance in the acephalous areas where the movement of local Africans into the higher levels of the chiefly structure for the first time created a vested local interest in the colonial bureaucracy and an effective channel for the direct expression of local discontent. This new participation in the formal political network seriously undermined the vicarious displacement of political sentiment previously provided by cult participation. Nyabingi offered no promise of a return to traditional autonomy for the local Kiga but rather an alternate pattern for centralization—one in which the monopoly of power remained in the hands of the alien *bagirwa*. The British, in contrast, had created new channels for status and mobility and given the promise of local self-administration. While the Kiga could not, in any event, hope to regain their traditional autonomy, the British at least offered a more viable channel for political expression.

This attitudinal shift, so critical for the dissolution of the movement, was further reinforced by the emergence of a local African elite. The substitution of new criteria for prestige and power, inevitable with the acquisition of positions of local prominence, directly undermined the indigenous traditions of privilege which had validated the claims of the *bagirwa* to political ascendancy. The colonial superstructure itself became the major vehicle for political participation. With this increasing identification with the colonial power, the prospect of cult dominance and the promise of a new order of political unity within an alien traditional idiom could offer little ideological competition to the perceived rewards of mobility and local recognition of the existing British system.

An additional weakness of the Nyabingi cult was inherent in its ideology: despite its magico-religious matrix, the cult remained secular in intent. Offering no passive or vicarious alternative to open resistance, its repeated failure to rout local British officials could only confirm the futility of open opposition and the irreversibility of the colonial process. Resistance to European occupation, where it occurred, reverted to the traditional acephalous idiom: to tactics of evasion or to independent acts of covert aggression. Although no efforts at open rebellion were organized after 1928, by the mid-1930's arson, an offense which lent itself admirably to the evasion of detection or prosecution, was being systematically employed against local authorities in Kigezi. Arson had been traditionally employed as an integral feature of the raiding complex, but this earlier context offered no precedent for its emergence as a major modality for political discontent. Its transformation suggests, however, the relevance of the strengthening colonial context and a need for increasing circumspection in defying British rule.

The sudden dislocation of the cult from its enduring role as a vehicle for political protest marked the end of co-ordinated opposition to British rule in Kigezi. No further effort was made to challenge the presence of Europeans; rather, local political energies, confirming the premise of European occupation, were channeled into a manipulation of and movement within the system itself. This stability and increasing efficiency of the district administrative structure as it moved into the 1930's, the increasing local tolerance of the many inconveniences and restrictions which its continuing presence implied, and the expansion of options for direct participation eroded both the original stimulus and conditions for local resistance.

With this attenuation of local resentment there was no longer a felt need for either an open or a vicarious rejection of the colonial superstructure. The polarity of focus, so critical to the endurance of the cult in both the precontact and early colonial periods, was lost in the growing congruence of colonial aims and African needs. Within this changing context the cult of Nyabingi could offer no viable alternative, either structurally or ideologically, to the process of colonial expansion. The abandonment of the cult was thus in a very real sense inevitable, for its relative weakness had been repeatedly demonstrated and the world which it promised was no longer real or desired.

PSYCHOLOGICAL STRESS AND

THE QUESTION OF IDENTITY:

CHILEMBWE'S REVOLT RECONSIDERED

ROBERT I. ROTBERG

In early 1915 a number of Africans led by John Chilembwe rose against
the established order of the Protectorate of Nyasaland, killed three
whites, wounded two others, and, for at least a brief time, threatened
radically to stem the growth of settler power. The course of the rising
and the social, economic, and political circumstances which preceded
it and made it possible are by now well known and are summarized
below. But the critical questions—precisely why its American educated
leader, hitherto a respected member of the community, fomented revolt, and what he and his followers intended by so doing—continue to
perplex students of this rising, of protest movements in Africa, and
of revolution everywhere.

Did Chilembwe seek to make himself king of Nyasaland in the
manner of Christophe of Haiti, Prester John (of the book by John
Buchan), or the hero of George Heaton-Nicholls's *Bayete!*? If victorious, what then? Or did he anticipate defeat and plan with that
contingency in mind? Did Chilembwe seek martyrdom and merely in-
tend his rebellion as a flamboyant gesture of protest? What did he
want? And why did he care? Were there psychological factors which
presupposed revolt? What, in sum, gave a sense of purpose to the rising
and sustained Chilembwe throughout the period of its gestation and
emergence?

These questions can probably never be answered indisputably.
Rebels sometimes make demands of authority in writing, justify their
actions in printed or diary form, or are called upon to explain their
deeds to a tribunal or a commission of inquiry. But for the Nyasa rising
of 1915 there now exist no explanations or tracts by Chilembwe, nor
is there reliable testimony by those of his followers who were later
summarily tried for participating in the conspiracy. Similarly, there

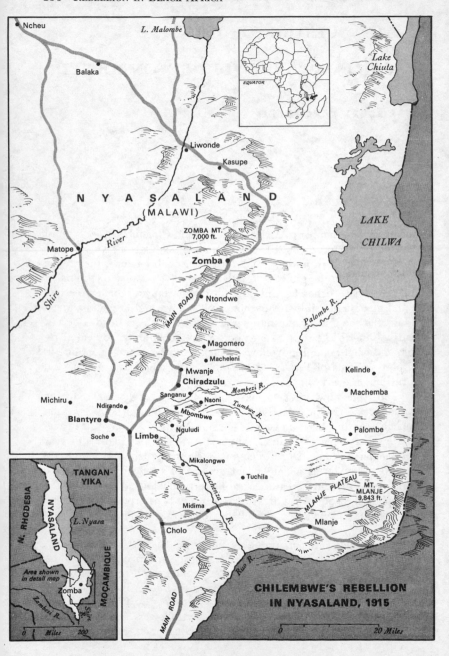

Ncheu

L. Malombe

Lake
Chiuta

Balaka

EQUATOR

Liwonde

Kasupe

N Y A S A L A N D

(MALAWI)

LAKE
CHILWA

ZOMBA MT.
7,000 ft.

River

Matope

Zomba

Shire

MAIN ROAD

Ntondwe

Palombe R.

Magomero

Macheleni

Kelinde

Mwanje

Chiradzulu

Michiru

Sanganu

Nsoni

Mombezi R.

Machemba

Ndirande

Mbombwe

Tumbwe R.

Blantyre

Nguludi

Soche

Limbe

Palombe

Mikalongwe

Luchenza R.

Tuchila

MLANJE PLATEAU

MT.
MLANJE
9,843 ft.

Midima

Cholo

Mlanje

TANGAN-
YIKA

Rio R.

N. RHODESIA

NYASALAND

L. Nyasa

MOÇAMBIQUE

Area shown
in detail map

Zomba

Zambezi R.

Shire R.

**CHILEMBWE'S REBELLION
IN NYASALAND, 1915**

0   Miles   200

0   20 Miles

MAIN ROAD

exist no first-hand accounts by persons who could claim an intimate acquaintance with Chilembwe or a real appreciation of his motives. On the other hand, there is no dearth of contemporary assertion and contemporary or nearly contemporary speculation. There are reminiscences by whites and at least two lengthy African views of the rising which, from internal and external evidence, hardly seem capable of having been manufactured. The reminiscences and one African account, that by Andrew G. Mkulichi, a rebel, were used by George S. Mwase in a book which has recently been published. Its detailed reconstruction of the events of 1915 depends in turn upon the testimony of Wallace Kampingo, another of the rebels. A reconsideration of Chilembwe's motives is also assisted by newly discovered contemporary data—primarily the papers of a mysterious African shopkeeper named Haya Edward Peters. Future advances in our understanding of the Chilembwe phenomenon will obviously depend almost exclusively on the finding of contemporary materials, if any, which are today unknown.

The main events of the rising are not in dispute. On the night of 23 January 1915, after a period of preparation that lasted no more than two months, the "battalions" of Chilembwe's small army of conspirators issued forth from the small church at Mbombwe, the headquarters of his Providence Industrial Mission. Some battalions went south to Blantyre and Limbe, the white-dominated commercial centers of the Protectorate. Another headed toward the estates of Nsoni and Midima. Two other patrols or platoons, for the term battalion grossly overestimates their size, effectiveness, and purpose, followed the twisting paths northward to the nearby vast estates of Alexander Livingstone Bruce. A message was also dispatched to Ncheu, 110 miles northwest of Mbombwe, where Filipo Chinyama had promised to foment a complementary revolt. Finally, Chilembwe sent a courier to German-ruled East Africa with a communication about the rising.

The rebels first drew blood at Magomero, the headquarters of the Bruce estate. There William Jervis Livingstone, the manager of the estate, and his wife were entertaining Mrs. Ranald MacDonald, the wife of a customs official. In a nearby house occupied by the custodian of the local rifle club's ammunition supply, were Mrs. Emily Stanton and Mrs. Alyce Roach. The four women were accompanied by five children. Duncan MacCormick, an estate employee, was alone in a third house. None had any forewarning of the attack, although their servants, at least some of whom later demonstrated their loyalty to the women and children involved, certainly knew for what purposes the battalion had come.

The rebels wanted Livingstone's head, and, after a slight skirmish, during which Livingstone was wounded, one of the attackers forced his way into a bedroom where Mrs. Livingstone was vainly attempting to revive her husband, and—she later recalled—"with an axe proceeded to cut off my husband's head." By this time MacCormick, alerted by his servants, had come to the assistance of the Livingstones. But the rebels met his advance with spears, and he died beside William Livingstone. Throughout the attack, however, none of the women and children at Magomero was in any way harmed or molested, and Mrs. MacDonald's attempt forcibly to halt the rebels' attack was ignored. In addition, aside from the arsenal, the existence of which had helped to prompt the attack, the rebels looted no property and returned to Mbombwe with only a few rifles, some ammunition, and Livingstone's head. It was placed atop a pole in the Mbombwe church.

While the attack at Magomero was taking place, the second battalion shed blood at Mwanje, another section of the Bruce estate. These members of the battalion speared Robert Ferguson, the stock manager, on his bed, but he managed to stagger a few yards to the house of the section manager. There John and Charlotte Robertson's preparations for bed were interrupted, and a running gun battle ensued until the Robertsons escaped into a cotton field. The Robertsons could never explain why they should have been attacked and Ferguson killed. The battalion may have hoped to find a cache of arms or may have intended simply to safeguard the line of retreat from Magomero. In any event it returned empty-handed to Mbombwe.

The raid on the isolated planters at Nsoni and Midima never took place, but telephone lines between Zomba and Tete and Blantyre and Mikalongwe were severed. The battalions which were primed to attack the *boma* in Blantyre and commercial establishments in nearby Limbe failed to act. Similarly, after vainly waiting for the Nsoni/Midima battalion to join them, the seventy rebels who had been instructed to break into the arms warehouse in neighboring Mandala were able to complete their mission with only partial success (seizing a few rifles and seven hundred rounds of ammunition) because supposedly loyal African watchmen and soldiers turned against them. The untended *boma* at Chiradzulu, a mere five miles from Mbombwe, was never threatened; the rebels likewise refrained from attacking the numerous whites who lived without protection on prosperous estates within a twenty mile radius of Mbombwe and Magomero; and the men of Mbombwe resorted to arms again only on 26 January when they severely wounded Father Swelsen, a Roman Catholic priest, and set his Nguludi mission on fire. It is impossible to guess whether the rebels under Filipo Chinyama really intended—as Mwase reports—to make their way southward to join Chilembwe; before they could even attack the Ncheu *boma* an alert administrator learned of their intentions from several loyalist chiefs and arrested Chinyama and company without a struggle. Nor is it possible to say whether or not Chilembwe and Chinyama expected their initiative to stimulate a mass uprising among the peoples of southern Nyasaland. Only thus could the rebellion have succeeded, but Chilembwe spent the days of the revolution meditating atop a hill near Mbombwe. He seems, furthermore, to have prepared no line of defense and to have failed to fortify his mission station. More surprisingly, although the possibility of failure was discussed, no systematic retreat was planned or put into effect.

The uprising was short-lived. By 26 January hastily raised white volunteers had pressed an attack on Mbombwe, where they were resisted only for a day. Many of the rebels fled, or attempted with little success to mingle with noncombatant villagers; Chilembwe himself was finally persuaded to leave his hill and seek refuge in neighboring Moçambique; and, after the expenditure of much dynamite, whites managed to destroy the thick-walled church at Mbombwe. On 3 February Chilembwe was killed by a small patrol north of Mlanje, and, by the end of March, forty rebels had lost their lives on the scaffold or before firing squads and about three hundred had been imprisoned.

The ease with which the rising was suppressed immediately encouraged confident drawing of conclusions about its origins: Why, observers and antagonists asked themselves, had Africans risen so unexpectedly? What moved the rising's presumably fanatical leader, of whom few had hitherto heard? And what had he and the rebels expected to achieve?

General answers to the first question proved easiest to supply. The attack on Magomero obviously implied hostility toward Livingstone and the Bruce estates. It was accepted in settler and official circles that Africans who had worked for the estate or lived within its three hundred square miles might justifiably have complained about the way in which they had been treated. Livingstone's rule had been especially iniquitous and objectionable, and he had in a wanton manner destroyed prayer houses of the Providence Industrial Mission. Even the official commission of inquiry, whose report could hardly have been expected to be critical of settlers, felt compelled to say that "Livingstone's treatment of natives was often unduly harsh and apart from this the general system of estate management was not satisfactory." The members of the commission and their contemporaries were also forced to acknowledge that whether on or off the lands owned by Bruce, Africans felt systematically discriminated against, were subjected to severe curtailments of their personal liberty, and almost always were treated by whites with disrespect. Subsequent investigations have substantiated these accusations and emphasized the extent to which Africans resented their cruel rejection by the official society of white-ruled Nyasaland. Their social and psychological grievances were real and keenly felt, and are not to be underestimated.

But the existence of social and psychological grievances is insufficient to explain with what intent Chilembwe transformed a widespread and rather discontinuous energy of disaffection into the actuality of revolution. The then Governor of Nyasaland was naturally the first person (of whom we have any record) to commit his conclusions to writing. On the day of Chilembwe's death he reported to the Colonial Office that the various papers and books which had been seized in Chilembwe's house "prove and disclose a wide and well-organized movement to attack and massacre the whites." A few weeks later the official responsible for the administration of the Blantyre district probably spoke for many of his colleagues when he opined that "John Chilembwe wanted to become King of Nyasaland." (The Yao chief, Malemia, believed that Chilembwe wanted to be "the Governor.") Unlike some observers, however, this administrator advanced the paradoxical but perceptive explanation that Chilembwe "and his educated accomplices must have persuaded themselves that there existed a general disaffection towards Europeans which would result in a widespread rising following immediately on his first attack on the white men . . . [but] with the exception of the attack on Magomero there can never have been a more irresolute and half-hearted rising. It seems clear to me that there existed no real desire to kill Europeans among the bulk of John Chilembwe's followers. . . . My own belief is that, with the exception of the ringleaders, no one knew what Chilembwe contemplated, and the bulk of his followers did not know for what they were called out. That they were animated by no common grievance against the Government or Europeans as a whole I feel sure."

The commission of inquiry, whose members were all local men naturally sympathetic to their peers, finally presented its official report early in 1916. The commission decided that "The objects of the rising were the extermination or expulsion of the European population, and the setting up of a native state or theocracy of which John Chilembwe was to be the head." But it failed to define any of these terms or to demonstrate the nature of the information which indicated such unequivocal conclusions. Indeed, presumably because such a conclusion was in no way controversial, the commissioners saw no need either to supplement or modify their bald statement. If today it begs innumerable questions, the chief of which must be to reconcile Chilembwe's methods and the scale of his operations with his possible goals, then it reflected the locally acceptable stereotype and, in ruling circles at least, was never openly challenged. Nyasaland, moreover, was embroiled in war against the Germans, and most whites were readily prepared to accept the commission's findings as definitive. Sir George Smith, who was still the Governor of Nyasaland in 1919, saw no reason to modify his original views, or to take issue with the commission, when he submitted a chapter on his country to Sir Charles P. Lucas's *The Empire at War*, a five volume compilation of essays from the far-flung colonies of the Crown. "The movement," Smith wrote of Chilembwe's rising, "was designed [unquestionably] for the massacre of whites in the Shire Highlands . . . and for the suppression of white rule." Smith also believed that "however ill conceived . . . the rising was full of potentiality."

During the two decades between World Wars I and II, Chilembwe's rising retained some local notoriety. Certainly the administration was alert for any recrudescence of similar activity, and the Criminal Investigation Division of the protectorate's police force maintained a steady surveillance of those of Chilembwe's followers who had been released from prison. They also scrutinized the activities of African churchmen, particularly those of separatist persuasion, and watched all other educated Africans as a matter of routine. But no whites questioned the orthodox interpretation of the rising—indeed, there was no compelling reason why any should have—and beyond Nyasaland's borders even the historical fact of the uprising was little known.

However, a medical officer in Kenya, Norman Leys, had served in Nyasaland and was concerned to explain the nature of African grievances in the former colony, as well as to set the Nairobi riots of 1921 in a fuller context. He understood the problems and aspirations of Africans far better than many of his white contemporaries and appreciated the many factors that drove Africans to rebel (and yet approved of the brutal suppression of all revolts). The short chapter on Chilembwe's rising in his *Kenya* was thus written with a modicum of compassion and the advantage of a degree of hindsight. Leys derived his summary—for it is no more than that—from the report of the official commission and conversations with the Rev. Mr. Robert Hellier Napier of the Blantyre Mission and "many of the survivors of the rising" who were in prison in Zomba. According to Leys, Chilembwe's inspiration came from the Old Testament; every week he preached sermons "in which the example of the Jews in their national struggle with Egyptians, Philistines and others was held up for their admiration and imitation." Chilembwe's plan "was to get the people on the estate to murder their masters, and then to bring about a general rebellion. He had a list of all the Europeans [then 821] in the country, of whom some were to be killed out of hand; others, including the women and children, were to be expelled from the country; while a few, men and women, were to be allowed to remain as teachers, but without political authority." The great majority of the rebels, Leys believed, were "serfs surrounded by people living rent-free." Although Chilembwe, he wrote, "no doubt dreamed of an Africa for Africans . . . the bait he tempted his followers with was land of their own, and release from the necessity of work without wages in order to pay rent and taxes." Like his predecessors, Leys essentially agreed that Chilembwe had sought to destroy white rule and become king of Nyasaland. And this was the view that by and large prevailed until 1958.

African testimony and writings have been more equivocal than those of whites. Their conclusions give pause to those who would readily accept a simple, direct explanation of Chilembwe's behavior. The first public intimation of Chilembwe's attitude toward whites and the efficacy of rebellion came in August 1914 when a frightened man approached Philip Mitchell, then a raw recruit to the Colonial Service who was temporarily in charge of the Chiradzulu *boma*, with a confusing story about the intentions of John Chilembwe. By the time that Mitchell had become Sir Philip and had governed Uganda and Kenya, he could remember little about this obscure incident on the eve of World War I. It seems, however, that the man must have been one Eugenio of Matuta village, an African teacher in the employ of the Roman Catholic Montfort Marist Fathers Mission at Nguludi. A later recollection of Eugenio's testimony by Bishop Auneau of the Mission —that Chilembwe "intended to kill all the Europeans of the country, as well as those Africans who would not join him, and then make himself spiritual and temporal head of Nyasaland"—seems repetitive of the stereotype and less acceptable than Mitchell's immediate report to L. T. Moggridge, his superior in Blantyre: "A boy from the Nguludi Mission has made a long rambling statement, the gist of which is that the Azungu [whites] are said by John Chilembwe to be going to attack the natives in November and that before they get a chance the natives must attack the Azungu. They are to go to Zomba and make the Boma bugles blow the alarm in the middle of the night, while John Chilembwe's people squat outside the doors of the European houses and kill the owners as they come out on hearing the bugle."   Neither Mitchell himself nor his successor, although they cross-examined Africans assiduously, censored Chilembwe's correspondence, and kept their ears to the ground, managed to confirm Eugenio's story or to learn anything more about the supposed conspiracy. Milthorp, Mitchell's replacement, merely gathered that Chilembwe was telling Africans not to work for whites, but in Milthorp's view rebellion was not being contemplated. Indeed, on several occasions Milthorp and Moggridge, the Blantyre Resident, assured the Governor, who for his part was prepared to deport Chilembwe on the slimmest evidence of suspicion, that there was "little to be feared from this man." Furthermore, Moggridge, blinded by common prejudice, was confident that "Our native is a very poor hand at conspiracy and concealment; if there are more than two or three in the business it will certainly be given away. . . ."

After the rising, statements were collected—it is not known in what form, under what circumstances, or by whom—from a number of African participants and the white survivors. Lupiya Zalela (alias Kettleo) reported that "They . . . agreed to bring the war on Saturday and kill all the Europeans first, so they went to Magomero to kill the Europeans. Mr. Livingstone was killed because he did not pay us well for our work. . . . Chilembwe sent messengers to various churches saying 'The Europeans are to kill the natives on Monday, 25 January; What shall we do? Tis good that we begin the war and kill the Europeans before they begin.' The people agreed." The testimony of Duncan Njilima, who was immediately afterward executed for high treason and for being an accessory before the fact, agrees substantially: "I went to John Chilembwe . . . and he said 'The Europeans want to seize and kill all natives this year. I want all natives, before the Europeans come, to attack and kill them.' I refused and said . . . 'what will you take with you to fight?' John Chilembwe said that there were boxes of ammunition at Magomero. 'Many people will go to Magomero to take the rifles and ammunition.' . . . 'We will take sticks.' " Abraham Chimbia recalled that Chilembwe had said that "the Europeans were making slaves of us and getting us killed in war." Mrs. Alyce Roach said that she had been given a note (the author is unspecified) to take to the Chiradzulu *boma*. It said: "tell all white men that the chiefs of all tribes have agreed to kill them because they have so cruelly robbed us of our Mother land." These are, in sum, statements of a defensive as well as an offensive character and say nothing directly about Chilembwe's ultimate aims. But then, too, their contents are in essence based on hearsay of a very incomplete kind.

Two personal statements by contemporaries of Chilembwe are of great importance despite the fact that they were made from memory many years after the event. Kalindi Morrison Malinki worked with both Joseph Booth, Chilembwe's first mentor, and Chilembwe himself. He subsequently became Nyasaland's first African Seventh-day Adventist pastor. Sometime during the early 1950's he recalled that "Things went well for a few years when, later, Chilembwe hated the European. His hatred grew more bitter that he definitely made up his mind to destroy all the Europeans in Nyasaland. But, as he could not do all this by himself, he at once got busy interesting all his believers and his friends to join him in his plan. 'The European is here to make you his slave for ever, let us get rid of him,' he told them. One day John Chilembwe came to my house. 'Why do Europeans trouble us?' he asked. 'Let us plan to kill them all!' "

The second statement is of an entirely different character. Entitled "Maziko a Prov. Ind. Mission. Chiradzulo. Nyasaland. 1900. A.D.," it was compiled from memory in 1951 by Andrew G. Mkulichi, one of Chilembwe's followers, and contains a fairly full account of Chilembwe's life and influence. According to this source, after Chilembwe's famous letter of November 1914 had failed to elicit any stir of recognition of African grievances on the part of the government, Chilembwe feared that he would soon be arrested and killed. "He then began strong teaching" counseling revolt, and read out, among other portions of the New Testament, Acts 20:32: "And now brethren, I commend you to God, and to the word of his grace, which is able to build you up, and to give you an inheritance among all them which are sanctified," and finally strengthened his followers with the words: "We ought to suffer persecution. . . ." Mkulichi also reported that Chilembwe frequently reiterated three points: "I hear the crying of my Africans. My people are destroyed through lack of knowledge. It is better for me to die than to live." If the gist of this account—not all of which has been quoted—is credible, Chilembwe courted martyrdom, not a kingdom, and only acted out of despair, not avarice. Mkulichi's account narrows Chilembwe's fear of being killed by whites to a specific point in time, thus moderating the otherwise paranoid dimension circumstantially attributed to his behavior by the few Africans who made statements immediately after the rising.

Both of these statements were among the many elicited especially for the pioneering study of Chilembwe by Shepperson and Price. In the course of their very thorough survey of the rich and disparate evidence, they advanced a number of hypotheses to explain Chilembwe's behavior. First, to them it was a harmful simplification to specify the aims of the rising as no more than anti-European and pro-independent-African government. "No doubt these were the objects which Chilembwe and his lieutenants, as well as the majority of his convinced following, set themselves, if the Rising should prove successful. Yet it is by no means clear that Chilembwe believed it would be successful, and one aspect of the Rising, as a symbolical gesture to show that Africans in the Protectorate would not always accept passively the spate of changes and discriminations which the rush of European rule was heaping on them, [was] . . . suggested. It was one way—perhaps the only way—of forcing upon the government and settlers of the Protectorate an independent African point of view. Thus the aims of the Rising appear to have been twofold: first, if successful, the creation of an African state in Nyasaland, with strongly theocratic elements and selected European guidance; second, if unsuccessful, a gesture of protest . . . against what were conceived as the intolerable aspects of European rule." On the point of "selected European guidance" the authors subsequently reiterate—on the basis of what evidence is uncertain—that Chilembwe's concept of the future Nyasaland was not multiracial, although "he apparently considered that that state which would emerge from a successful rising would accommodate some Europeans as mentors and specialists." In their concluding chapter Shepperson and Price go on to say that Chilembwe and his followers were "confused in their aims: they wanted both to destroy and to preserve; to stage both a demonstration and a revolution; to assert a traditional dignity by martyrdom, and by the same activity to mould a new community." They make the important distinction that the prospect for which Chilembwe began to fight was "one of founding a nation rather than of restoring the fortunes of the tribes." At another point in their analysis the authors emphasize the equally critical conclusion (also obvious, but often overlooked) that Chilembwe "wanted to break the European monopoly of the power, wealth, and dignity which their culture conferred, not to reject that way of life."   Unlike their white predecessors, Shepperson and Price refused to accept a simple reading of Chilembwe's character. They examined it with a full awareness of and deference to its complexity, and, from a number of different angles, saw how Chilembwe might well have wanted to make a gesture as well as to oust his rulers. Their variety of rich sources led in no conclusive direction, however, and they were thus forced to accept the validity of both main postulates while indicating a slight preference for the possibility that Chilembwe consciously played the precarious role of martyr.

Fortunately a reconsideration of Chilembwe's aspirations need not rest with Shepperson and Price's admirable, if wisely ambivalent, conclusions. The full text of George Simeon Mwase's "A Dialogue of Nyasaland, Record of Past Events, Environments and the Present Outlook within the Protectorate" which was originally written in 1931–32, has now been published. Based upon the evidence of a leading participant in the rising, it contains a graphic account of the events leading up to the rising, and the rising itself, that can hardly have been invented.   Without question it provides the fullest African explanation of Chilembwe's motives and aims. Mwase, for example, flatly says that "John had no intention of rebelling against the Government itself. . . . His personal aim was to fight white Planters, Traders, and other white settlers within the country." He grieved for his country and his fellow

Africans, but determined to act only after his famous letter to the *Nyasaland Times* failed to bring promises of amelioration. The conspirators, Mwase wrote, "all came to the conclusion, that by not answering us on our request, means death on us." They all said, Mwase reported, that "it was better for all of us to die, than to live and see all these troubles"—the last two words possibly referring to World War I. In early January (Mwase supplied a precise date) the conspirators held a decisive meeting. There they decided "'to strike a blow,' or else . . . to be buried alive alternately." And it was on this occasion that Chilembwe specifically referred to the example of the abolitionist John Brown, "who after losing his hope, in succeeding the request in writing . . . he determinate to strike a blow and lose his own life, than, as he said, [it] was too good for him and was ['] out of sight and reach.'" Mwase then recorded: "John said, this case stands the same as that of a Mr. John Brown. . . . 'Let us then strike a blow and die,' for our blood will surely mean something at last." (Somewhat later in his narrative, Mwase specifically says that Chilembwe is the Mr. John Brown of Africa, and also compares him favorably with William Prynne, the Puritan pamphleteer, and Sir Roger Casement, the Irish patriot.) Subsequently Mwase quotes Chilembwe as saying "I did not mean you to succeed and defeat whitemen, no, not at all, that is not my idea even when I am standing here now. This [action] is only a hint to the whitemen, that the way they treat our country men and women is to grieve the whole country, and on behalf of all our country people, we choose to die for them."

Chilembwe's "instructions to his army," as given by Mwase, strengthen the above suggestions about the intentions of the leader, intensify the impact of Mkulichi's much briefer account, and reinforce the suspicions put forward by Shepperson and Price.

> You are all patriots as you sit. Patriots mean[s] to die for Amor Patria. This very night you are to go and strike the blow and then die. I do not say that you are going to win the war at all. You have no weapons [guns?] with you and you are not at all trained military men even. One great thing you must remember is that Omnia Vincit Amor so for love [of] your own country and country men, I now encourage you to go and strike a blow bravely and die.
>
> This is only way to show the whitemen, that the treatment they are treating our men and women was most bad and we have determined to strike a first and a last blow, and then all die by the heavy storm of the whiteman's army. The whitemen will then think, after we are dead, that the treatment they are treating our people is almost [most] bad, and they might change to the better for our people. After we are dead and buried. This blows means "non sibi sed patria."

According to Mwase, Chilembwe willingly sought martyrdom. "He knew at the beginning that his idea of striking a blow on a whiteman meant his death." Chilembwe had no weapons; whites had many. His army was small and untrained. Mwase compared his action to that of a person, armed only with a maize stalk, who intrepidly and absurdly attacks a lion at his prey. He wanted glory, says Mwase—"He wanted to win heroic, and nothing else." Furthermore, he specifically wanted to draw attention to the grievances of his people by protesting, and, after failing to do so by his letter, the only way in which he could draw attention to his protest was by attacking the government with a "maize stalk." "He did," Mwase began a long parable of explanation,

as the old story say, that in a place, somewhere in the North, a lot of monkeys found plenty of fruits food and they were enjoying and living upon that food. One day a huge elephant came over to that forest, where, after entering into the fruit forest, instead of eating the fruits with monkeys, the elephant began to knock and cut down the fruit trees and chewed even the roots of the trees. This kind of action, the elephant repeated often times. The trees were finishing falling. One day the elephant was again doing the same thing. One of the monkeys approached the elephant personally, and ask him to stop felling down the fruit trees, as they, the monkeys, had no other food to live upon—and told the elephant the better way was for him to eat the fruit of the trees in the same way they were eating, by plucking off the fruits only, and have the trees to yield more fruits for next year, and so forth. The elephant paid not a slightest attention to that, now he made a worse of felling the trees he was doing. Monkeys being a small kind of animals, never went on with the matter, although the matter was a grave one, but through fear, he went away.

Next day the monkey came again and sat on one of the fruit trees in the forest, just by the side of the elephant road. The elephant again came passing the same road, a poor monkey then gave a deadly slap on the elephant tail, that slap made the elephant look behind and saw that the slap had been inflicted on his tail by a tiny monkey. He caught him, and asked him, what he meant by it. Monkey replied, I did not mean anything Sir. [The elephant asked:] Why and what made you to slap me? I am too tiny and weak, [the monkey said,] to go on discussing with you and I thought it the best, to give you a signal of my poor slap, that you may understand that the action of felling fruit trees do us a great harm; and I choose to die by being tramped by you, than to die with hunger. The elephant said, you are a fool, poor little monkey, you knew you have no strength to fight me, so as you have made up a fool of yourself, by touching me with you tiny hand. I will now crush you into powder. The monkey was then crushed and finished.

Next day the elephant passed that road again, and when he arrived near that tree, where that monkey was, remembered that slap which he received from a tiny monkey, and for what the tiny animal bravely slapped him, and when he saw the rest of monkeys about eating the fruits from the trees, he thought, if I will fell more fruit trees, surely, these tiny monkeys will look at me as a bad man, though they have no words to speak or power to fight with me. So the elephant at last became [took] pity on the little animals and never fell more fruit trees, but he kept eating in the way the small animals were eating. At the end, the elephant became a big friend and a protector of the small animals."

Mwase's account lends color and circumstantial evidence to the case for a gesture rather than a bid for power. But it can be argued that Mwase, who wrote in 1931–32, may well have wanted to put a more acceptable gloss on Chilembwe's motives for patriotic reasons. Mwase had already engaged in the desultory politics of self-assertion, and he may have felt that the advancement of educated Nyasas had been inhibited by the government's opinion of Chilembwe as a crass, self-serving opportunist. Mwase never once considers whether Chilembwe accepted the inevitability of failure. But this may simply be ex post facto reasoning, and, even if Mwase did not see the inherent contradiction, he was clearly troubled by Chilembwe's willingness to invite assistance from the Germans. Mwase does not attempt to explain why Chilembwe, if he wanted merely to make a gesture, bothered to co-ordinate his plans with Chinyama, and why Chinyama (according to Mwase) was expected to march south from Ncheu to the Blantyre district, attacking planters in the Zomba district en route. Additionally, the reader is devoid of means to discover on what grounds Mwase asserted his belief in Chilembwe's search for martyrdom. The instructions and statements which he quoted, however, contain too many plausible components to have been concocted wholesale. It has been shown that the rebel Wallace Kampingo was Mwase's primary informant,   and it is an allowable assumption that Mwase renders Kampingo's memory (however accurate or inaccurate it may have been) with a high degree of faithfulness. Certainly few Africans of (in the Western sense) limited educational attainments and experience—for Mwase was no more advanced than many of his contemporaries—would, despite the marching song, have known enough about John Brown to forge a new myth with such seeming verisimilitude.

Before deciding the extent to which Mwase's attractive and romantic hypothesis should become the orthodox interpretation, it is essential to scrutinize the whole body of evidence as well as the conclusions of the record. Moreover, it is especially important that whichever explanation of the intentions of Chilembwe wins favor accords well with what we know of the latter's personal history and his psychological makeup. Unfortunately, of Chilembwe's formative years we can learn very little. He was born in "the time of Livingstone"—during the 1860's or early 1870's—to a Yao father and a Cewa (or possibly a Mang'anja) mother. Chilembwe later, as a student in America, said that his father was a "king," but this was the fanciful talk so beloved of an expatriate. His mother, however, had previously been married to a Yao with some chiefly connections, and she herself bore a name with historically regal overtones. She may conceivably have set Chilembwe on the road to prominence by precept, or by reminding him of a real or presumed heritage. Indeed, according to Mkulichi's account, Chilembwe's prenatal behavior foretold greatness. Chilembwe had twisted and turned in the womb to an unusual degree and was thus, in his mother's view, intended to "turn" future events. In this connection there is some scientific evidence that maternal emotional stress increases fetal activity and leads to reduced birth weight and irritable, hyperactive infants. Furthermore, infants reported by their mothers to be very active as fetuses were somewhat more advanced on motor test items than those reported to be less active in the fetal stage. Or, more probably, does this reported recollection of Chilembwe's mother merely signify a later attempt by biblically knowledgeable Africans to equate Chilembwe with John the Baptist, his putative namesake? Passages from Luke, particularly 1:41 ("And it came to pass, that, when Elisabeth heard the salutation of Mary, the babe leaped in her womb; and Elisabeth was filled with the Holy Ghost.") are analogous, and Mkulichi, or even Chilembwe himself, may have wanted to suggest links between the two Johns. Chilembwe would often have pondered the relevant remainder of Luke, particularly 1:48-53 and 76-80, and could himself have used this supposed affinity with the first John to win waverers to his side in 1915. Had his mother not said that he had emerged into the world feet first—an unnatural and precocious sign?

A few years after his birth, Chilembwe and his family moved from Sanganu, in the Chiradzulu district, to what became Blantyre. By the accident of this residence Chilembwe—conceivably thrust forward by an ambitious mother—became a student and catechumen of the Blantyre Mission of the Church of Scotland. This event took place about 1890, or a few years before, and may have implied a conscious desire by Chilembwe or his parents to learn more about the ways of the whites who had so recently (missionaries arrived in 1876, planters followed, and the Shire Highlands became a British Protectorate in 1889) settled in their midst. As his biographers aptly described the milieu, "Chilembwe spent his early years in an atmosphere of great insecurity and change. It was an atmosphere full of the keenness of the contrasts between the new gospel of peace and brotherhood which the missions were preaching and the evident injustices and disturbances of both European and African society at a time of rapid social change. The new education which the missions had brought with them provided much of the stimulus and the means for observant Africans like Chilembwe to apprehend these contrasts."

In 1892, in the midst of this ferment, a missionary of unorthodox persuasion arrived on the scene to challenge the Blantyre church. He was Joseph Booth, a British fundamentalist of apocalyptical religious vision. After a commercial and agricultural career in England and the Antipodes, he had heeded the evangelical call and, soon thereafter, entered Nyasaland with a determination to establish a self-supporting Baptist church on lines pioneered by William Carey in India. From his Zambezi Industrial Mission on the outskirts of Blantyre, Booth attempted to spread the egalitarian ideas that immediately made him anathema to the established Scottish missionaries and to the colonial administration.   He criticized the comfortable life led by European missionaries in the midst of African poverty, paid Africans somewhat higher wages than did the mission or the government, and soon attracted a small but devoted following. In this group, which included several potential Scottish converts, was John Chilembwe. Whether Booth's personality, wages, or message, or some dissatisfaction with the Scots, wooed Chilembwe is not known. Booth's daughter recalled that he "had heard of Father as being a kind, white man." He came with a note which read: "You please carry me for God. I like to be your cook-boy."

It is clear that Chilembwe and Booth were soon *en rapport*. He became Booth's faithful house servant (Booth had recently become a widower), and in that capacity also cared for Emily and John Edward, the evangelist's young children. As his knowledge of spoken and written English improved, he interpreted for Booth, was baptized, and later taught in schools of the Zambezi Industrial Mission. He became the mainstay of the new church as he was the linchpin of Booth's household. Emily remembered Chilembwe's qualities: "Without his faithfulness and dependability I doubt very much if I could have survived, or if Father could have completed . . . the buying of land for a mission station. . . . Father was able to leave me in his care. He was kind and infinitely patient."   Sometime after Chilembwe's death, Booth wrote of their first days together: "The writer doubts if any human being he has known has had a greater influence on himself than this same Native Youth. His many touching acts of kindness and thoughtfulness during the first 18 months of the writer's residence in Nyassaland, before any other White Comrade assisted. . . . Certainly the writer and his little daughter being alone would have died but for Chilembwe's never wearying tender help. . . . He joined me in a time of Distress and Sickness . . . [and] soon won my heart more than I could have believed possible."

There is no doubt that Chilembwe was influenced beyond measure by what was, for the time and place, a most unusual contact with a white household, and through it, with a corner of the West. Guided by Booth, Chilembwe could not help but appreciate that the typical British approach to colonial problems was not invariable. Booth was among the earliest whites to enunciate a clearcut doctrine of "Africa for the African"; indeed Chilembwe joined him in 1897 in proposing an African Christian Union of Nyasaland, the objects of which were to be "equal rights, political, social, and economic, for Africans as well as Europeans; the development of African education along the technical lines of the European world; independent African activity in all economic fields; a just land settlement; the encouragement of a pro-African press and literature; and the growth of independent African Christianity." By this time Chilembwe had, if the term is not too loaded, become an évolué with perhaps some appreciation of the precariousness of his position between traditional and white society. Already the few whites who looked upon Nyasaland as their home resented and feared the emergence of Western-educated Africans. A color bar was in the process of erection. Indeed, even if Chilembwe had not gone to the United States, his association with Booth and the isolation that often oppresses the marginal men in any society might themselves have provided the necessary inspiration for the makings of a revolutionary.

A profile of the American experience, to the extent that we can recapture it, is essential for an understanding of the possible motives of 1915. Booth asserts that Chilembwe "volunteered" to go with him to the United States in order to disprove Arab-disseminated rumors (then circulating among the Yao) about the fate of the African slaves who had been transported to the United States. Many Yao apparently believed that "for hundreds of years Whites had taken shiploads of slaves to U S A & other places & eaten them there, for they never came back." But even if this widespread attitude of doubt provided the main motivation for Chilembwe's voyage abroad, it is also evident that Booth (who presumably paid for most of Chilembwe's passage) wanted very much to exhibit Chilembwe before the committees and church groups to which he expected to appeal for funds. And either Chilembwe alone, or both jointly, may have decided that Chilembwe's stature and potential for good would be enhanced by further study in an American institution of higher learning. In any event, they traveled together in 1897 via London and Liverpool to New York, Richmond, and Baltimore, later visited Washington, Brooklyn, and Philadelphia, and by early 1898 Chilembwe, supported by New York Negro Baptists, had been enrolled as a student in the Virginia Theological College and Seminary in Lynchburg, Virginia.

His experiences in western Virginia, and wherever he traveled along the eastern seaboard, could hardly have lessened whatever antipathy he may already have harbored toward whites. In Richmond, mobs of young white men followed and frequently stoned Booth and Chilembwe for walking together, sitting together on the same public park benches, and living in the same Negro household. In Virginia, as elsewhere in the South, Negro voters were systematically being deprived of their suffrage by the poll tax, literacy requirements open to interpretation, and other recently introduced legislation. Segregation, sometimes accompanied by violence, was then being extended into new areas of routine and endeavor. And lynching was a common occurrence. Although little direct evidence survives, Chilembwe could hardly have escaped some confrontation with these harsh facts of Negro existence. In the same way, he could not have avoided becoming acquainted with the different methods utilized by Negroes to respond to the prevalence of white power. He probably heard or read of the slave rebellions. He conversed with a number of the leaders of the independent Negro churches, may have been influenced by his discussions with John L. Dube, the experienced and later militant proto-nationalist, religious separatist, educator, and publisher from Natal, and was probably conversant with the radical ideas of some of the men who subsequently founded the National Association for the Advancement of Colored People.

It is unclear, however, what Chilembwe studied, or whether he followed any set course during his two years in the Lynchburg college. The nature of his reading is unknown, although his biographers reasonably suppose that it may have included the well-known autobiography of Frederick Douglass. It is, in fact, sensible to argue that the image that recurs in Mwase's account—that Chilembwe urged his followers to "strike a blow and die"—derives from Douglass. In 1892 Douglass had published a final, completely revised version of his popular autobiography. An analysis of John Brown, a central figure in the author's life, occupies sizable portions of the second part of the book. Douglass dissects Brown's character, motives, and strategy in a way that may well have appealed to Chilembwe. He also refers specifically to a conversation he had had with Brown before the raid on

Harpers Ferry and, in so doing, he uses the very form of words that—if Mwase is to be believed—became the *leitmotiv* of the rebellion: "Our talk was long and earnest; we spent the most of a Saturday and a part of Sunday in this debate—Brown for Harpers Ferry and I against it—he for striking a blow which should instantly rouse the country, and I for the policy of gradually and unaccountably drawing off the slaves to the mountains, as first suggested and proposed by him." Chilembwe may somehow also have known of Brown's conversation with Mrs. Mary Stearns in Boston: "Oh," he said, "if I could have the money that is smoked away during a single day in Boston, I could strike a blow that would make slavery totter from its foundations." But whatever the source of inspiration for the particular and admittedly obvious image, Chilembwe could only with difficulty have avoided learning of Old Brown's raid on Harpers Ferry. It is not very far from Lynchburg, and the raid, celebrated as it was in song and poetry, was widely if erroneously credited with having precipitated the Civil War, the emancipation of the slaves, and the welcome years of reconstruction. Louisa May Alcott had christened Brown "St John the Just"; for Ralph Waldo Emerson, Brown had made the "gallows glorious like the cross," and Henry David Thoreau described Brown as "an angel of light." At the time of his deed, Julia Ward Howe had told her sister that "The attempt, I must judge insane, but the spirit *heroic.* I should be glad to be as sure of Heaven as that old man may be, following right in the footsteps of the martyrs, girding on his sword for the weak and the oppressed. His death will be holy and glorious—the gallows cannot dishonor him—he will hallow it."

Negroes of Chilembwe's acquaintance may conceivably have viewed the deed with a greater sense of proportion, but Chilembwe may still—as Mwase asserts—have incorporated the folk myth into his own psyche. Certainly John Brown was a folk hero in late nineteenth-century America; that he had struck a great and heroic blow for freedom and liberty, and that martyrdom was a just reward, were widespread sentiments. As late as 1931 Mwase—if his own understanding of Brown's actions was in any way compatible with that of Chilembwe—believed that by being against slavery and fighting his own government, Brown's name "won a great fame. Up to this time all the military troops march on with a song of Mr. John Brown actions and deeds, although his actions and deeds were seen as criminal offences. Many years after, wise people examined them, and found that they were worth while. So they published them out, and made it known to everyone, and after all they formed a song out of his actions and deeds. The song is still living now. . . ."

Although he was awarded the degrees of A.B. and B.D. *in absentia* in 1901, Chilembwe returned to Nyasaland in 1900 (the date is in dispute, and his own deposition gives "Feb. 1900" as the date of the opening of the Providence Industrial Mission) as an ordained representative of the National Baptist Convention. The events of the subsequent fourteen years would provide grist for a number of analytical mills but, as with so many facets of Chilembwe's career, the existing evidence is more tantalizing than conclusive. For the first few years, assisted by American Negroes from the National Convention, he certainly concentrated on the difficult problems of establishing his unique mission. Gradually he transformed a collection of mud huts into a proper station, opened a chain of out-schools (he reported seven in 1914), constructed the solid station church, planted crops, and gained adherents throughout the Shire Highlands and Moçambique, where he occasionally preached. Chilembwe also seems to have turned his station into an outwardly Western community; he insisted upon European affectations and the wearing of clean, neat Edwardian attire. Chilembwe's African biographer commented favorably upon his sobriety and his habits of industriousness. "He liked to see his country men work hard and prosper in their undertakings, also to see them smart, such as Negro fellows he had seen in America." Outwardly, at least, Chilembwe accepted the techniques of advancement so favored by the black bourgeoisie, preached no disturbing millennial doctrine, and, when whites put their impressions on paper—which was rarely—the Chilembwe of this period was viewed in a respectable light.

It is arguable that Chilembwe initially believed that the attainment of African power and of enhanced social and political opportunity depended upon the ability of Nyasas to demonstrate commercial ability and responsibility. It was with such ends in mind that he helped in 1909 to establish the Natives' Industrial Union. Its objects were said to be "the promotion and protection of Negroes Christian work in the Country, the collecting and recording of commercial information and . . . the establishment of a Court of Arbitration. Communication with the public Authorities on subjects affecting the Commercial and Planting Community, or such other things as occasion may require." A kind of co-operative was envisaged, a five per cent dividend ("or thereabout") being half-promised. Whether the Union ever functioned as a co-operative, however, is not ascertainable. We have records in English of meetings throughout 1909, but no account of the business of or discussions at these meetings. It is also assumed that the Union continued to exist through at least 1911, when its name became the African Industrial Society; its purposes seem to have been as nebulous as those of the Union. But again no positive evidence is available. Was it a "talk shop" in the manner of the later welfare associations? Or was it a façade for a conspiracy of some kind? All we know is that Chilembwe participated in some of the meetings during 1909 and may have been instrumental in organizing the Union (along lines sketched by Booth years before). In a letter to the mysterious Haya Edward Peters which could just barely refer to conspiracy as well as to the Union, Chilembwe said: "I want to remind you, that you must stand as a man, and be not discouraged or be coward enough, but stand in God's His own will. Please don't you be tired to preach the gospel of Native, Industrial, Union to every Christian man and to every Christian women. You can reach them by writing to them, and telling necessity of being a member, of the said Union. I think the future of the Christians is very largely depends on true understanding that when Christian join with Christian, and are blought [sic] in continous contact with men of intellectual and spiritual strength; it will benefite both part. Should also enterpert the meaning of the greate intercessory prayer, in the same literal way. that they all may be one, that the world may believe."

Chilembwe's name was not, perhaps for good reason, on the list affixed to the earliest invitation (of 9 April 1909) to Africans to join the Union. Peters seems originally to have had the idea of a Union, and he was joined by Joseph Bismark, an African businessman, A. M. Chisusi, an African photographer, James G. Kuuji Mlanga, and Justin K. Somanje, whose name was later deleted. Two weeks later, at the first meeting of the Union, Bismark took the chair, and among the new members present were Cedric Massangano, headmaster of the Blantyre Mission; Thomas M. Massea; Harry K. Mate[i]cheta, who was later ordained by the Blantyre Mission; Asher M. Matipwile, possibly a relation of the Yao chief, Moses Matache; and Nelson Kabweza. At the second meeting on 15 May, Chilembwe, who became chairman, and John Gray Kufa Mpantha joined the others and several new recruits. The yearly dues were set at 12/- (which was later to become £5), Bismark was appointed treasurer, and an argument ensued, interestingly enough, about photographing the members. Chisusi wanted to practice his profession, but the members "strongly pointed out that photos should not be taken." But by the end of June, Morris Chilembwe; John Wesley Mlanga; Ardwell Mlenga; Ruben N. Funsani; "David Livingstone," a sometime colleague of Chilembwe during their days with Booth; Kalindi Morrison Malinki, the Seventh-day Adventist; D. B. O. (a relation of Filipo?) Chinyama; Charles Scott Kwikanda; and Stephen Nsomo had also joined. It is true that many of these men were involved in the uprising of 1915, and the most prominent among them formed the innermost circle of the cabal. Nevertheless, there is no reason to assume that these men were scheming, or that they were doing any more than muttering criticisms of the established regime. Chilembwe did tell Peters that "everything is hard on us," and then went on: "Please don't you think that it requires [sic] to have more than hundred members of the said union meetings. How many have we now let me know all particles?" But the intent of his message may be more innocent than its mystery would suggest.

The key to an understanding of Chilembwe's actions and thoughts during the six or seven years before the uprising probably lies with a solution to the conundrum of Haya Edward Peters. Very little was known about Peters until 1968, when Bridger Pachai discovered that the real name was Peter Mlelemba. He was born in the Blantyre area in about 1875, thus making him a contemporary of Chilembwe, and attended the Blantyre Mission School, perhaps with Chilembwe. He completed his studies, however, at the Zambezi Industrial Mission at Mitsidi. Later, during 1905–6, he was employed by the British Central Africa Company (Kabula Stores) and is subsequently reported to have mined mica in the Kirk Range of central Malawi with a white businessman. When this venture failed, Peters (properly Mlelemba) purchased (it is not known how he obtained further capital) the Nangafuwe Estate near Ndirande on the outskirts of Blantyre. He sold timber, grew chillies and tobacco, and ran a small store. He was among the two or three leading indigenous businessmen in the Blantyre area. By 1914 he also had a little school for fifty boys and girls, but lacked training in the Scriptures. He claimed to be studying by correspondence with a firm in London "in order to help my brethren." His father died in 1910 at Nangafuwe, and there is correspondence about family and business matters between Haya Peters and a brother named J. B. Warren Peters.

The use of a European-sounding name was not uncommon among the educated class of Nyasas; Bismark, Gray, Isa Macdonald Lawrence, Charles Domingo, and several other évolués were all known by their non-African names. Furthermore Mlelemba seems to have had a light complexion. He wanted to be recognized as an assimilado, and positively refused to be known by his African name. Hence the adoption, not only as a nom de plume, of the name Peters. But traces of all of these other men appear in missionary records, contemporary correspondence, and the surviving official records. Only the Peters clan escaped notice and even avoided being implicated in the uprising, largely, it seems, because Haya Peters himself was then on an elephant hunting expedition along Malawi's northeastern border with Moçambique. When Peters learned of the uprising (it is still not known whether he anticipated a rising, but Pachai cogently believes that he did not), he fled through Moçambique to German East Africa where he was eventually captured by the British command. Later he was allowed to proceed to South Africa. Some years later Peters returned to Nyasaland and was employed as a clerk in the Blantyre *boma*. He was murdered in 1940 near Blantyre because of some domestic quarrel.

If we cannot as yet precisely delineate the extent to which Peters participated in the planning of the rebellion, we can at least seek to estimate the extent of Peters's influence upon Chilembwe's ideological development. From a reading of their correspondence it appears that Peters was the more forceful and the stronger of the two—he clearly dominated Chilembwe—but this appearance could be explained by the peculiar nature of their financial relationship (for which, see below, 366), and/or by the fortuitous circumstance that our image of Peters is derived almost entirely from the construction and tone of Chilembwe's outgoing letters. No letters survive from Peters to Chilembwe. Nevertheless, the sense of their relationship seems evident, and Chilembwe certainly treated Peters's ideas with profound respect. The earliest extant letter from Chilembwe to Peters concludes: "I had not thought, that here in Africa can be found few heads so wise as you & [Domingo]. Certainly your Schemes are the source of spiriturs Illumination in this dark country and your words not with . . . standing are wonderfull preservation of this benighted people. I may die tomorrow but the trueth remaineth that you shall be counted one of the Africa sages. Believe me God is able."

This letter may contain, as do later ones, a hint of conspiracy, but if so the rising was a far more calculated and premeditated exercise than has generally been accepted. Moreover, the only extensive expression of Peters's views indicates that he was a man of forward, emancipatory, but hardly revolutionary, views. The "Rough Rules" is in Peters's hand, not Chilembwe's (although the ideas could have been those of either, or even of Joseph Booth), and attached thereto is an explanation of the importance of the Union which seems to have been the text of a sophisticated speech delivered by Peters at an early meeting of the members of the Union. It is again in his unmistakable hand (although his style had somewhat altered by 1914) and is of uncommon interest:

If a black man becomes a lawyer a Doctor a minister or an ordinary teacher, his professional duties would not ordinary bring him in a touch with the portion of the community, but rather confine him to his own role. Industrial education, however, would soon recommend itself to the white Nyasaland. This distorts my real meaning. All such training has its place and value in the development of a race. Mere training of the hand without mental and moral education would mean little for its welfare of any race, all are vital factors in the harmonious plan, but; while I do not propose that every individual should have hand training, I do say, that in all my contact with men, I have never met one who had learned a trade in youth and regretted it in manhood, nor have I ever seen a father or another who was sorry that his children has been taught trade. There is still doubt in many quarters as to the ability of the negro, unguided, [and] unsupported, to hew [out] his own path and put into visible, tangible, indisputable forms the products and signs of civilisation. This doubt cannot be extinguished by mere abstract argument, no matter how ingeniously and convincingly advanced. Quietly, Patiently, doggedly, through summer and winter sunshine and shadow, by self sacrifice, by foresight, by honesty and industry, we must reinforce arguments with results. One farm bought, one house built, one home nicely kept; one man the largest taxpayer and depositor in the local Bank, one school or church maintained, one factory running successfully, one truck garden profitably cultivated, one patient cured by a negro Doctor, one sermon well presented, one office well filled one life cleverly lived—these will tell [more] in our favour than all the abstract eloquence that can be summoned to [plead] our cause. Our pathway must be up through the soil, up through swamps, up through forests up through the streams and rocks; up through commerce, education and religion! In my opinion we cannot begin at the top to build a race any more than we can begin at the top to build a House. If we try to do this, we shall reap in the end the fruits of our folly.

Did Chilembwe share this belief in the efficacy of a gradualist approach? Did he thus accept inwardly as he espoused outwardly that notion of change which would least disturb whites and the ideology of colonial rule? Did he thus identify with his oppressor? Or did Peters and Chilembwe, from whom Peters may conceivably have obtained the ideas and very words for his speech, simply adopt as their rationale the appealing and stirring (but in no sense radical) views of America's leading and most celebrated Negro? There can be no doubt that Booker T. Washington inspired Peters's speech to the members of the Union. The message and the very construction are unmistakably stamped with the imprint of Washington's lush oratory. Indeed, a careful comparison of the above text and Washington's speeches and writings reveals what Peters may not have told his colleagues—that nearly every word had first been uttered by Washington. If Chilembwe were influenced by Peters, it is evident that these thoughts of Washington influenced his outward conformity far more than the shape of his inner conflict and the subsequent urge to rebel. On the evidence of 1915, Nat Turner and William E. Burghardt Du Bois were far more Chilembwe's men than was Washington.

It is easier to demonstrate the effect upon Chilembwe of other aspects of his dealings with Peters, particularly the psychological stresses that are revealed by their correspondence. Sometime in 1908, when Chilembwe was (according to his own statement) "pennyless," he decided to open a little store. From Peters he borrowed £50, and apparently also promised to pay interest on the unpaid balance of the loan, a sum which amounted to 1/- per pound per month. But £50 proved insufficient to build and stock a store, and Chilembwe went bankrupt. Only then did he begin to appreciate the leech-like quality of his creditor. Tenaciously Peters clung to the scrap of paper which Chilembwe had signed; monthly he dunned Chilembwe, eventually, over about six years, extracting not only the principal, but a grand total of £42 interest—much of it in turn begged from the National Convention and other American friends. There is no doubt that Chilembwe was harried mercilessly by Peters, with whom he nonetheless remained friendly: for example, from 1909 Chilembwe began pleading for time and some sympathy. "If you really wish to help your poor people, Let us limit this you shall not lose every penny." "Brother, trust in God, and also in me. . . . Please have faith on me." Again "I hope you will not forget to remember that when a man havn't got money he cannot create money." "I know next December was our agreement and it will not go beyond that, but the time of your grace is needed you had been so good in the beginning toward this first African Church, and I hope you will be the same to the end. You understand me that it is motto in my heart to live honestly before God and my fellow countrymen." In 1912 when £23 was still outstanding and Chilembwe was forced again to seek help in the United States, he wrote with an even heavier heart than before: "The remainder I am searching and I shall pay you only give me time. My word I value and if you not value yours I am not responsible. . . . Pray for me that I may not fail, for the money in my heart I value nothing. For I have weighed the world and its riches and find nothing. Comparing the love I got for my people and our God. And as for you my dear friend I owed a great thanks I shall never forgot the kindness you showed me in this world and in the world yet to come. . . . I remain in prayer that God may raise some friends to loose me the chain prepared for my neck. God bless you."

Of what oppression were the links in this chain forged? Chilembwe was never freed-from his worries about money, the correspondence continuing in a similar vein through March 1914, and in 1913 Peters threatened to take his debtor to court. "To go to the law with me My dear Bro. Peters," Chilembwe advised, "we will gain nothing it will be simply to mock ourselves." But money was only the most obvious of Chilembwe's many anxieties. The chest complications which had hastened his departure from the United States, and which had troubled him since, grew particularly severe after about 1909. His sight also began to fail. Continuously he complained of feeling unwell. In 1911 he wrote plaintively to Peters: "My Dear Brother as usual I am suffering with the Asthma and being on heaviest weather and atmosphere being so high has coursed a dreadful pain in my system so that I had been trying the medicine from both white [and] black Doctors. But proved resultless till I give up for using the medicine for fear it will poison me. . . . I am almost too weak but in the spirit there is a hope of long living." At his death he was emaciated and cut a very poor figure.

It would not be amiss at this point in our discussion to consider the possible psychoanalytic interpretation of Chilembwe's problems. Despite the paucity of hard data, the insights of psychoanalysis may at least be suggestive. Certainly if we are to make the fullest possible use of the available evidence, it is necessary in this case to attempt to go beyond the inherent limitations of a strictly documentary approach.

It has long been accepted that in many patients asthma, which was first described in clinical detail in the seventeenth century, can be a severe psychosomatic disorder. Immunologic sensitization is suspected of invoking an initial attack of bronchial asthma, but the exposure of sensitized persons to sensitizing allergens does not always produce an attack, and individuals often exhibit asthmatic symptoms when they are not exposed to the allergens. Emotional stress often stimulates an attack, and the frequency and severity of asthmatic attacks is clearly related to the state of the patient's emotions. Furthermore, chronic emotional disturbance can prolong the symptomatology despite the best medical care. All we know, albeit at secondhand, of Chilembwe's childhood is that he may have been unusually close to his mother, conceivably even overdependent. (We have no information about his father, his father's role, or his father's presence or absence in the childhood home. It is unlikely, however, that Chilembwe would have seen much of his father during the years of his youth; his mother's society stressed matrilineality and emphasized no decisive role for fathers.) If this is so, it conforms to our knowledge of the non-physiological dimension of asthma. Franz Alexander, whose findings are widely accepted, says that the nuclear psychodynamic factor "is a conflict centering in an excessive unresolved dependence upon the mother." As a defense against such an infantile fixation, a variety of personality traits—aggression, ambition, hypersensitivity, and so forth—may develop. Asthmatics have been described as anxious and insecure, and a classic report indicated that bronchial asthma occurred when the patient's security was threatened or when there was a temptation to act in a way which would cause the mother's love to be withheld.   Unfortunately, we know too little about Chilembwe's formative years and the nature and timing of his first attacks to decide whether the above clinical findings apply directly to his case, or even whether reference can be made to Western findings when a retrospective analysis of African psychopathology is being attempted. It is nevertheless very tempting to accept the relevance of further research, the conclusions of which do not depend on a purely psychoanalytic interpretation of the presumed childhood relations of Chilembwe and his mother: it has been shown that the repression of aggressive feelings and the internalization of hostility is often associated with a high incidence of asthma, and that severity and frequency of attack are linked in a crude but positive way with the magnitude of the hostility repressed.

Even if it is premature to suppose that the incidence of asthma by itself led to rebellion, it is not unwarranted to suppose that a host of personal afflictions, each by itself inconclusive, tugged fitfully at the sinews of Chilembwe's spirit during the fateful few years before the uprising. Collectively they would have oppressed a troubled mind and encouraged a dramatic, all-redeeming response to affliction—especially when the doleful social conditions prevalent in the Highlands and the real troubles of his parishioners would only have magnified the impact of the afflictions and increased the stresses to which Chilembwe was subject. It is also worth wondering whether the rebellion occurred when Chilembwe was in the throes of what Erik Erikson, in analyzing the psychological gestalt of Martin Luther, has called a "crisis of generativity." It occurs "when a man looks at what he has generated, or helped to generate, and finds it good or wanting, when his life work as part of the productivity of his time gives him some sense of being on the side of a few angels or makes him feel stagnant." Luther suffered physically, or psychosomatically, during this stage, as did Chilembwe, but it may be even more important that Chilembwe believed that his own end was near. The act of rebellion, then, may in Chilembwe's eyes have been invested with the attractive glitter of redemption. For him—at a time of psychological crisis—it may have been seen as an obvious, even the only, alternative. After all, his preachings and his written protestations had produced no amelioration of white attitudes, on the northern front Africans daily lost their lives, and action was the only clear alternative to stagnation. In a more generalized way, if Chilembwe were indeed succumbing in 1914 to the stress of his mental and physical circumstances, then the act of rebellion contained within it the seed of psychic liberation. He had withheld his feelings for some time, at least in terms of the dominant white society, and rebellion provided an outlet—a "safety valve"—as well as a means of expressing hostilities. By the end of 1914, tensions had clearly accumulated to a dangerous level.

It is also relevant to inquire whether Chilembwe, in the clinical sense, may have identified with his aggressor. He had unquestionably adopted white values and standards, as Mwase makes clear. Chilembwe tried to dress well and to adhere to Western conventions of behavior. He strove for a respectability which—within his own milieu at least—he seems to have achieved. He married a woman who, according to several accounts, was of mixed parentage—a half-caste. And there is a somewhat prurient letter to Peters that indicates Chilembwe's interest in other girls of mixed blood: "Now concerning the half-cast [sic] girl mentioned in your letter I regret Sir, to say Walker has arrived yesterday with a tedious report that girl is used by a whiteman . . . and that the girl has already conceived. And it leaves me in hope that you will try another chance." Nevertheless, there is no evidence to show that Chilembwe's identification was pathological. He does not seem to have been truly submissive in the "Sambo" sense, nor can his identification be equated with the transference analyzed in the classic studies of concentration camp experiences—except in the sense that resignation exemplified by a willingness to be killed, "to strike a blow and then die," is submissive. But it is at least suggestive that identification with the aggressor has been defined as representing, on the one hand, a preliminary phase of superego development (which Elie Cohen and others have shown can be altered and/or resumed under extreme conditions later in life) and, on the other, an intermediate stage in the development of paranoia. A person "introjects some characteristic of an anxiety object and so assimilates an anxiety experience which he has just undergone. Here, the mechanism of identification or introjection is combined with a second important mechanism. By impersonating the aggressor, assuming his attributes or imitating his aggression, the child transforms himself from the person threatened into the person who makes the threat." Furthermore, "reversal"—the transformation of acceptance into aggression—is said to complete "what introjection and projection have begun, and the result is the development of paranoid delusions," which would help to explain African testimony about Chilembwe's state of mind on the eve of the rebellion. Did Chilembwe, having identified, project the hostility which he himself suffered back upon the obvious aggressor?

If psychological factors contributed to the decision to rebel, then it is arguable that the very act of rebellion was more important to Chilembwe than the immediate consequences of that act. Chilembwe's state was such that he could easily have persuaded himself—especially

after the outbreak of World War I and the refusal of the government
to heed his protest—that oppression of Africans and the spirit was
imminent, that his own life had in any event reached a point of no return, and that by sacrificing his own life in a good cause he could
achieve something at last. Whether or not Chilembwe's spirit had
plumbed the depths of despair, the example of John Brown—especially as seen through the popularly distorted prism—would probably
have seemed worthy of emulation. Mwase's account, the recollections
of Mkulichi, the fact that Chilembwe meditated atop Chilimangwanje
hill throughout the critical days and nights of the rebellion, the symbolic taking of Livingstone's head (the precise reason for doing so is
uncertain), the failure to attack other isolated planters, the way in
which the white women and children were well treated and used as
messengers, and the fact that the rebellion was so half-heartedly organized and involved so few Africans—and presupposed no widespread
tribal revolt—all tend to substantiate the hypothesis that the rising of
1915 was intended as a gesture, as the "only way to show the whitemen," in words Mwase attributed to Chilembwe, "that the treatment
they are treating our men and women was most bad." Recall too, that
Chilembwe was credited with saying: "They whitemen will then think,
after we are dead, that the treatment they are treating our people is
[most] bad, and they might change to the better for our people [a]fter
we are dead and buried."

   But is it legitimate to dismiss the conclusions of the commissioners
of inquiry, and other contemporary or nearly contemporary white ver-
dicts so cavalierly? Does not some of the African testimony collected
after the rebellion discredit Mwase's reconstruction? And how are we
to reconcile the planned attacks on Blantyre, Limbe, and so forth, and
the second front that was supposed to be opened up by Chinyama,
with a putative gesture? Moreover, a "much thumbed" military manual
—the nature of which is, however, unspecified—was found in the
Mbombwe church after the uprising, and there is evidence that Chilembwe trained stretcher bearers and planned the storage of guns.   If
the gesture were meant to fail, would Chilembwe have even bothered
to raid the arsenal in Blantyre or to sever telephone lines? Then, too,
there is the letter to the Germans: A few days before his followers
rose, Chilembwe sent Yotam S. Bango, a courier, through Moçambique
with a letter—no copies of which have ever been found—which the
Nyasan authorities assumed had been intended to solicit the assistance of the German regime in the struggle against the British government. Whether by design or not, Bango delivered the message to the
Bezirksamtmann of Tunduru who, in turn, according to an ambiguous
letter from him in Swahili that Bango conveyed back to Nyasaland,
claimed that he had transmitted Chilembwe's message to the Provincial

Commissioner in Lindi (who seems to have received it) and the Governor in Dar es Salaam.

There are only three ways of reconciling the divergent strands of evidence. Either Chilembwe wanted to overthrow white rule but was realistically prepared to have his actions interpreted merely as a gesture of protest; was determined to protest in such a way that the whites would take notice but also hoped that he might, God willing, by some fluke succeed and become king of Nyasaland; or, eschewing any ambition to erect a theocracy on the ruins of British Nyasaland, simply wanted to maximize (or be seen by his followers as trying to maximize) the effectiveness of his protest. Mwase's evidence accords best with the last proposition and least well with the first unless we are prepared to assume that Chilembwe deliberately misled his followers or that Chilembwe wanted one thing and his disciples another. The psychological evidence strongly supports the third proposition. And since nothing emerged at Bango's trial, or in the Nyasaland records, which hints at a conspiracy, Chilembwe may merely have written of his plans in order to gain German acquiescence if the rising happened to succeed. He may not have asked for guns or ammunition. The existence of a military manual and the cutting of telephone wires need not imply anything other than a desire to enhance the possible effectiveness of a protest. Nor does a second front necessarily imply an aggrandizing rather than a reforming zeal. Indeed, Chinyama himself may have been operating independently, that is, he may have rebelled for reasons quite distinct from those of Chilembwe and simply co-ordinated the two movements in order to enhance their overall impact.

The socio-economic conditions then prevailing in the Shire Highlands obviously would have given the suggestion of rebellion an immediate appeal to upwardly mobile Africans of the emergent middle class, landless immigrants from Moçambique, and employees of white landowners. But rebellion as an instrument of protest could not have appeared to these different groups as either the only or the most promising of solutions to their collective dilemma. In order to foment revolt, a charismatic figure was necessary who could persuade disparate groups of possible followers that rebellion would provide the only sensible way of alleviating their self-perceived discontent. It is likely that Chilembwe, who radiated (newly discovered?) sources of incandescent illumination, reminded his possible recruits of the overweening nature of white oppression and of the conceivably dismal future that awaited Africans under continued colonial rule. Such arguments could have been powerful, yet it still seems probable that only the conjunction of two factors gave them an overwhelming appeal. The outbreak of World War I and the refusal of the authorities to heed

Chilembwe's written protest were in themselves ominous acts; they tolled the bells of doom for Africans, or at least would have been perceived in that manner by persons already disturbed by their fate. It is also worth suggesting that decisions based on such collective perceptions could only have been precipitated by the declarations of a charismatic leader whose own perception of reality had become unavoidably distorted and/or heightened. The rebellion, as has been argued elsewhere, would probably not have occurred when and as it did had the world war not broken out, but equally—as the discussion of Chilembwe's psychology has implied—only the state of Chilembwe's mind and spirit, with its possible manifestation of the syndrome of reversal (given the descriptions of his paranoia), encouraged him to equate the outbreak of war with the imminence of existential doom and thus to provoke a call to arms.

Finally, can we ever know precisely what Chilembwe intended to achieve by his call to arms? If, lacking an unambiguous testament, we cannot, it seems evident that Mwase's words must carry great weight. From a psychological point of view his description alone speaks to Chilembwe's condition better than any case which one could construct for an intended theocracy. From what we know of the character and course of the uprising itself, it seems inconceivable that Chilembwe could have expected that he would succeed in overthrowing the established order. Certainly with the bulk of the Protectorate's army away on the northern front, that he and his followers could have done much more than they did is obvious. They could easily have massacred whites in some number in their isolated farm houses and, by enlisting the support of the servants in Blantyre, in the houses in town. They could easily have held the white women and children hostage, but they refrained from so doing. If rural Africans had truly risen (the masses failed to participate in any way and it is wrong to argue that Chilembwe acted on behalf of, or was in the vanguard of an aroused peasantry), the Protectorate would have been indefensible until loyal troops could have been released from the war. But nothing was done along these lines, nor, if we except the rather garbled testimony of Norman, even planned. His followers need not have themselves wanted martyrdom (in the eyes of John Gray Kufa the prospect would not have seemed very inviting), and, in the final analysis, this duality of intention could well have overshadowed and confused Chilembwe's personal quest for martyrdom and psychological redemption. He did, however, want to become the Mr. John Brown of Africa, and thus struck a resolute, if very premature, blow for freedom in colonial Africa.

THE GUSII REBELS

AUDREY WIPPER

Resistance to alien control in southwestern Kenya was first demonstrated in 1905 and 1908 when the dominant Gusii* staged two revolts. Only after disastrous confrontations with modern weaponry did the indigenous people change to more passive forms of resistance. Prominent among these were millennial cults.

Of special significance was the earliest sect in the area, the cult of Mumbo, which had its beginnings during the first decade of British occupation.† A pan-tribal pagan sect, Mumboism prophesied the early

This analysis is limited to material gathered mainly from administrative records. I visited Kisii in June 1966 and spoke wth several ex-chiefs who had been in charge of the district when Mumboism was at its height. I also spoke with the local authorities and some of the inhabitants. In this way I was able to check certain information and acquire more.

The original draft of this paper was presented at a Conference of the East African Institute of Social Research, Makerere University, Kampala, Uganda, in January 1966. Considerable revisions have been made, and data collected through interviews added.

* The Gusii, a pastoral-agricultural people now numbering more than 500,000, belong to the Bantu-speaking language group. Composed of seven autonomous tribes that recognize Mogusii as their ancestor, they formerly banded together to wage war on the Kipsigis. Otherwise, each tribe went its own way and fought over cattle, women, and territory. In addition to the common ancestor shared by all Gusii, each tribe recognizes its own founder.

† The simple spelling for tribal words is used. Instead of adding different prefixes to distinguish different forms such as "Nyamumboites" or "Omamumbo," the word "Mumbo" is used throughout the paper.

departure of the Europeans and the coming of a golden age during which the elect would be blessed with abundance and the wicked overthrown. In its symbolism, Mumboism was nativistic, as it rejected European customs and advocated a return to the old prophets and the old ways. Its message stressed the lost glory and dignity of the tribe that were to be re-established in the millennium. From another and more revealing perspective Mumboism was both revolutionary and utopian, rejecting the colonial regime, tribal authority, and traditional mores, and introducing new norms and leadership roles. Although it engaged in sporadic collective protest, the cult was concerned mainly with prophecies, dreams, ritual, and ecstatic behavior.

Mumboism has often been presented in a stereotyped way that obscured much of its basic content. The colonial administrators and the missionaries saw it simply as an atavistic, irrational, vicious movement, grounded in perversions and superstitions. Albeit in a more restrained manner, this negative view has been carried over to the academic world. Thus, B. A. Ogot overlooks any aspects of the cult that do not fit his description of it as "fanatical and non-programmatic . . . [a cult whose] leaders preached complete rejection of everything European and a return to the African way of life." John Lonsdale, another historian, writes of the cult's "reactionary appeal . . . the rebellion had to be backward-looking, rejecting all things European. . . . Mumbo was a political aberration. A return to the Old Africa was not yet the key to the future." Little evidence was, however, presented for these allegations, and no serious study of the cult was undertaken.

Therefore, in an attempt to understand the nature of Mumboism, this essay will explore its message and activities, the basis of its support, and the way in which the agents of social control reacted toward it. Two propositions are basic to my argument. They are presented as assumptions from which some of the more particular statements follow: (1) Discontent and protest are manifested in many forms and when one fails another will, other conditions being equal, be tried; (2) For discontent to result in protest, general grievances need to be sparked by particular grievances.

arteries of communication and cut off from contact with the West by lack of European settlement, it was an area whose inhabitants continued in their traditional ways of life for a longer time than tribes in more settled regions. By 1938, for example, there were still no political associations in the area and the tribes had little contact with other tribes. They were therefore slower than either the Luo in Central Nyanza or the Kikuyu in Central Province in articulating political opinion. Even in 1949, Philip Mayer noted that "outside the immediate neighbourhood of the township and of the two main mission stations, Christians are few and literacy is rare among adults."

It was into this isolated area that, in the early 1900's, the British attempted to extend their control. The reaction was a protest which found its center in the Kisii Highlands, also known as Gusiiland. Located some fifty miles south of the equator and some thirty miles inland from Lake Victoria, the Highlands were bordered on the south by Tanzania; on the east by the District of Kericho, the tea-growing country of the Kipsigis tribe; on the southeast by the vast plain of the nomadic cattle people, the Masai; and on the west and north by the Nilotic Luo. Softly rolling hills, a pleasantly cool climate, and fertile, rain-drenched valleys make the Highlands a delightful green oasis amid the semi-arid lowlands of the west and the hot savannahs of the east.

A Gradual Awareness

Three factors in particular contributed to the region's gradual awareness of an outside world, undermined the basis of traditional life, and set the stage for the development of millennial movements: (1) British penetration and political reorganization; (2) the missions; and (3) the Carrier Corps and forced labor.

1. British Penetration and Political Reorganization

British administration was not established in South Nyanza until 1908. Their first efforts sparked local rebellions, which led to two punitive expeditions, in 1905 and 1908. These dealt harshly and effectively with the rebels, the 1905 affray being described as "not so much a battle as a massacre." Both confrontations ended in the Gusii's total defeat.

When a message arrived in 1905 of a Kisii revolt (Europeans at that time referred to the Gusii as "Kisii"), a detachment of one hundred African police under W. Robert Foran and a company of the Third King's African Rifles under Captain Jenkins were immediately dispatched to quell the rebellion. Foran vividly described the encounter:

Then came word that the Kisii were in open revolt. Almost immediately a small punitive force was sanctioned, though reluctantly by Sir Charles Eliot [the Commissioner of Kenya from 1901 to 1904]. . . .

The tribesmen did not understand the power of modern weapons and had yet to encounter the white man in combat. They boldly attacked the small force of 200 askaris with masses of spearsmen. Captain Jenkins formed [a] square and gave battle. He let the attack have a good dose of lead, but this did not halt their more determined advance. They ran straight up to the rigid wall of fixed bayonets. Their losses were great. The machine gun was kept in action so long during this sharp engagement that it became almost red-hot to the touch. Before the Kisii warriors were repulsed, they left several hundred dead and wounded spearsmen heaped up outside the square of bayonets. This was not so much a battle as a massacre, but wholly unavoidable under the circumstances. It was an urgent case of decimating that determined attack or else being completely wiped out by the Kisii warriors.

The lesson was effective. The Kisii withdrew into the hills, while we buried their dead and succoured the wounded. Our casualties were negligible, only a few askaris being slightly wounded by spears or arrows. We camped in a commanding site near the scene of the fight, and confidently awaited the outcome of events. Early next day the leading chiefs came in and surrendered unconditionally, the tribe being sentenced to pay a heavy fine in cattle and sheep for their past misdeeds.

Foran goes on to describe the 1908 revolt.

On the march between Karungu to Kisii I observed that the latter tribe, the Gusii, were displaying obvious signs of unrest. [It had been decided to move the district administrative center from Karungu on Lake Victoria to Kisii, a distance of about fifty miles inland as the crow flies.] They deserted their villages and crowded the hill-tops at our approach; while all the warriors were fully armed. Straws on the wind, but showing which way it blew! Trouble was definitely brewing. I reported what had been seen to Northcote, the acting district commissioner at Kisii Boma [Swahili for a compound, in this case referring to the administrative headquarters] and he promised to go out next day to investigate what was troubling the tribe. . . . [An interlude of one or two days passes.] I was in pyjamas so put on a dressing-gown and went across to his bungalow. Ainsworth [the Provincial Commissioner] was very agitated. He told me a runner had come through from the Kisii Boma that afternoon, reporting the Kisii were in open rebellion, killing Indian and Somali traders and that Northcote had been speared dangerously in the back while out in the district investigating the state of affairs about which my letter warned him. Immediately he received my note, Northcote mounted his mule, collected half a dozen askaris, and set forth to probe the cause of the unrest

among the tribesmen. The Kisii, seeing how small was his escort, suddenly attacked. A spear thrown by one of the warriors struck the district commissioner in the back, severely wounding him and only just
missing the spine. His men opened fire, drove off the Kisii, and then
carried Northcote back to the Boma. . . .

Ainsworth ordered me to collect all available police, stores and
ammunition for a month, also the necessary porters. I was to march at
dawn, or earlier if possible, to the relief of Kisii Boma, which was reported to be surrounded and being attacked by the warriors of the
tribe. . . .

[In Kisiiland] every village was deserted and the warriors massed on
the hill-tops; but they made no attempt to interfere with our advance.
They had not forgotten their experience when attacking the 1904
[correctly 1905] column under Captain Jenkins. The closer we got to
the Boma the denser became the masses of Kisii spearmen; yet they
still hesitated to dispute our progress. . . .

[Later, after the Gusii had asked to surrender] we were astonished to
see heavy clouds of smoke arising from the neighbourhood of the road
to Kendu, followed by the sputtering of machine-guns and rifle-fire.
. . . [Foran had sent a message to the commander of the Kisii Expeditionary Force en route to Kisii informing him of the tribe's willingness to surrender and that they were now peacefully returning with
their livestock to their villages. To his amazement this information was
ignored. "Another medal cheaply won," remarked a British officer on
learning that the Expeditionary Force was going to fight anyway.] We
made our way towards the headquarters of the Kisii Expeditionary
Force to report ourselves and receive instructions. The [Kings] Africa[n]
Rifles were putting in some strenuous work—burning villages, devastating standing crops, capturing livestock and hunting down the bolt-
ing warriors. It was tough luck on the latter, for I have no doubt they
were under the impression that the tribal surrender had been accepted
and no war would take place. . . .

While waiting for a chance to report ourselves we heard that the
main column had already burned a great many Kisii villages, as well as
capturing over 4,000 cattle on their march from Kendu [Kendu Bay on
Lake Victoria] into the country of the tribe. . . . Meanwhile the main
column pursued the Kisii about the country, burning villages, destroying crops and capturing both prisoners and livestock. . . .

On the way back to the Boma a large body of Kisii warriors again
boldly attacked, forcing us to open fire upon them with rifles and ma-
cine guns. We heard afterwards that twenty-five men were killed in
that short, sharp engagement. They followed us almost up to the outposts around the Boma, only withdrawing when we fired three volleys
over their heads.

A series of telegrams conveyed the results of the expedition to the

Colonial Office in London where, for some time, there had been concern over the handling of punitive expeditions which, in the absence of official policy, had been left pretty much to the man on the spot. On February 1, 1908, a telegram received by the Colonial Office read: "Result of operations in Kisii to 28 January cattle captured 5,636 sheep and goats 3,281. 100 Kisii killed. No further casualties on our side. Operations suspended as several clans wish for peace. Kisii reported generally demoralised." Two days later a telegram reported the number of dead Kisii had increased to 160 and that the commanding officer hoped soon to meet the main body of Kisii. At that point Winston Churchill, the Colonial Undersecretary, intervened:

I do not like the tone of these reports. No doubt the clans should be punished; but 160 have now been killed outright—without any further casualties, and the main body has not yet been encountered. . . . It looks like butchery, and if the H. of C. gets hold of it, all our plans in E.A.P. will be under a cloud. Surely it cannot be necessary to go on killing these defenceless people on such an enormous scale.

Churchill then sent a telegram to Sir Donald Sadler, the Governor of Kenya.

Much regret to observe large numbers of Kisii killed in recent operations. Rely upon you to confine bloodshed within narrowest limits consistent with safety of force and restoration of order. Impress immediately upon O. C. that every effort should be made to induce the enemy to submit peacefully after the most severe lesson they have received and mercy should be extended to all not personally concerned in original outbreak. I shall expect a full report upon any causes of discontent which may have provoked rising.

Churchill's suspicions turned out to be correct. A letter from Northcote to his father two days after his attack stated that the incident had been exaggerated—it was only the Kitutu who had attacked—and that far too severe repressive measures had been used. Lieutenant Colonel Mackay, the commanding officer, later sent in a report that confirmed what the previous telegrams had indicated:

From the date I commenced active operations to the end of the expedition on 6 February 1908, the enemy suffered heavily. They lost over 7000 cattle captured and 5000 sheep and goats were taken, many living and cattle Bomas were burnt while over 200 casualties were inflicted on the enemy, who were completely demoralised fleeing with their families into the Kavirondo country for personal safety.

This controversial episode was not allowed to drop with Churchill's admonitions, but was carried on by R. Popham-Lobb, another British official, who had for some time been incensed over the tactics employed by punitive expeditions. Popham-Lobb calculated the losses suffered in six operations in Kenya during a five-year period (1902–6) to be 2,426 Africans killed as against the administration's loss of 179 killed and wounded. He estimated that since the number killed and wounded was probably three times the number killed, the "enemy" had suffered casualties forty times as great as had the administration.

Popham-Lobb dispatched a long report to the Colonial Office a year after the event, in which he urged close scrutiny and supervision of military operations. He attacked the colonial administration and used the 1908 expeditions as a prime example of needless slaughter:

> The whole episode betrays a degree of administrative ineptitude and a vicious misuse of force on the part of the Administration which deserves the gravest censure, and a Governor so lacking in a sense of his responsibilities with regard to native races under his care that he is able to see in the result of such methods only a "complete success" . . . .

Despite Popham-Lobb's attack, no investigation was undertaken and no punishments were meted out. This was due in part to the lateness of Popham-Lobb's report, for it was considered unwise after a year to reopen the whole question. Instead, a set of Lugard's "Instructions for the Control of Expeditions" was sent to the East African authorities for their consideration.

From the above documents, the following conclusions can be drawn:

1. Spears and shields were no match for machine guns, bayonets, and rifles. When their villages were burned to the ground, their crops demolished, their livestock captured, their warriors killed, and their prophets shown to be impotent in the face of a much superior force, the Gusii suffered the humiliation and demoralization of complete defeat. Pacification showed the futility of armed resistance and closed off the possibilities of revolt and direct challenges to the colonial power.

2. Neither the 1905 nor the 1908 revolt was a haphazard skirmish that happened to occur when a spear slipped or a gun went off. Both were premeditated and planned, determined, and persistent on the part of the Gusii.

3. These military expeditions must have proved a shattering ex-

perience for this hitherto unmolested tribe; they furnished a rude awakening to the realities of foreign conquest. Not only did they lay the basis for British rule in South Nyanza, but they gave Africans a first contact with Europeans which must have made the Europeans appear to be objects both of fear and hatred. Is it any wonder that with such a violent beginning, British rule should, in turn, have been violently attacked some fifty years later?

4. Since the Gusii had indicated a desire to surrender, the very need for the 1908 expeditionary attack can be seriously questioned. The commanding officer probably found, after his troops had marched miles across difficult country, that he had a company of trigger-happy soldiers itching for some action. The attack suggests that considerable truth lay in Sir Charles Eliot's contention that punitive expeditions were often needlessly waged by British officers who were hungry for medals.

Evidence suggests that the military seized upon a minor incident to show the Africans brutally who was master. Northcote's spearing appears to have been used as an excuse to perpetuate widespread destruction against a whole community regardless of its participation in the disturbance. Out of all proportion to the danger involved, the military decided on the systematic employment of violence to establish beyond doubt the insurgents' utter powerlessness. Nor was this an isolated incident. Popham-Lobb, Churchill, and other officials knew only too well that these tactics were being used consistently in the colonies.

5. The geographical location of the revolts almost assured the involvement of the Bogonko clan. Kisii (the administrative center) was situated in the middle of Kitutu Location, an area occupied by the Kitutu tribe. Ainsworth's reports clearly singled out the Kitutu tribe as the protagonists. He stated as a matter of fact that the trouble was confined to the Kitutu: "In a few words, it is evident that the Kitutu did not want a station near them. They resented the white man intruding amongst them. They were extremely ignorant and isolated, and the witch's medicine showed it was bad for them if the European remained, and that it was good for the Kisii that he should die." In the Kitutu tribe the Bogonko was the largest clan, comprising more than half of the location's population. Since it was also the most powerful clan, its warriors probably led the attack. Subsequently this area was to become the center of Mumbo activity. (The various links between protest by revolt and the reasons for Bogonko support of Mumboism will be traced in a later section.)

With the advent of the British, Gusii society was politically re-organized: the villages where the young warriors had lived while making forays upon a neighboring tribe's cattle were abolished; allegiance to clan and tribe no longer entailed military duties; territory was divided on the basis of tribal units with the result that the seven Gusii tribes were allocated to seven subunits known as locations, an administrative unit like a county, and central authorities were introduced into a traditionally chiefless society. In making these changes, the British used the indigenous structure, placing chiefs and headmen responsible to them in charge of areas roughly coinciding with tribal units. Usually the chiefs were chosen from traditionally powerful clans whose right to rule was accepted by the people; sometimes, however, out of ignorance, the British would appoint an individual who had secured their favor but whose credentials marked him as insignificant in the eyes of his fellow Africans. Other times, rival contenders from within the same clan or between two powerful clans contested the chieftainship. "Government backing [and threats of dismissal] replaced the consensus of the elders as the sanction for chiefly action, the scope of such action being immeasurably widened by Government's requirements." Thus a basis for inter- and intraclan rivalry was engendered.

Under the new system, the chiefs had wide powers—some traditional, some new—and considerable autonomy in the management of the locations. Each reported directly to the District Officer and District Commissioner. During Mumboism's most active period, the chiefs also held judicial powers (until the African Tribunal Courts were established in the 1930's, and even after that informally they exercised wide judicial powers). They provided not only advice and warnings but meted out punishment. Commenting on the scope of chiefly power, R. A. LeVine wrote:

> Location chiefs, who act as constables and informal courts of first instances, go far beyond their formal powers, incarcerating young men for insolence to their fathers, threatening legal sanctions against husbands who neglect their wives, punishing their personal enemies with legal means at their disposal. Gusii judicial leaders do not fear the adverse opinions of their fellowmen because they know that their judicial authority is respected and even feared by the entire group. Chiefs and Tribunal Court presidents are the most powerful individuals in Gusiiland; immoderate criticism of them to their faces is considered impolite as well as simply unwise.

This concentration of power meant that the chiefs could act autocratically and few would dare to challenge their action.

Much prestige also came to be attached to being in a chief's employment. His retinue included a host of assistants: clerks, elders of the tribunal court, tribal police, headmen, personal bodyguards, and, as befitted an important person, any number of household retainers. Assistants often took advantage of their position and ordered people about on matters having nothing to do with the government of the location.

Most chiefs were wealthy before taking office, but if they were not they soon rectified this condition. While a chief did not have the actual right to appoint personnel, he was in a key position to influence choices. Nor did chiefs fail to exercise this influence, as can be seen by the many officials who were their kinsmen. Obviously, a chieftainship was viewed as a political plum, a position that could be used to enhance an individual's as well as a clan's power, prestige, and wealth. Thus the office of chief was much sought after, and its loss could well foster envy and bitterness on the part of the unsuccessful.

Militating against any direct challenge to the chief and governmental officials was the authoritarian structure of Gusii society. Command relationships were a part of everyday life, a person of higher rank being entitled to order a lower-ranking person to do his bidding in any sphere. Thus, wealth, prestige, and political position traditionally endowed their possessor with broad powers of command. As LeVine put it, deferential behavior on the part of lower status persons was pronounced and had been that way in the past as well: "A soft voice and downward glance constitute traditionally proper demeanor for someone talking to an elder, chief, or other figure of importance."

2. Impact of the Missions

As the power and authority of the administrative center was extended to the hinterland, missionaries followed. In reaction, a number of semi-religious, semi-political sects developed in Gusiiland. They formed a loose network of small, locally organized groups with little or no co-ordination except for shared anti-European sentiments and a belief in a millennium when their prophets would return and banish the foreigners forever. In a very general way, these sects resembled each other in their organization as well as in their belief in the god Mumbo and various indigenous prophets.

The first missionaries to arrive, the Seventh-day Adventists (the Adventists), landed at Kendu Bay and opened a mission station nearby at Genia in 1907. The second group, the Mill Hill Fathers (the Fathers), founded a mission at Nyaribari near Kisii in 1911. Besides introducing Christian teachings which challenged the basis of traditional thought, the missionaries also opened schools and hospitals. As elsewhere, their educational efforts produced a group of young men who became increasingly divorced from indigenous social control. Year after year, the annual reports noted the growing rift between the students and tribal authority. The 1921 Report, for example, stated: "The mission boys appeared inclined to impose on newcomers in an endeavour to get support for an attitude of independence from tribal authority . . . any attempt [must be prevented] on the part of the mission boys to regard themselves as a separate community." The 1924 Report complained that the mission adherents "are too much inclined to consider themselves as a class apart and consequently entitled to different treatment from other natives and to a certain extent to be outside the authority of ordinary native law and custom." In 1926, S. O. V. Hodge, the acting District Commissioner, wrote that the elders "complain of the lack of respect shown by mission boys to their elders and betters. This is repudiated by the boys themselves who in their turn complain of the drunkenness, laziness, and unprogressiveness of the older generation." Thus the cohesion of tribal society was weakened since many of the new Christians believed that in shaking off old communal obligations they had rid themselves of tribal control. Not only did they refuse to make tax and bride-wealth payments, but they scorned the authority of chiefs, elders, and headmen.

No doubt the rivalry between the Adventists and the Fathers was still another factor that disturbed Africans since their differences were more obvious than their common ground of Christianity, and, although open disagreement among the missionaries themselves rarely came to the fore, disagreement among their converts was often violent.

3. The Carrier Corps and Forced Labor

The third factor of change was the recruitment of men for the Carrier Corps. This aroused the inhabitants of Nyanza to the events occurring around them and gave thousands of men new experiences and ideas. What happened was that, with the progress of World War I, it had become necessary to recruit porters to transport equipment for the German East Africa campaign. A large portion of the responsibility fell upon Nyanza. The task of acquiring porters for the Corps, referred to as "a suicidal system of supply," was with great reluctance undertaken by John Ainsworth and, according to Lord Cranworth, it "nearly broke his heart" for "he was not unaware of the privations and casualties which must inevitably be suffered by those he loved. . . ."

Carrying heavy loads through tsetse- and mosquito-ridden swamps and over sun-baked savannah in humid tropical weather was one of the toughest, most grueling assignments of the war. Ainsworth estimated that of the 162,000 Africans recruited for military labor, 24,000 died—although other estimates of the number dead were much higher and the government's conservative figure was strongly criticized.

Nyanzan porters served with distinction and their effort was singled out as one of the factors that helped to win the war. They were affectionately eulogized in the following paraphrase of Kipling's "Gunga Din."

> Oh, the Lindi road was dusty
> And the Lindi road was long
> But the chap w'at did the hardest graft,
> And the chap w'at did most wrong,
> Was the Kavirondo porter with his Kavirondo song
> It was "Porter njo hapa!" [Porter, come here!]
> It was "Omera, hya! Git!" [Omera, come on!]
> And Omera didn't grumble,
> He simply did his bit.

The experience of the Carrier Corps—which was not forgotten—had a profound effect upon the Africans' attitudes toward employment. A district annual report states, for example, that in 1914 many young men had been tricked into coming to the district station to "cut grass," whereupon they had been seized and sent off to the Corps. When rumors spread in 1938 of an impending second world war, the Gusii displayed anxiety and hardly anyone turned up for the annual administration-sponsored sports meet. Even after a lapse of twenty-four years no Gusii intended to be so deceived again!

It was also no secret that the administration forced young men to leave the district and seek work in other areas. Although leading colonial officials attempted to stop this practice, individual District Commissioners appeared to have had considerable leeway in the administering of their areas. Thus, the District Commissioners of South Nyanza in 1915 and 1920, respectively, wrote: "Lately in order to fulfill Labour requisitions, force has had to be applied i.e. the young men have been rounded up during the night"; and "There is no use in blinding the fact that the majority of this labour [5,000 men] was not voluntary—it was ordered out by Chiefs and Elders, under instructions from me, in the hope that once the young men have taken the plunge, and find that they do not die in masses, and are not starved and ill-treated, there will be a more or less steady flow of voluntary labour in the future.

Origins and Development of the Cult of Mumbo

The exact date of Mumbo's origins is hard to pinpoint. There is a legend that Onyango Dunde, a Luo of Alego Location (which lies on the eastern shore of Lake Victoria), was given the message in 1913. One evening when sitting in his hut, Onyango was accosted by a gigantic snake so big that when it stood on its end in the lake, its head reached into the clouds. (One version has the snake coming from the clouds.) The snake swallowed Onyango and then regurgitated him, unhurt but shaken. This appeared to have been the snake's way of obtaining Onyango's attention because it immediately began to speak:

> I am the God Mumbo whose two homes are in the Sun and the Lake. I have chosen you to be my mouthpiece. Go out and tell all Africans— and more especially the people of Alego—that from henceforth I am their God. Those whom I choose personally, and also those who acknowledge me, will live forever in plenty. Their crops will grow of themselves and there will be no more need to work. I will cause cattle, sheep, and goats to come up out of the lake in great numbers to those who believe in me, but all unbelievers and their families and their cattle will die out. The Christian religion is rotten [mbovu] and so is its practice of making its believers wear clothes. My followers must let their hair grow—never cutting it. Their clothes shall be the skins of goats and cattle and they must never wash. All Europeans are your enemies, but the time is shortly coming when they will all disappear from our country.
>
> Daily sacrifice—preferably the males—of cattle, sheep, goats, and fowls shall be made to me. More especially do I prefer black bulls. Have no fear of sacrificing these as I will cause unlimited black cattle to come to you from the Lango, Masai, Nandi and Kipsigis. Lastly my followers must immediately slaughter all their cattle, sheep and goats. When this is done, I will provide them with as many more as they want from the lake.

Having spoken thus, the snake disappeared into the lake, and Onyango set out to spread Mumbo's words. He soon gathered a fairly large following.

From Alego Location in Central Nyanza, Mumboism spread quickly to neighboring locations and thence to South Nyanza, carried by some mission-trained men in the absence of the Adventist missionaries. (The Adventist mission, though staffed mainly by Canadians, had its headquarters in Hamburg, Germany. During World War I, the missionaries were all interned.) Mumboism's millennial message fitted in well with Adventist teachings such as "Watch and pray, for the end of the world is at hand." The District Commissioner of Kisii spoke of a new religion, "Mumbo," making its appearance in his district in 1914–15.

The sect's existence became patently evident on September 19, 1914, when the Germans invaded Kisii from what was then German East Africa and the British vacated the town in order to mobilize resistance and return. Believing Mumbo's prophecy that the British would soon depart, the local inhabitants mistook their temporary exodus for the millennium and looted the town and the neighboring missions. They ransacked all the government buildings and houses, the missions of Nyaribari, Nyanchwa, and Asumbi, and the trading centers of Riana and Rangwe. District Officer P. M. Gordon recorded the event:

> Thus it was that the Africans who gathered on the surrounding hills to watch the battle of Kisii, and as evening fell, saw the rival forces draw off to the north and south, felt assured that the prophecy was fulfilled. The Europeans had gone forever! . . . Their works, their offices, and Missions must be cast out. In this spirit of frenzy the empty Missions and trading centres, and offices were plundered, sacked and burned. The sight of the [King's] Africa[n] Rifles marching back in good order the following morning must have been a severe shock.

Even the heavy fine of three thousand head of cattle levied by the administration and the dispatch of many Kisii to work outside the location did not kill the movement. The following year, the chiefs reported an increasing number of adherents. Again many were sent out of the district to work.

In the years from 1915 to 1920, the cult spread rapidly, causing the British anxiety. As the District Commissioner put it in a letter, if the sect were left unattended "in an affair of this sort incalculable harm may be done and the position in time become so bad that the whole district be utterly inflamed and disorganized." Not knowing with what it was dealing, the administration questioned the chiefs and missionaries and sent informers into the sect's schools.

In 1920 another group, closely resembling Mumbo, was reported. It had been started by an old woman, Bonairiri of Kitutu Location, and it believed in the return of the prophet Zakawa. Zakawa was a great Kisii medicine man and prophet who, when the Uganda Railway was begun, had collected the Kisii, gone to the site of the present district headquarters, and prophesied where the police lines, the hospital, the office, and the District Commissioner's house would be built. He had also prophesied that over the course of years the young men would be disarmed and prove a greater source of revenue to their parents than the girls (who brought a bride-price), because they would receive wages for their work. He had also predicted the departure of the Europeans. When most of his prophecies came true, Zakawa's reputation as a seer was established. Whether he had actually uttered these prophecies is immaterial, since everyone believed that he had. Later his influence was enhanced by a belief that he was still alive: apparently he had died during a great beer-drink around 1902 but because he had not had a regular funeral, it was thought that he had not truly died and would return.

At the outset, Bonairiri sought permission from the chief to start a school where she could instruct her followers. The chief took her to the District Commissioner who refused her request. In mid-October, 1920, the chief reported that Bonairiri had collected a small group to whom she was preaching Mumboism. The administration dispersed her school. In November, it appeared that she had been joined by exponents of Zakawaism.

With the addition of Zakawaism, the movement was strengthened. In December 1920 District Commissioner H. E. Welby reported that all the people of Kitutu location were attending Bonairiri's school and that most, especially the old men, believed in Zakawa's return. Two days before the predicted reappearance of Zakawa and the departure of the white man, the District Commissioner, worried about Mumboism's rapid growth and the restlessness that it was causing, disbanded Bonairiri's school and rounded up the ringleaders. Consequently, Bonairiri was found insane and confined to a mental institution; her husband, Owura, whom Welby described as "chiefly responsible for the ready adoption of the dangerous part of the teaching"; her son, Marita, said to be "the most active agent in spreading the dangerous part of his mother's and father's teachings"; and Ongeri, the son of Maraa, the witch doctor responsible for the spearing of District Commissioner Northcote during the 1908 rebellion, together with another woman, were in 1921 all deported to Lamu, an isolated Arab town about eight hundred miles away on the coast of Kenya.

Repression, however, did not mean the end of the movement. During the 1920's there were outbreaks of Mumboism in Karochuonyi, Kasipul, and Kochia locations of South Nyanza. In 1927, the District Commissioner of Kisii wrote that the natives of Majoge Location were resurrecting Mumboism and that it was spreading rapidly to Bassi, Nyaribari, and Kitutu locations. (These locations form the northeastern section of South Nyanza and border one another.) The administration made the ringleaders move their huts into Kisii village where they could be watched. In 1931, the Local Native Council passed a resolution forbidding the practice of Mumboism.

However, the District Commissioner expressed the fear that should there be a serious famine or some other calamity the cult would recruit many followers and trouble would ensue. And as predicted, it was in the early 1930's, during a serious economic depression brought on by drought, famine, and an invasion of locusts, that the last widespread resurgence occurred. Thus, in 1933, the chiefs and members of the Local Native Council reported an alarming spread of the cult into all areas of South Nyanza. The climax was reached in November at the District Sports Meet when twenty armed young Mumboites defied the order of the senior Kisii chief to disperse. The nine ringleaders were promptly arrested and, after a judicial inquiry, deported to Kipani (another isolated settlement on the Kenyan coast). Within a few months, little was heard of Mumboism.

The movement did not die out completely, however. There was evidence of its activity in 1938 and 1947. Finally, in 1954 during the Mau Mau emergency, it was proscribed. But in 1963 Ogot estimated that there were still about five hundred practicing Mumboites: my own investigations in June 1966 revealed that the cult was extinct. Local people could recall its existence but none knew of any recent activities. When asked whether any members were still alive, several mentioned Marita, Bonairiri's son, but no other name was given. Ex-Chief Musa Nyandusi wrote in January 1967, "Marita Ogwora is the only survivor who is alive, others were old and died. Since they were arrested by the British Government, they never practised their cult."

During its time, Mumboism had its geographic center in the district of Kisii in the locations of Kitutu, North Mugirango, Nyaribari, Bassi, Majoge, and Wanjare; it had also spilled over into the neighboring locations of Gem, Kasipul, Karochuonyo, Kochia, and Kaniamwa. It had even recruited members as far away as the Luo location of Gwassi, on the shores of Lake Victoria.

Two general observations can be made about Mumboism's pattern of development. First, its growth coincided with years of agricultural depression. Its greatest activity occurred immediately after World War I and in the early 1930's, both periods of serious hardship when people pressed by drought and famine sought supernatural help in controlling the elements. Of these periods, Lonsdale wrote:

Traders took advantage of concerted tax-drives to lower the prices offered for African cattle, huts were occasionally burned to encourage payment, and widows, unlike those in Tanganyika, had to pay the full rate of tax on their huts. Inefficient tax-registers and collection in both the reserves and settled areas not infrequently led to double-payment of the taxes of migrant workers.

Second, the movement developed erratically. There were sudden flareups when membership expanded greatly—churches were built, schools opened, and feasts held. These florescences sparked government concern, and it would respond with repression, causing the sect to lie dormant for some time only to blossom forth in a nearby area with another leader.

Little is known about the actual organization of local groups. Sometimes the Mumboites built their meeting places on hilltops, at other times they met in their home compounds in a hut set aside for this purpose. The following describes such a meeting place:

. . . The meeting place of the cult consisted of a beautifully swept enclosure adjoining the High Priest's Boma and capable of seating some two hundred people. From the next boma to that of the High Priest ran a made path, four feet wide and trenched at the sides. . . . The enclosure was surrounded by a well-built dry stone wall. In the centre was a little semi-open hut about six feet in diameter, finished with white mud. . . . There was no door, it appeared symmetrical all round. . . . In the centre of the hut was a phallic altar-post, bearing traces of blood-stains. . . . The High Priest's daughter produced some unpleasant animal relics from a hole in the wall in the enclosure. In the Western corner a bush plant (Nyaluthkoth) had been planted. . . . In the Eastern corner was a small length of inner wall covered with dry grass, from which a shrub was growing so as to leave a covered but hollow space between the walls.

The members were divided into two orders. The first order, the priests, were older, established men, usually the head of a *boma*, who were "called"—by being possessed—in a way similar to Onyano, the founder. It was believed that the spirit of Mumbo wandered the land until it found a suitable person to enter. Supposedly invested with supernatural powers that enabled them to cure all kinds of illnesses and even resurrect the dead, such people were in great demand. The second order consisted of the priests' dependents and any others who wished to join.   Members were also distinguished on the basis of their tasks, be it sect leader, evangelist, food provider, teacher, prophet, or any of a variety of ritual specialists.

Message and Activities of the Cult

In order to try to explain the sect's tenacity despite administrative repression, let us look at its message and basis of support.

First of all, its message. Mumboism articulated an aggressive stand against foreign domination: "The Christian religion is rotten; all Europeans are your enemies." The movement proclaimed a set of values to which all "true Africans" should adhere, and it attacked the administrators as bearers of false values. The British were charged with being alien intruders and corrupters of the traditional way of life, and the chiefs with being agents of the intruders and traitors to that way of life.

The chiefs were treated with particular contempt. For example, at the District Sports Meet after twenty Mumboites in warriors' garb openly defied both the senior Kisii chief and an important Luo chief sent by the District Commissioner to stop their dancing, District Commissioner E. R. S. Davies reported:

> . . . I believe that they have all intrigued against the authority of the chiefs and headmen and deliberately hindered them in carrying out their duties by insults and threats, and claiming greater powers . . . When I arrested Muchirongo the day after the meeting of Mumboites at Kisii, I heard him abusing the chiefs, some of them individually by name and all of them collectively in a way that showed me that such teaching was dangerous to peace and good order, and inciting enmity between his followers and government. He and those who thought like him were without doubt intriguing against constituted power and authority . . . Moreover the chiefs are evidently afraid of it and realize that they are the special objects of hatred and scorn.

Given the powerful position of the chiefs, the authoritarian structure of Gusii society, and the fact that the order had come directly from the District Commissioner, this defiance was particularly bold and disrespectful. Also, its conspicuous style—the men being decked out in fighting attire (perhaps symbolizing the former revolts) and participating in traditional dances (perhaps denoting loyalty to traditional values)—suggests premeditated action designed to antagonize as well as to convey a message.

The millennial dream was the movement's chief tenet; with minor variations, it was held in common by the different local groups,   and appeared in the prophecies, visions, and dreams of cult heroes, both living and dead. It promised the destruction of the colonial order: the present world was soon to undergo a great cataclysm at which time a terrible vengeance would befall the enemies of the Mumboites, all of whom—the administrators, missionaries, and chiefs—would be overthrown and a kingdom of the Mumboites established.

Several versions recounted how this transformation was to proceed. In one, all water would be turned into blood and only Mumbo's followers would have drinking water, provided by him. All white people would disappear, leaving the Africans as sole survivors. In another, the founder was to be snatched up into heaven by fire, from whence he would dispense food to his followers. A third story recited how a certain Abachi tribe (an unknown tribal name) would descend from the north and exterminate the white man with sharp knives. Even the exact number each Abachi would kill (twenty white men apiece) was specified. Another story that circulated during World War I and had some basis in fact predicted that the Germans were soon to invade and cut off the arms of men in clothes, presumably Europeans and Westernized Africans, and particularly chiefs and mission converts. The Mumboites would escape unscathed because they were the Germans' friends. Still another story recounted that Zakawa's return was to be followed by days of darkness and a plague of locusts, after which the white man would be no more, and Zakawa, together with a sect priestess, would occupy the district headquarters. Given the frustrated ambitions of the Bogonko clan it is not surprising that the apocalypse they envisioned was both catastrophic and violent.

What was the Mumboite utopia to be like? As with the Marxian utopia only the barest outlines were specified, but in contrast to that utopia, work was not given a prominent place. It was, in short, to be a life with an abundance of material goods, a relaxed happy life free from worry in which the Mumboites could smoke *bhang* (Indian hemp) as much as they wanted. They would be blessed with an unfailing supply of sheep, cattle, and goats and their unattended crops would grow plentifully. Food would be showered upon them from heaven or arise of its own accord from Lake Victoria. They would be reunited with their dead, especially their great warriors and prophets and their god Mumbo. The crippled would be cured.

When was this paradise to be reached? Although the date was not usually specified, it was believed to be near at hand. There were reports that the Mumboites were buying lamps, in preparation for the end of the world when all would be dark. Some faithful followers, believing Mumbo's promise of food in the millennium, stopped cultivating their gardens, a few killed all of their livestock as he had ordered, and others refused to comply with the government demand for road construction, saying that since the Europeans were soon to leave, roads would no longer be needed.

One of the most revealing aspects of this dream was its reversal theme. In the promised land the superior-inferior positions of the Europeans and the Africans were to be reversed; the poor were to become rich and the weak strong. The politically dominant would suffer terrible punishments: They would die, be damned, be turned into monkeys, have their arms cut off, or be eaten by the great snake Mumbo. This theme appeared in a number of stories. For instance, part of the myth stated that actually the black man had been created first and white man second but that Zakawa and Mumbo had purposely put the white man over the black. Zakawa's sorceries were also credited with originally bringing the white man to Africa. This situation was soon to be righted with the return of Zakawa and other prophets, who would banish the white man forever. No information is available as to why this topsy-turvy state of affairs had originated, but in similar sects it came about, so the explanation goes, to test the black man by trials and tribulations—a purification through suffering. Only those who had truly followed Mumbo's edict—"Go tell all Africans . . . that henceforth I am their God"—would be saved.

It was not only within the cult that this theme predominated. Similar stories circulated elsewhere in South Nyanza. For example, a rumor that gained some currency among the Gusii and Kipsigis during World War II was that of the "Queen's dream." The Queen of England was said to be really a prophetess who dreamt that a black baby with wings would be born. The social order would then be reversed and the black races would take command. In an effort to prevent the baby from being born, the government was supposed to be trying to make the Africans sterile by distributing European blankets and tea, which were believed to possess magical properties that could bring impotence. What the cult did was to take such rumors and stories and give them form and coherence by linking them to a set of related ideas.

Whatever else they did, these stories certainly portrayed the blacks' dislike of the whites, and they transferred the power to determine men's destinies to the black man. Since he will occupy his rightful position, he will control instead of being controlled. The reversal theme can be viewed as an effort to come to terms with the fact that the white man possessed superior ability to cope with the physical environment and had far greater material wealth than the African. This myth transformed the humiliating aspects of defeat into virtues, for Mumboism credited its own prophets with having put the African into a subordinate position. The colonial era, soon to be terminated, was to be considered merely an interlude in the chain of events leading to the assumption by the Mumboites of their predestined superior position.

In spite of Mumboism's blatant rejection of Christianity and white men, Christian influence is, however, evident in its teachings. Bonairiri preached that woman came from the rib of man. The millennial concept appears to be derived from Christian eschatology since there is no mention in either traditional Gusii or Luo religion of a Day of Judgment, there being rather the traditional principle of retribution whereby evildoers were punished here and now. The belief that the Mumboites would be provided with food by their god at the millennium is reminiscent of the Lord supplying manna to the Children of Israel during their progress through the wilderness to the promised land. Though a traditional custom, the sacrifice of animals may well have been reinforced by the Old Testament practice. A number of precepts such as one will go to heaven by praying to Mumbo, one should not steal, one should not insult people, one should honor the aged, and one should not go about naked, have a Christian flavor about them. Although some of these practices were part of traditional life, the very fact that they were singled out as explicit rules suggests Christian contact.

The "origins" story (Mumbo the sea serpent swallows Onyango Dunde) also sounds as if it came straight from the Old Testament account of Jonah and the whale. A Luo tale, however, also tells of an important elder being swallowed by a sea serpent. Mumbo's legend may be based either on Luo or Biblical cosmology, or it may have originated independently. Probably, however, since there were parallels between the Christian and traditional myths, these parallels became the basis for a new one.

The strongest Christian influence is, however, in the concept of Mumbo. Did the Gusii, the main supporters of Mumboism, have any similar ideas? Or even more relevant, did the tribe in which the myth originated, the Luo, have such an idea in their traditional beliefs? The Gusii are said to have had a snake god called Kiboyi. According to LeVine the word *Nyasaye*, which is equivalent to our concept of "luck" or "fortune," is often heard among the Gusii, who believe that it is a Luo word diffused via the missionaries. Events over which an individual has no control are attributed to *Nyasaye*. However, absent from Gusii thought is any notion of a creator-spirit.

Whisson maintains that the concept of a creator-spirit was present in Luo cosmology before the Christian idea of a creator was introduced. *Nyasaye*, however, is a Bantu rather than a Nilotic term, and the Luo, like the Alur (another Nilotic tribe), appear not to have had a clear idea of a personal god until they came into contact with the Bantu. To some extent *Nyasaye* was equated in Luo thought with the sun. It was considered a good thing for all people to be out of bed by dawn, when simple supplicatory prayers were offered to the rising sun. An old man might say "Rise well for me that I may be at peace." Younger people might ask that a good prospective mate be brought to their notice during the day. Similarly, prayers were offered at night as the sun set. *Nyasaye* was seen not only in the sun but in other large and extraordinary phenomena—in the moon, in large rocks, in big snakes, in elephants, and in awe-inspiring objects of nature. The creator-force was not personalized in any way. It belonged to the cosmology of a nomadic people to be worshipped wherever men were, not only in a temple or in a sacred grove.

Mumboism seems to have taken from the indigenous religion the idea that the creator-spirit dwells in Mumbo. However, in Mumboism the traditional view of a vague life-force that fills wondrous objects is gone; in its place is the omnipotent Christian figure who clearly promises eternal life to his followers and damnation to unbelievers. Here the Luo creator-spirit has changed from a depersonalized force into a personal god with the attributes of the God of the Old Testament. He is a commanding and demanding patriarch who requires exclusive worship from his children and lays down rules that must be followed: "I am the God Mumbo . . . go and tell all Africans . . . that henceforth I am their God. Those whom I choose personally, and also those who acknowledge me, will live forever in plenty . . . but all unbelievers and their families and their cattle will die out . . ." Hence, a new culture form emerged from combining indigenous and Western ideas.

Mumboism often also turned to the past for inspiration: fresh meaning was imbued into tribal ways; old dreams were animated with a new vitality. Since Mumbo had ordered a return to the old ways, the converts were directed to reject the new religion of Christianity, to sacrifice daily, let their hair grow long, wear clothes of skins, and never to wash. Old tribal dances were revived. The most venerated Gusii warriors and their most militant anti-British leaders were claimed by the movement. Zakawa the great prophet, Bogonko the mighty chief, and Maraa the instigator of the 1908 rebellion became its symbols, infusing the living with the courage and the strength of past heroes.

Furthermore, leaders bolstered their own legitimacy by claiming to be the mouthpieces of the deceased prophets, an effort in which their descendants were especially successful. Nyamachara and Uriogi, the sons of Zakawa, for example, revived a belief in their father's return, as a result of which, pilgrims came to their village bearing gifts of livestock, and some even reported that they had seen Zakawa. In a similar vein Ongeri, the son of Maraa, spread his mother's teachings, and Nyakundi, the son of Bogonko, established himself as the medium of communication with both his father and Zakawa. Thus, with the progeny of Gusii heroes supporting the movement, blood ties as well as symbolic links with the past were established. Here was an especially powerful group whose prestige and authority could well be used to arouse, strengthen, and weld the various disunited cults into solid anti-British opposition.   The legitimacy conferred by the ancestors—especially the Gusii heroes—was of particular significance because among the Gusii ancestor spirits are the major supernatural beings.

However, the cult's advocacy of a return to the old ways can be given different interpretations. Identification with indigenous values obviously meant the rejection of Europeans, especially of the missionaries who insisted upon the wearing of clothes and on cleanliness. But the rejection of European clothes was probably also connected with the chiefs' practice of employing as assistants youths who dressed in European or Swahili apparel, "the donning of which is popularly supposed to increase their cerebral powers."   Usually these boys had obtained an elementary education, a knowledge of Swahili, and were converts to Christianity. They were useful to the chiefs on two counts: first, they could translate from the vernacular into Swahili (many chiefs could not); second, they had become acquainted with Europeans, and chiefs in working with the British preferred assistants who had some knowledge of the white man's ways. Consequently, the youths held a position of status as associates of chiefs, missionaries, and administrators. Thus, if the chiefs were viewed by the Mumboites as European lackeys, doubtless the mission converts were viewed as equally contemptible. In addition, the youths' behavior was not likely to endear them to their tribesmen. With their knowledge of the outside world they could qualify as sophisticates among their illiterate countrymen. There were countless complaints about their "swelled heads" and one can imagine how obnoxious some were in lording it over their fellows. Therefore, the cult's rejection of European clothing may also have been tied up with its refusal to recognize these youths' claims to superiority.

To sum up, Mumboism's stories, myths, and prophecies represented the wishes and dreams of peasants for wealth, happiness, freedom, and the punishment of their enemies. Here was a way of coping with a world in which they lived but which they did not understand.

Having in some ways been catapulted into the twentieth century, for which their traditional beliefs had not prepared them, they were at pains to explain it. Beginnings of doubts about the efficacy and veracity of their indigenous beliefs were met by the cult's provision of answers to the pervasive questions of the times. The answers, concocted of traditional and Christian teachings, claimed legitimacy by rejecting Christianity and resurrecting the old prophets while, at the same time, utilizing certain attractive features from what was viewed as the West's powerful religion. The message of Mumboism was a skillful attempt to reconstruct a disintegrating world by combining traditional and Western ideas and thereby obtaining the best of two worlds.

The cult's ideology also attempted to restore pride in traditional ways and promised a new self-respect based, in part, upon downgrading Europeans and upgrading Africans. It provided an explanation and a ray of hope in a promise of a better tomorrow. In the words of one District Commissioner: "The melancholy fact remains to be stated, that a large number of men and women in this district do find, at any rate, spiritual and physical satisfaction in these base fraudulent practices." Hence, the ideology represented first and foremost a way of righting the colonial system with all of its inequalities and injustices, and thus provided the means to adapt to a rapidly changing social order.

Given these beliefs, what were the means which the Mumboites employed to bring their millennial dreams to fruition? They appeared to rely heavily upon magic and ritual to solve their problems: if the proper rite were performed Mumbo would bless them. Priests sacrificed to Mumbo to ensure protection against drought and invasions of locusts. The usual practice was to present a priest with a sheep or goat which he sacrificed to Mumbo with the prescribed oblations. Sometimes it was specified that such offerings should be black, at other times white. Feasts were held periodically. Together with their integrative function, they may have symbolized the disappearance of economic privation during the millennium. The priests also performed ceremonies to appease the spirits, control the elements, cure sickness, and restore life.

This concern with magic was rooted in traditional beliefs. Illness, death, and various kinds of disaster were dealt with by sacrifices and oblations which were carried out by a host of supernatural specialists: professional sorcerers and witch-smellers in the area of medicine, rainmakers and hail-stoppers for weather protection, magical detectors for theft control, and other part-time experts who executed rituals for removing different kinds of curses and providing protection against specific misfortunes.

Resistance to the British appeared to be largely symbolic, as in the refusal to wear European clothes or to eat European food. It was believed that no harm could come to anyone protected by a Mumbo cloak and cap of skins. District Commissioner Campbell obviously understood the significance of Mumbo garb when he wrote:

> As regards the men . . . I personally interviewed them all and they professed Mumboism. Each was wearing a "mumbo" cloak of goat skins sewn together also a hat of skins. . . . I am glad to say that for the time being my action has squashed the movement as those who foolishly paid cattle etc. to the teachers now see those men in prison awaiting trial and in consequence of my having burnt their cloaks and hats before their eyes I do not anticipate any immediate recrudescence among the Kisii.

With the government's efforts to repress the sect, resort was had to less obvious signs of membership. One chief, for example, who would not be able to admit membership and keep his job, wore a badge of goatskin under his ordinary clothes. This was a most appropriate symbol since the British had let it be known they did not favor the wearing of skins. These tactics had probably been abetted by Maraa's counsel. According to ex-Chief Ooga, however, Maraa after the revolt of 1908 changed her tack, exhorting her people not to fight the Europeans by force because God had told her during the night that the Europeans would go. God himself was going to fight them and the people should trust in Him. They should also try new ways—of talking and cleverness—to rid themselves of the foreigners.

Ecstatic behavior—"being possessed"—which was manifested by trembling, uttering a stream of unintelligible words, and falling down, was also much in evidence. Assistant District Commissioner S. H. Fazan reported that an informant had described possession as follows: "Mumbo comes when dark clouds are in the West. He possesses people and makes them tremble. Sometimes he comes at night when a man is asleep. Signs of possession are trembling and speaking unintelligible words." Possession is still practiced among the Gusii, sometimes being linked to sun worship as well. *Abarogi* (diviners) become possessed when they shake gourd rattles during the initiation of a new diviner.

Possession among the Mumboites could also have been influenced by its Luo membership. According to Luo beliefs, spirits live in people most of the time and, when not possessing someone, return to their several homes, in the sun, in trees, rivers, or in the mythical water snake, Mumbo, whose home was Lake Victoria. These spirits, *juogi,* were believed to give the person possessed the power to prophesy and, after suitable experience, the power to cure people possessed by the same kind of spirits. In all likelihood, possession, whether it was purely Gusii in origin or Luo-influenced, was reinforced by the Christian practice of "receiving the spirit," and the traditional powers given the possessed were extended to include the miraculous powers of Jesus Christ. Although I have no direct evidence of this connection, such is the case in a present-day sect—Legio Maria—which originated in a nearby area.

The Mumboites were great smokers of *bhang* and consequently were harassed by law enforcement officers. An informer reported that they smoked secretly during specific hours set aside each day (4 and 5 A.M. and 7 and 9 P.M.), probably with a guard posted, and hid their pipes on the mountain during the day.

It is interesting to note that the cult also made several attempts to abolish both female and male circumcision, in 1920 ordering that it be suspended for nine years. Apparently the order was carried out, at least in Kitutu and North Mugirango locations, for the year 1921. But dissatisfaction with this arrangement led to its resumption the following year. When, in 1922, many children died during the period of seclusion, their deaths were attributed to the violation of custom in 1921.

This was an attempt at a radical innovation, especially when it was tried as far back as 1920. Writing about the Gusii in 1959, LeVine stated:

> Although fairly progressive agriculturalists, they are behind other Kenya Bantu tribes in westernization, owing partly to isolation and partly to cultural conservatism. One of the major foci of this conservatism is the initiation cycle, involving genital operations for boys and girls. . . . Although missionary activity and the use of European clothing have altered the ritual content of the initiation to some extent, and school attendance limits its duration for some boys, there has been no general trend against initiation in Gusiiland, no long-term indication that its universality and cultural significance have been impaired.

And that was written nearly forty years after this initial attempt!

Circumcision is among the most important events in the life of the Kisii. The ceremony marks the assumption of an adult role with its rights, duties, and higher status. It is an integral part of the whole fabric of mores, customs, and practices that order traditional society. Philip Mayer, in a detailed study of the initiation rites, describes the community's involvement:

. . . the initiation cycle is woven into the life of the neighbourhood
in such a way that nobody remains altogether unconcerned. Children
too young to be initiated themselves are occupied in carrying food or
running errands; . . . The older boys and girls, who have already
been initiated but are not yet married, play a very important part, indeed, apart from the actual operation and the adults' beer parties, they
organize and carry out most of the rites and celebrations themselves.
. . . The young married people are less closely involved, but ma-
turity brings the right to be entertained at the beer-drinks with which
all parents celebrate their respective children's entry into and emergence from seclusion. Among the old people, some will be needed to
take part in the ritual, for instance, in blessing the novices at the end
of seclusion and burning the bedding.

Had this order been followed important changes in Gusii culture
and social relations would have ensued. Boys and girls well below the
usual age might have been circumcised, and if they had failed to fulfill
kinship and other obligations of adult status the meanings of initiation for the child and his family could have been substantially
altered. The age-grading of children would also have been disturbed
and, if a considerable number of prepubertal boys and girls had
waited the nine years to be circumcised, some would have indulged
in sexual relations and offspring would have resulted, thereby vio-
lating the mores that initiation must precede sexual activity. Besides,
Gusii distinctiveness is maintained by their language and culture
rather than administrative autonomy. Circumcision is one of the most
important customs integrating all Gusii and setting them off from the
surrounding Luo. The order to abolish circumcision, therefore, was
strongly anti-traditional.

It is also possible that incest and the "communal enjoyment of
women" may have been practiced, as these activities are mentioned in
five separate accounts.   The most reliable data came from an old man
convicted of incest with his daughter in 1938 and sentenced to two
years' imprisonment with hard labor. He gave as his reason his membership in the cult.

A strong argument can be made for dismissing such allegations.
First, there is a paucity of evidence. Second, the Gusii lived in a generally hostile and suspicious environment where malicious gossip was
rife.   And third, given this milieu, together with the administration's
need to justify its repression of the sect, it would not be surprising if
many accusations were exaggerated. On the other hand, to dismiss the
accusations prima facie might lead to overlooking a significant dimension in the development of protest. What is needed is to look beneath
the rhetoric to investigate each accusation for whatever truth there may

be in it. In reference to sexual practices the questions to be answered are: (1) did the population, in general, regard them as deviant and (2) did the Mumboites engage in them to a greater extent than non-members?

The answer to the first question can be stated quite simply: for the Gusii, marriage provided, and still does, the only acceptable sexual outlet. All other relationships were regarded as deviant, although viewed with varying degrees of disapproval. Feelings of sexual avoidance and embarrassment between persons of adjacent generations were at the core of Gusii morality. They were strongest between father and daughter or daughter-in-law, next strongest between father and son, less between mother and son, and weakest between mother and daughter or daughter-in-law. LeVine does not spell out the taboos governing the father-daughter relationship, but, having elaborated the father-son relationship, he states that the former is even stricter. Hence, father-daughter incest would be abhorrent to the Gusii. It was viewed as an affliction caused by ancestor spirits which must be propitiated by sacrificing an expensive animal like a sheep or a goat.

No information is available on what the ambiguous phrase the "communal enjoyment of women" entailed. However, according to tradition, sexual relations were surrounded by norms of privacy. Adultery, especially on the part of the wife, was believed to bring severe supernatural sanctions, and premarital sex, though engaged in, was not approved by the older people. Girls had misgivings and feared gaining the reputation of a "slut" and young men did not consider it proper to fornicate with girls whom they intended to marry. Thus both incest and "communal enjoyment" were regarded as deviant by the Gusii.

As for the second question, evidence suggests that at least some Mumboites indulged in these practices. Scholars have written about sex as an area of particular tension for the Gusii. LeVine and Mayer have noted the aggressive sexual behavior of both men and women.

Obviously not all Gusii were satisfied with the established norms, least of all youths whose sex life was stringently curtailed and whose sources of adventure and status had been cut off. Since young people were prominent in the cult, it is reasonable to expect that they would push for new arrangements. Therefore, given a culture area with less than satisfactory norms which impinge, in particular, upon an age group prone to experimentation, it would not have been surprising if deviant practices had developed.

No data are available on how widespread these practices were, whether they were carried out as part of the ritual, and if so, what were the accompanying beliefs. Since the movement was composed of small, autonomous groups, it provided ample scope for each to go its own way. The possible significance of this behavior will be discussed later.

Basis of Support

Tribal support for Mumboism came mainly from the Gusii and a few Luo and Kuria. Aside from tribal affiliation, were there any special categories or strata of people for whom the movement had special appeal?

The core of support for Mumboism appears to have come from the Bogonko clan, the largest and wealthiest clan of the Kitutu tribe. This tribe consisted of seven alien clans linked to the dominant Bogonko lineage, whose allegiance had been bought by providing them with cattle for bridewealth. The political structure of the Kitutu developed from mutually benefiting patron-client relationships founded on the warrior tradition. In the era immediately prior to the British occupation, the Bogonko clan was at the peak of its prestige, having subordinated the seven alien clans to itself and having formed the beginnings of a "state" system with a hereditary chieftainship. This was the most advanced system of political authority, in the sense of a centralized, hierarchical structure clearly demarcating the political from other spheres, to be found among the seven Gusii tribes. Some of its elders were even recognized as authorities not only within the clan itself but throughout the whole tribe.

When the British came, the position and influence of the Bogonko clan suffered. It is submitted that they became the leaders of protest against the colonial regime, as the center of Mumbo activity was in Kitutu Location where, as previously stated, more than half of the population belonged to the Bogonko clan. Furthermore, the clan was well represented in the Mumbo sect, Bogonko being a cult symbol and his son, Nyakundi, having been imprisoned for Mumbo activities. It is also submitted that the resentment of the Bogonko clan was primarily *political*, arising from their resentment over the administration's by-passing of their chief (possibly because of the clan's support of the revolts). This has been noted by LeVine. Indeed, the Bogonko's lack of general grievances has been pointed out in numerous sources. In contrast to the Kikuyu situation, for example, there was no acute land shortage among the Gusii and the Luo of South Nyanza. Nor did economic grievances seem to have been root causes. And general anti-British sentiments cannot serve as sufficient explanation because all Kenyan Africans experienced the same system of colonial rule, and some protested and others did not.

But it can be argued that alien rule impinged on some to a greater extent than on others; and that those who felt its burdensome aspects more were consequently more highly motivated to protest and, if need be, to suffer the consequences of their militancy. In the case of the Bogonko clan, the members appear to have used general anti-British sentiments to further their own political purposes.

Numerous data support this hypothesis—that the grievances were mainly political and clan-based. Thus, the choice of symbols—Bogonko, the clan's great warrior, and Maraa, the *laibon* (ritual leader) who ordered the spearing of the District Commissioner which led to the 1908 revolt—emphasizes political protest. In addition, one may note that support for Mumboism also came from people who had something to lose under the British system, for example the tribal ritual specialists for whom there was no room in the mission churches. Thus, though the mission churches could provide a place for the priest-like head with a set of customary duties, they excluded the charismatic prophet who sought to cure psychological and physical disorders. In Mumboism, where there was an emphasis on communicating with the supernatural, possession, and the curing of illnesses, there was room for this type of leader.

There were also those who aspired to a new role in a changing society. Thus, a surprisingly large number of leaders were women: Bonairiri, the chief exponent of Zakawism; Kibiburi, considered a dangerous agent by the administration and deported to Lamu; Obondo, mentioned in administrative correspondence as a future priestess; and Okenyuri, the wife of a cult leader described as "the most attractive agent who works the mystical and oracular interviews with Mumbo," and Maraa. Traditional society has many middle-aged or elderly female diviners. This is the most important role a woman can occupy outside the family and, although a respected position, it does not endow her with extraordinary powers or prestige. The cult may have adapted this role to that of priestess.

Young men were especially prominent in the cult. Chief Orinda, in charge of a location where the cult was strong, said: "The sect consists only of young men. There are no old men in the sect or practically none." Unmarried girls joined the sect. Chief Mahangain reported that the elders were refusing to attend *barazas* (public meetings) and "that the young men are preaching to the effect that it will only be a short time before white men go, that they will have a free fight, and it will be a case of the survival of the fittest. This sounds as if the young were openly challenging the elders' authority.

There is an apparent inconsistency here. Earlier, we noted that the District Commissioner had stated in 1921 that Zakawaism was especially attractive to the old men and that almost all in Kitutu Location had joined. Here (in 1919), we note that chiefs say that only young men join and hardly any older people. How is this discrepancy to be explained? It could be that the composition of the membership varied by area or by time, or that Zakawaism had a particular appeal for older people, because of its links with the great Gusii prophet, that Mumboism, in general, did not have. Lacking evidence, we can only conjecture.

Why did women and youths support the cult? What was there in it for them? At the heart of the traditional authority system were the ancestors and the elders. In death as well as in life the ancestors were regarded as being intimately bound up with the welfare of the clan. Only the elders, because of their close lineage relationship to the ancestors, were able to ascertain the ancestors' will and, when necessary, make the required propitiations. This gave them much power and permitted them to exercise strong social sanctions. One of the functions of ancestor worship was to keep respect and power in the hands of the elders who, because of their wisdom, were believed to possess the necessary attritubes of authority.

But the cult established other criteria for leadership. In keeping with its reversal theme, youths and women, both occupying low status in the traditional authority structure, figured prominently as leaders. They claimed greater powers than the elders. They communicated with the ancestors, interceded on behalf of the members with other supernatural agencies, and made many of the decisions that in traditional society belonged to the elders. Thus, in rejecting age and sex, two major attributes of traditional leadership, and in introducing new norms and leadership roles, the cult in essence rejected tribal authority.

Both mission and Mumbo youth were rebelling against tribal authority, and some of the latter were engaging in activities highly disapproved of by the older generation. Joining either the movement or the mission provided new activities, and both supported, even if unintentionally, rebellion against tribal authority. Both groups attracted young people and, although the Mumboites clearly disliked the educated mission students, the cult recruited many of them. Two choices were presented to young people: (1) to join the cult which was to take an aggressive stand against the foreigners and to defy the chiefs and elders; or (2) to join a mission where one could become literate and perhaps acquire a job with the administration. Joining a mission had the added advantage that one was not forced to leave the district to go to work. One group of young people chose to accommodate to the colonial system while the other chose to reject it. Although any number and combination of factors could have accounted for the difference in choice, it is possible that geographical proximity was the crucial factor. Did it simply depend on whether the mission or the cult was closer to the individual's home? As evidence is lacking, we can only speculate.

The cult therefore recruited a clan with political grievances; people whose traditional positions were threatened by the incipient order; and those who, like women and youth, were laying claims to new roles. No doubt as in any amorphous, heterogeneous movement, the psychologically unstable, the shiftless, and the malcontents joined, but they do not appear to have formed its mainstay.

Attitudes of Agents of Social Control Toward Mumboism

In examining the nature of the sect and its development, a crucial dimension is the way in which the agents of social control—British administrators, chiefs, headmen, tribal police, and missionaries—saw it and dealt with it. Once the sect had established itself as anti-British, the administration used a number of repressive tactics to eradicate it. Deportations, imprisonments, fines, forced labor, and a variety of harassments were employed whenever the sect appeared to be gaining members.

By and large, the administration viewed the cult leaders as exploiters of credulous peasants—as persons who manipulated an environment of superstition and fear for their own ends. District Commissioner Hodge said:

> Apparently the reason for the cult springing up again was that Onkenyuri and Omwega had most of their cattle confiscated after the previous Mumbo trouble and thought that now was a suitable opportunity of restarting the cult and thereby again amassing stock. The fee for becoming a Mumboite is a goat—a higher grade in it requires a cow.

And, in 1934, the District Commissioner of South Nyanza, E. R. S. Davies, stated:

> The general opinion which I form on the present evidence is that the promoters of the movement and their devotees are parasites addicted to *bhang* smoking who want to obtain food for nothing and have used unscrupulously certain prophecies of the past and a fear of locusts, over which they are believed to have power. They on the other hand claim to be teachers of a true religion persecuted by the chiefs who attribute evil and sedition to them.

Some administrators even feared that the Mumboites would cause another uprising. District Commissioner Campbell wrote: "I think that there is little doubt that most have been preaching sedition, though it may be difficult to get evidence." Later in the same letter he reported that Chief Nsungu had said: "It is exactly this sort of thing that might lead to the murder of an officer and another Kitutu War" [an obvious reference to one of the Kisii revolts]. In the previous year the District Commissioner had written: "There is no question but that Mumboism may become an extremely dangerous political force. . . . If such warnings are totally neglected there is a possibility of the events which occurred at Blantyre being repeated in this Protectorate." (In 1915, Africans led by John Chilembwe had revolted near Blantyre, formerly Nyasaland, now Malawi. The revolt had lasted less than two weeks and been completely crushed, yet it was a portent for other colonial administrations.)

The hostile reaction on the part of the administration naturally hardened the sect's view toward it. Men were often arrested, detained, and deported on mere suspicion and on charges that would not have been upheld under normal conditions in British and American courts of law. For instance, a District Commissioner in a letter to his Provincial Commissioner admitted that he had insufficient evidence to have four people deported. He wrote " . . . it is difficult to get any weight of evidence against individuals of actual sedition." Nevertheless, they were deported.

In spite of its repressive tactics, the administration did not present a monolithic front in its handling of the cult. It stressed a pragmatic approach and attempted to abide by the rule of law, even though often disregarding civil liberties. An interesting case occurred in 1918 when District Commissioner Campbell sent some Mumboites out of the district on a project using compulsory labor. The Provincial Commissioner wrote:

> The Assistant District Commissioner here reports that you have sent in a batch of 28 men under escort for work at Magadi. As you are aware labour is not to be forced even for Government purposes without the sanction of His Excellency. Neither Chiefs nor District Commissioners can deport men from their Districts except they are being transferred from one jail to another under warrant. In the circumstances, I am ordering the return of the men and shall be glad of an explanation.

In defending his action, District Commissioner Campbell wrote:

> In this matter I feel bound to say that I consider the headman acted with extraordinary loyalty and energy. It requires some pluck on the part of a chief to boldly tackle a wholesale and vicious movement such

as this, surrounded by superstition, illwill and mysterious "dawa" [magic]. In acceding to their suggestion to send the riff-raff out to work and try the teachers it seemed to me and still does that in the interest of Government, the step taken was a wise one and that under the Native Authority Ordinance Section 5 (1) and (2), 6 (1) a legal one. I cannot agree that sending men such as these to Magadi for six months work for good wages can be described as "deportation" and when natives in a reserve are misbehaving themselves I do not understand how the operation of sending them out for a few months work can be placed on the same footing with "forcing labour" when all and sundry have to be called upon. . . .

The Provincial Commissioner then wrote both John Ainsworth, the Chief Native Commissioner (the highest official in charge of native affairs) and the acting Chief Secretary to report the District Commissioner's action. The Chief Native Commissioner wrote the acting Chief Secretary supporting the Provincial Commissioner's reprimand; he too viewed the District Commissioner's action as *ultra vires*. In his letter, the chief Native Commissioner displayed considerable knowledge of Mumboism and, since he felt that it was neither a political nor a subversive cult, he suggested ridicule instead of repression.

Personally I failed to detect in it any disloyal or harmful tendency and formed the opinion that to take official notice of the matter was likely to do more harm than good. Sometime ago, I saw some of the so-called teachers and followers when I came to the conclusion that the best way to deal with the subject was to ridicule rather than take serious notice of it. . . . Personally I deprecate any repressive action by the Government until and unless we are satisfied that the cult has become such as to lead to disloyalty or that it is dangerous to peace and order in the districts concerned.

Any hasty or ill-considered action in a matter of this description is likely to create an impression in the native mind that the Government fears the teaching when it becomes imbued with exaggerated importance and may on that account alone become highly desirable.

I believe that the best policy is to keep in touch with any such movement as this and allow it to have full scope until we are satisfied that it is necessary to take steps to deal with it. . . .

For their part, acting as agents of the administration responsible for law and order, the chiefs and headmen viewed the sect with hostility. If it disrupted the community, they were required to deal with it, and it was they who were blamed for not forewarning the District Commissioner. Administrative records report: "All the Kisii chiefs and many of the Luo chiefs . . . were unanimous in advising the suppression of the cult" and "The trial [of Mumboites] was well attended by the general public. About 150 assessors (chiefs and tribal elders) recommended the deportation of the eight accused and the imprisonment for six months of another." Even if they had sympathized with the cult, the chiefs as civil servants could not afford to let the administration know it. The evidence confirms, however, that they were anti-cult. They had much to lose if its goals were achieved; the cult's elect and not the administration's appointees were to be the potentates in the new order. Thus, having accommodated themselves to British rule and standing at the top of the native authority structure, they were certainly going to look askance at any group that advocated a change.

Not unexpectedly the missionaries were also against the cult. Father Scheffer of the Asumbi Catholic Mission wrote the District Commissioner fully supporting his action in sending the Mumboites out of the district on work projects. His view was consistent with the missionary perspective.

> I have heard reports to the effect that Mumbo people, taken by you, have been sent back from Kisumu. What a pity! Mumbo people were responsible for all the looting in September 1914. They were responsible for a good amount of trouble to their respective chiefs at the time the latter were recruiting government labour.
>
> At the present they still are opposed to the progress of civilization and from information received they are an immoral and drunken lot.
>
> One of their many prophecies was that in 1914 when the crops would be in the *wasungu* [white man] would leave the district. This very phophecy made some people think that Mumboism was of German origin and if I had anything to say in the matter, I would stamp out anything of that kind, and the manner I would try to stamp it would be to make them see something of the world. It would convince them that the *wasungu* had come to stay and they would have to submit to the higher authority.

It is not surprising that the missionaries were against Mumboism since the missions probably lost many members to the sect. Although there is no information available on how many of the members of Mumbo had formerly belonged to a mission, other independent sects in Kenya have posed serious threats to missions.

By and large, then, the agents of social control viewed the cult negatively. They wanted peace and stability, whereas Mumboism continually provoked unrest and lawlessness. The sect upset established ways: youth challenged chiefs and elders, women challenged men, and the sect challenged foreign domination and traditional life. It is difficult to say whether the repressive tactics of the colonial power actually brought an end to the cult or whether it died out because of, among other things, the failure of its millennial prophecies.

Our image of the early phase of the colonial era has been formed by the writings of European administrators and missionaries, since it was their views and evaluations of tribal life that have been disseminated. They defined the cults as consisting of "deluded," "hysterical" people under the sway of a leader whose "diseased brain" was centered on self aggrandizement. Action was thought to be motivated by "the black and blood-stained forces of sorcery and magic stirring the vicious hearts of wicked men."

Whether or not any of these accusations is true, it should be noted that the history of sects and other nonconforming groups shows that new and different groups whose ways and motives are unknown tend to be regarded by the established order with suspicion and, at times, outright hostility. That such suspicion was largely inappropriate in the instance being studied here is clear for the following reasons:

1. Doubts about the veracity of many accusations were voiced from the lowest to the highest administrative levels. Chief Orinda stated frankly that he did not like the people of Mumbo but continued:

> On the other hand much that has been said against them is not true. They cultivate like other people and they do not kill stock, and they give no trouble at all when they are wanted for work. They come to work at once. Their teaching is good. They teach men not to steal, or use insulting language, or to laugh at old men, or to walk about naked.

An informant, sent to one of the sect's schools, reported:

> I don't know that they do any harm except to say that the *wasungus* will soon return to their own country. They do not kill all their cattle in preparation for the millennium. They have little feasts at their bomas from 10 days to monthly intervals and occasional big ones for which they foregather at Betis' boma. [They had been accused of killing all their cattle in preparation for the millennium. Probably some of the more fervent believers did, but the more prudent did not.]

While most administrators viewed the sect as dangerous, retrogressive, and a menace to law and order as well as to morals, a few refused to characterize it as all bad. Assistant District Commissioner Fazan, after investigating the sect, wrote:

> . . . most of them have stock, and they cultivate shambas. They all either wear clothes, or more than one goat skin, so that they live up to the precept not to go naked. A man called Wadi, who is the chief of Chief Orinda's retainers and has most of the actual work of collecting porters to do [for the Carrier Corps], states that the Mumbo people give no trouble whatever, and that their readiness to turn out for government labour is conspicuous. For my part I can add the testimony that I have more than 40 of them confined in my camp at the present

moment. None of them are reported to have resisted the summons to appear, and nobody has made any attempt to escape. Therefore they do not seem to me to be intractable.

I investigated a charge of assault (or grievous hurt) against them and found that the persons who brought the charge were more culpable than the persons charged. The persons who brought the charge were mission boys.

By the foregoing remarks I do not mean to vindicate Mumboism. I am aware that a large amount of damage has probably been caused by it. But it is possible that the attitude of the persons concerned may be loyal in one place and disloyal in another.

I should not even like to say they are not disloyal here, but I have found no evidence of it.

2. The administration's accusation that the Mumboite rituals exploited credulous Gusii does not stand up to examination. A comparison of their fees with those charged by the *omari* (witch-smellers, the traditional practitioners), shows that the Mumboites charged the usual fee, a cow (worth about $42) or a goat or goat meat ($5). On the other hand, the issue of who was a true or false prophet, a true or false witch doctor, is complex and beyond the scope of this paper.

3. While it is true that the Mumboites smoked *bhang*, so did many others in Nyanza. John Ainsworth, Provincial Commissioner of Nyanza in 1908, commented on this practice:

> All the Kavirondo, particularly the Luo are great smokers of tobacco which is grown in this country. . . . It is also a custom amongst the men at times to smoke *bhang* obtained from a species of Indian hemp which is cultivated in the country for this purpose. *Bhang* smoking produces a state of semi-madness or intoxication. . . . Some few months ago I instructed all DC's to call in all chiefs and inform them of the dangers of *bhang* smoking and point out to them that a great deal of crime in the country was due to its use.

In 1921 Senior Commissioner H. R. Tate wrote: "*Bhang* smoking and witch-craft are prevalent all over the District and are difficult to stop." Anyway, the administration's belief that *bhang* encouraged the outbreak of hostilities because of its aggression-arousing tendencies is debatable. *Bhang* may release aggressive tendencies or it may produce a state of euphoria.

4. It is true that the cult looked to the past by calling upon its heroes for support and inspiration, so in a symbolic sense it can be called "retrogressive." There is no evidence, however, that incest and the communal enjoyment of women were ever part of the approved traditional life. The smoking of *bhang* was indulged in by other Gusii. Unless "retrogressive" is used in some absolute moral sense, it appears to

have little meaning here. Rejection, rather than regression, is a more suitable designation. The cult could not banish Europeans but it could symbolically reject them—particularly the mission converts. Instead of "regressing" to the old ways, the movement rejected or attempted to reject several important tribal mores: circumcision and the authority of the elders.

With these labels the colonial administrators and missionaries made the Mumboites appear basically different from the majority of Africans. They considered their protest childlike and primitive—irrational behavior aroused by the prophecies and incantations of witch doctors. These explanations detracted from the dignity and rationality of the African and served to exonerate the administration while bypassing the important question of whether, in fact, genuine grievances existed.

Failure to consider the time perspective in interpreting actions can sometimes lead to error. The Gusii were defeated in battle. For them to persist with this tactic would have been futile. Obviously an alternative to the spear had to be found. Groping for ways to cope with the formidable intruders, they turned to a belief in the millennium which had been promised by the powerful white man's religion. Under the circumstances this can hardly be construed as irrational conduct.

A Later Phase of the Movement

During the 1950's groups similar to Mumbo appeared sporadically. But none had any lasting impact. In 1952, a millenarian movement inspired by the Adventists emerged in various parts of the Highlands. When Mumboism was proscribed in 1954 another cult in the same area, known as *Dini ya Mariam,* was also proscribed. (*Dini* is the local word for sect and the literal translation was the Sect of Mariam.) Mariam Rogot of Kabondo Location was its chief protagonist. Accompanied by her husband, Paul Adika, she had wandered the countryside preaching her own brand of evangelism. She spoke of the imminent end of the world, carried out baptisms, and incited ecstatic behavior among her followers. *The South Nyanza Annual Report, 1954* described the group as follows:

Led by a half crazy woman named Mariam Rogot, this sect which originates from a small group of renegades from the Roman Catholic missions, displays a marked similarity to the Mumbo religion which had with difficulty been stamped out many years before. In June Mariam Rogot, her husband and one other were removed from the

District on Detention orders, and this prompt action had the required effect so that by the time the sect was formally proscribed in September the movement had almost died out and gave no trouble during the remainder of the year.

In 1958 Mariam and her husband were sentenced to a month's imprisonment for holding illegal meetings. On release they recommenced their preachings, whereupon they were restricted to Nyamira substation in the Kisii Highlands. Despite the optimistic note in the 1954 report of the cult's imminent demise, the 1959 report concluded with: "There is no doubt that Mariam still has disturbance potential particularly among the very emotional and less stable bodies of fanatical religious thought." And in 1960 it was reported that Mariam and Paul had been de-restricted early in the year and had remained relatively quiet. Their activities included preaching on a number of occasions and attempting to amalgamate three other sects.

Of a different order were the later visionary experiences and efforts to abolish circumcision originated by the Bogonko clan in and before 1957.   LeVine discusses the short-lived 1957 attempt and states that it was only the most recent example. Information is not available on earlier ventures.

The 1956 initiation ceremonies began as usual in October but instead of stopping as was customary in December, they continued on into January. The Gusii explained this strange occurrence by telling how a youth from the Bogonko lineage saw three old men with long hair, sitting in the middle of the Echarachani River drinking beer. They ordered him to return with his father and when he did, the old men said:

> We are tired of living in the water. You tell the people of Bogonko and Kitutu to resume circumcision of their children and continue until seeding time [April-June] then stop. This is to give us, the people of the water, a chance to circumcise our own children. Go tell all people in Gusiiland to obey that rule.

The old men disappeared and the father and son spread the story in Kitutu. This order was plausible because it came from a source that commanded respect: the old men appeared to be a composite of ancestor spirits and living lineage elders which would make them particularly powerful wielders of supernatural sanctions.

The following evidence links this episode to Mumboism and to the Bogonko clan:

1. The order was reported by a Bogonko youth and directed to the Bogonko clan.

2. This attempt to change the initiation cycle was opposed by the chiefs because of its association with Mumboism. When the chief of Kitutu Location heard of the vision, he immediately said it was an attempt by the Bogonko people to resuscitate Mumboism, and the elders took the same view. Since this occurred during the "emergency," when "Mau Mau" posed a severe threat both to the British and to the chiefs as civil servants, it is understandable that the chiefs should frown upon any renewal of a movement that had overtones of militant Mumboism. Furthermore, it is likely that the chiefs saw the instructions to abandon circumcision as a threat to the established order.

3. This event was not unique and did bear a striking resemblance to earlier Mumboism.

(a) The order to suspend circumcision was the same as that ordered by the Mumboites in 1920; even the same period of time, nine years, was designated. Thus in 1957, in spite of previous disastrous consequences, the suspension of initiation was patterned on an earlier effort.

(b) The 1957 attempt was carried out in a manner reminiscent of the origins' myth. In both cases, spirits making their home in the water issued instructions that if followed would have introduced a radical change in tribal ways. Besides, the instructions were issued through a medium. This pattern of oracular presentation was deeply rooted in tribal ways.

(c) Geographically, both places where the events occurred were historically significant. Kitutu is a traditional source of cultural innovation. The Echarachani River flows through an area where the heroes of Kitutu are celebrated in myth and song, and it is the region where Gusii military success and civil leadership reached their greatest heights in pre-British days. Furthermore, visions had been experienced at that particular river before. And Lake Victoria, the site of the previous revelation, has a prominent place in African folklore.

(d) The mouthpiece of the ancestors was a youth, and youths were important in the sect.

Interpretation and Conclusions

Let me present a possible interpretation of the evolution of Mumboism. As I have indicated, the evidence is patchy and insufficient; therefore, the explanation is speculative.

When the Gusii saw that there was no way to fight the administration militarily, the thoughts and hopes of some turned to the "other
world" of which the missionaries had talked: If only they worshiped
the true god and followed the proper rituals, their problems would be
solved. Hence, their political protest took the form of a new subculture with an ideology that advocated a withdrawal from the world of
action. Thus the turning inward to fantasy and to the world of the
senses.

As for specific action directed toward ousting the British or acquiring an education or engaging in any concrete projects that would
provide the means for the desired material goals, there was little.
Some evidence suggests passive resistance. There were complaints
that the Mumboites refused to comply with compulsory labor and to
pay their taxes. But, by and large, anti-British activity was limited to
sporadic collective protest, like the looting of Kisii in 1914, agitation,
and the symbolic rejection of the foreigners.

Mumboism presents a curious paradox: on the one hand, it glori-
fied the tribe, while on the other, it attempted to abolish important
tribal mores. How is this contradiction explained? Why did its members engage in behavior that ran counter to the moral sentiments of
those around them? Why did they pursue conduct that marked them
off as "bad Gusii"?

Although military defeat was humiliating for all Gusii, it was
even more so for the Bogonko clan, which, as has already been pointed
out, probably suffered the brunt of the destruction. To add insult to
injury, this proud and formerly dominant clan had to suffer the appointment of a chief from a subordinate clan. At the same time its
members were in a highly structured colonial situation that provided
few legitimate channels for the expression of grievances. So unlike the
other Gusii the Bogonko's feelings of hostility-aggression gave rise to
their continual protest in one form or another; first in Mumboism and,
when its millennial hopes failed to materialize, in attempts to abolish
circumcision and other tribal mores. The effort to abolish circumcision,
closely linked as it was to tribal identity, was particularly aggressive,
attention-gaining, and extreme, and perhaps mirrored the desperation
of a clan long bedeviled by feelings of bitterness and long prevented
from asserting itself. At first, its aggression was directed toward the
foreign rulers, but later it acquired a negativistic strain lashing out at
the tribal system itself and was marked by a shift from collective goals
to more individualistic, hedonic values.

This negativism may have been abetted by the growing land pressures that had begun to be felt by the 1950's. *The Kenya Population
Census, 1962* showed that the districts of Kisii, Kisumu, Nairobi,

and Fort Hall were the country's most densely populated areas. Hence, the tensions that gave rise to the earlier protest were exacerbated by economic pressures, well known to be particularly potent fomenters of unrest.

The general patterning of activities supports this interpretation. Narcotics, ecstasy, visions, and passivity fit together and reinforce each other. Escapism and passivity were encouraged by the smoking of *bhang* which, in turn, abetted visionary states. Religious ecstasy or possession was seen, in part, as communicating with ancestral spirits.

What was the nature of Mumbo? My understanding of the cult suggests that although many of the elements attributed to it were undoubtedly present, its major dimensions were different from those generally posited. I would argue that:

1. Its goals were utopian and revolutionary rather than traditional and regressive;

2. Its message combined and modified, in an eclectic fashion, strands from different belief systems. Given the peasants' view and understanding of the world, Mumboism represented an ingenious way of adapting to, and coping with, a new, complex, and confusing situation rather than a curious mixture of irrational ideas or a retreat into past beliefs;

3. Its members exhibited deep admiration of, and desire for, European material goods rather than a rejection of all things European;

4. Its activity gave evidence of deeply rooted patterns of behavior motivated by strong desires rather than meaningless, ephemeral, spur-of-the-moment action;

5. Its main support came from people with social and political grievances rather than from a motley collection of "riff-raff," "parasites," "drunks," "sodomites," and the insane and hysterical.

The movement held aloft a vision of a future life in which the oppressed would be elevated and the oppressors put down. It advocated radical change: hence it was, in important aspects, anti-traditional. It would reverse the power structure, abolish circumcision, and broaden clan and tribal allegiance to encompass pan-tribalism. This ideology did not aim to change the present order but to abolish it and usher in a new social order.

The Mumboites held highly ambivalent feelings toward Europeans which can probably best be epitomized as a love-hate relationship. Coupled with a deep admiration for Western man's technology and material goods was a deep hostility, for his very superiority had caused the devaluation of the tribal way of life. The underlying theme in visions, stories, and utterances was the longing of Mumboites for "all those wonderful things" which Europeans possessed. What the members really wanted was not a return to the old way of life but the life of the European, at least as far as material goods were concerned. In his vision of heaven, the priest, Mosi, found his entry announced by an explosion of light after which he approached God on a motorbike accompanied by five Europeans. Advocating in a few specific and highly symbolic ways a return to the past, the cult nevertheless represented a drastic break with the past. It looked to the past for inspiration, but to the future for a pattern of life. When the new order arrived, Muchirongo, Bonairiri, and Zakawa were not going to live in their mud and wattle huts; they were going to collect the tax, occupy the district headquarters, and, no doubt, drive the District Commissioner's Land Rover.

The leaders articulated deeply held sentiments common to the masses of peasants. Their hopes, wants, fears, and resentments were unchangeable factors; they persisted despite the appearance and disappearance of leaders. These sentiments usually remained dormant until a spokesman brought them to the fore by giving them some form and substance, even if a loose one, and, to our minds at least, one full of contradictions. In large part this explains Mumboism's tenacity and the administration's difficulty in stamping it out for, whenever the administration tried to chop off its head, it found itself battling a hydra. Groups sprang up here and there wherever a local prophet appeared. When one set of leaders was deported, others came to the fore. There was little organization which the administration could seize, the movement being what is sociologically called "expressive." People were bound together by an amorphous structure of shared sentiments and beliefs with little formal organization or program.

Mumboism was yet another attempt on the part of the Gusii to rid themselves of the foreigners. More specifically, it was an attempt on the part of a dissatisfied, ambitious clan to assert itself and to retrieve its former dominant status. The argument that support for the movement came from those with strong anti-British feelings needs to be qualified. It is a facile generalization that obscures both the complexity of the colonial relationship and the *quid pro quo* realities of the day-to-day struggle for power and dominance. It presents a one-sided view of the African-British relationship which vastly underplays the Africans' dexterity in handling the British. It is perhaps too obvious to point out that Africans, like people everywhere, are interested in power, wealth, and prestige. It should be borne in mind that British administrators were few in number and that they had to rely upon support from the indigenous leaders. From the first days of the British occupation alliances were made between the British and the African chiefs, who often helped the British to bring areas under their control while enhancing their own position by the subjugation of their traditional enemies with the help of the British.

In South Nyanza, it was not just a case of the British using Africans but of particular African rivals for chieftainships securing their positions by acquiring British backing. The British provided a new structure of power and prescribed rules within which the age-old power struggle continued. Those chiefs who learned early how to handle the British in order to achieve their own ends came out on top. Tribal and clan rivalry continued as it had for centuries, only now another, foreign, dimension had to be taken into account. Consequently, those clans and subclans whose positions were enhanced and whose claims were supported by the administration tended to be pro-British. One can hypothesize that had the British supported the Bogonko clan's claims to chieftainship, the Bogonko would have worked with the administration and, being dominant, would not have protested.

The first challenge to European authority in South Nyanza came from Mumboism. Its undisputed stance against alien rule indicated an uncompromising position. Its attempts to find new ways to cope with the foreign invaders were fumbling, experimental, and ineffectual. Compared with the Kikuyu and Luo who, by the 1920's and 1930's, were pressuring and petitioning the colonial administration and the British government to redress their grievances, the Gusii were politically unsophisticated. And, although Mumboism's protest eventually fizzled out because of severe repression and the dissipation of its energies upon individualistic, hedonistic goals, it still represents the beginnings of African political protest in Gusiiland, the articulation of grievances, and the building of embryonic trans-tribal allegiances.

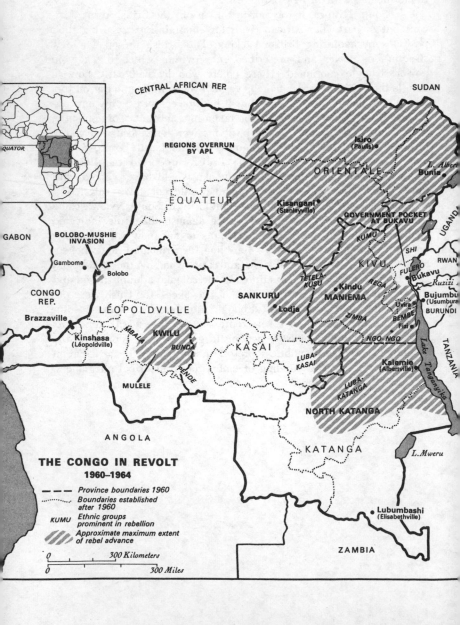

CENTRAL AFRICAN REP.

SUDAN

REGIONS OVERRUN
BY APL

Isiro
(Paulis)

O R I E N T A L E

L. Albert
Bunia

EQUATEUR

Kisangani
(Stanleyville)

GOVERNMENT POCKET
AT BUKAVU

GABON

BOLOBO-MUSHIE
INVASION

KUMU

SHI

RWAN

UGAND

KIVU

FULERO

Bukavu

Gamboma

Bolobo

CONGO
REP.

LÉOPOLDVILLE

SANKURU

TETELA-
KUSU

Kindu

MANIEMA

REGA

Ruzizi

Bujumbu
(Usumbura

BURUNDI

Brazzaville

Lodja

ZIMBA

Uvira

BEMBE
Fizi

TANZANIA

Kinshasa
(Léopoldville)

MBALA

KWILU

KASAI

NGO-NGO

BUNDA

Lake

MULELE

PENDE

LUBA-
KASAI

Kalemie
(Albertville)

Tanganyika

LUBA-
KATANGA

ANGOLA

NORTH KATANGA

L. Mweru

KATANGA

THE CONGO IN REVOLT
1960–1964

— — — *Province boundaries 1960*

.... *Boundaries established
after 1960*

KUMU *Ethnic groups
prominent in rebellion*

*Approximate maximum extent
of rebel advance*

Lubumbashi
(Elisabethville)

0   300 Kilometers

0   300 Miles

ZAMBIA

REBELLION AND THE CONGO

M. CRAWFORD YOUNG

Insurrection engulfed the Congo (Kinshasa)* in 1964. The tides of rebellion swept away central authority in five provinces out of twenty-one, and in portions of eight more. At high-water mark in August 1964, the complete collapse of the Kinshasa regime appeared a real possibility. Rebel success created the image of unified purpose and revolutionary promise. Only in its subsequent phases of decay and disintegration did the basic characteristics of rebellion become fully evident: a dramatic lack of cohesion, a disparity in purpose and perception, and a remarkable range of phenomena incorporated into the syndrome of insurrection.

The object of this essay is to examine the rebellion from 1964 to 1967 for those dimensions which place it in comparative perspective. In doing so, one immediately encounters the fundamental fact that the Congolese rebellion was not a single movement, but a series of parallel, partly overlapping dramas, which do not have one history, but several. Therefore, as a preamble, a highly compressed synopsis of the rise and fall of the rebellion will be offered to enable the reader to "place" the analysis which follows. Subsequently, we will consider the accumulation of an insurrectional potential, the stratification of values and

* In 1966 and 1967, the place names of a number of Congolese cities were altered. In this essay, we have exclusively used the current names. The changes are as follows: Kinshasa (ex-Léopoldville); Kisangani (ex-Stanleyville); Lubumbashi (ex-Elisabethville); Bandundu (ex-Banningville); Mbandaka (ex-Coquilhatville); Isiro (ex-Paulis); Kalemie (ex-Albertville); and Lukasi (ex-Jadotville).

Another alteration since the rebellion has been the consolidation to eight of the twenty-one provinces existing in 1964–65; in this essay, we retain the twenty-one as labels of convenience.

participation, patterns and limits of diffusion, exercise of powers in zones under rebel control, and the process of disintegration.

Rebellion: A Brief Summary

In the Congo, barely perceptible symptoms of rebellion first appeared in mid-1963, at the crest of a wave of relative euphoria: the country had been reunited; it seemed to have survived the disastrous events of 1960. Economic upsurge seemed to be accompanying a slow but steady improvement in Congolese administration. Not the least of the paradoxes to follow was the fact that the first violence appeared in Kwilu, the province which had been widely advertised as a "pilot province" and a local incarnation of the recovery process. Actually, in spite of the smiling surface of events, two important developments were already at work which were to help to precipitate insurrection. One was the declining ability of the Adoula government to absorb or provide outlets for opposition. Thus, though paralyzed by the utter fragmentation of political groupings, Parliament had provided a forum for the expression of opposition and a reasonable guarantee against arrest through parliamentary immunity. The decision, in September 1963, to adjourn Parliament indefinitely was therefore an important encouragement to rupture. The second development was the prospective withdrawal of United Nations forces by June 1964, a factor to which we shall return later.

The second half of 1963 saw two groups taking a dissident position. The first was the result of the efforts of Pierre Mulele, who had in July 1963 returned to the Congo after more than two years abroad, spent in part in China and Eastern Europe. Immediately upon his return he had gone to his home province of Kwilu and there begun the organization of a rural maquis. And at the beginning of October, a number of political figures who had been associated with the Lumumbist alliance in 1960, and the Kisangani Gizenga government in 1960–61, crossed the river to Brazzaville, where a *Conseil National de Libération* was proclaimed. The Mulele maquis and the *Conseil* were entirely separate efforts, although some *Conseil* elements subsequently claimed a link with Mulele.

The first violent incidents occurred in January 1964, with Mulelist insurgents attacking government outposts, mission stations, and, in some cases, palm oil mills and other company installations. By the end of January, large parts of Idiofa and Gungu territories were under siege. On 5 February, the chief of staff of the *Armée Nationale Con-*

golaise, Colonel Eugene Eleya, was ambushed and killed by a poisoned arrow. Army reinforcements were rushed to Kwilu; they succeeded in reopening the roads, and holding the towns of Gungu and Idiofa. By April 1964, the army had clearly gained the upper hand. But despite the complete lack of modern arms for Mulelist insurgents, and lack of access to external supplies, many months passed before the army was able to isolate the partisan bands and administrative reoccupation could occur.

As for the *Conseil,* it had initially concentrated its hopes on a coup in the capital and on external diplomatic and material support. Solicitations were made to radical African governments and to the Soviet Union and China; some modest financial support was forthcoming with a more abundant supply of advice. A coup in November 1963 narrowly failed; for a short time Sûreté head Victor Nendaka and army commander General Joseph Mobutu were captured. By the end of 1963, a series of camps had been established in Congo (Brazzaville), where ideological instruction and rudimentary military training were given primarily to residents from Kinshasa, Kwilu, and the Lac Léopold II area. A campaign of urban terrorism in Kinshasa was initiated in 1964 and reached a peak in May. The attacks consisted mainly of plastic bombings of public places carried out by commandos based in Brazzaville. But the bombings were insufficient in scale or duration to have a major impact. The last armed incursion from the Brazzaville base occurred in July 1964, when a small group from one of the Gamboma complex of insurgent camps seized the small towns of Bolobo, Kwamouth, and Mushie. The invasion lasted only six days; this band had disappeared by the time military reinforcements arrived.

Meanwhile, insurrection was making spectacular progress in the eastern Congo. Gaston Soumialot, in 1960 Lumumba's lieutenant for the Maniema area, in February 1964 arrived in Bujumbura to establish a *Conseil* office. He had traveled widely in the area between Kalemie (North Katanga) and Kisangani, had served as a provincial minister in the Kivu-Maniema government of Adrien Omari in 1961, and had spun a network of political relationships throughout this zone. His initial breakthrough came in linking to the broader cause of rebellion a local chieftaincy dispute among the Fulero, a small but strategically situated ethnic group living in the Ruzizi plain, along the Burundi frontier, and in the surrounding mountains. The first armed clashes in the eastern Congo occurred in April 1964. However, the crucial event was the seizure on 17 May of the town of Uvira. This opened the way to the Burundi border, and became a point of diffusion for insurgent initiatives. Fizi, at the heart of Bembe country, was captured ten days later, the Bembe rallying as an ethnic community to the rebellion. At the same time, two army battalions were routed by rural insurgents equipped with only a handful of firearms.

North Katanga was the next focus for dissidence. The backdrop for insurrection in Kalemie, then the North Katangan provincial capital, was a factional dispute within the provincial government between Jason Sendwe and Prosper Mwanga Ilunga. Both had been Balubakat (the dominant political party in the North) leaders in 1960, and were identified with the Luba resistance to the Tshombe regime in Katanga from 1960 to 1962. However, in late 1962 a split had developed which, by 1966, dominated all North Katangan political life. Sendwe had the support of the central government, but by May 1964 he led a virtually paralyzed provincial administration. In an atmosphere of total demoralization, an uprising led by Balubakat "youth" occurred on 27 May, fomented by a small group of young Luban leaders who had established liaison with Soumialot in Bujumbura. The national army units initially remained inactive, expecting the "youth" to be joined by a rebel force from the exterior. However, two days later, when the promised rebel army failed to appear and instigators of the uprising were unable to direct it, the army suddenly turned on the insurgents. A restored Sendwe government undertook a pitiless repression in the three weeks that followed. On 18 June, a small rebel column under the command of General Nicolas Olenga arrived from Fizi. The national army units simply evaporated: the bulk of the government troops had commandeered a train the evening before, and ordered three European railwaymen to conduct them to safety.

At this time, the remainder of North Katanga proved a veritable suction pump, the vacuum created by the disappearance of government authority providing unanticipated opportunities for expansion. Baudouinville was captured by forty-five men on 19 July. (The rail line, after the flight of the army, was used by withdrawing Europeans and, finally, by members of the Congolese civil administration who feared assassination by insurgents.) Small insurgent bands followed up this initiative, establishing a superficial and ephemeral suzerainty over most of North Katanga during July. In this zone, the population remained passive and indifferent and the rebel bands were mostly drawn from outside North Katanga.

Soumialot arrived in Kalemie on 28 June and briefly established an insurgent government claiming authority for the eastern Congo. However, by early July the center of gravity was shifting to the Lumumbist heartland in Maniema. The insurgent army, the *Armée Populaire de Libération*, which had first taken shape in the Uvira area in late May, coalesced in early July as a military force, faithfully replicating the structure and nomenclature of the national army. The popular army advanced along the old Zanzibari trade route from Fizi via Kabambare to Kasongo, which fell 15 July. Kindu was taken on 24 July, and the Lumumbist capital of Kisangani came under rebel control on 5 August. Thereafter, rebel columns fanned out in all directions, gorged with the armaments abandoned by the fleeing national army, vehicles confiscated from traders and companies, and money seized in the banks. During the six weeks which followed, all of Uele and Kibali-Ituri were overrun. One column following the north bank of the Congo River penetrated as far as Lisala, then the capital of the Middle Congo province, and another reached Boende, in Cuvette Centrale. Most of Sankuru was briefly overrun in September, and one group penetrated as far as Sentery in Lomami.

A major turning point occurred between 15 and 20 August, when General Olenga and a motorized column of six thousand men assaulted Bukavu. Government forces, reinforced by hastily remobilized Katangan gendarmes, held their ground, and the popular army suffered its first serious reverse. The balance of force was tipped by the decision, made under duress at the last moment, of Mwami Alexandre Kabare, paramount chief of one section of Shi, to back the central government. Because of repeated conflicts with Kinshasa-supported provincial authorities, Kabare had contacts on the rebel side, and Olenga had had reason to hope for his support. The Kabare chieftaincy lay athwart the approaches to Bukavu, and the Mwami's warriors decimated the insurgent invaders. An important central government redoubt along the eastern frontier, including portions of Central Kivu and North Kivu provinces, thus remained.

The zenith of rebel self-confidence was marked by the proclamation of 5 September of a revolutionary government in Kisangani under the leadership of Christophe Gbenye. (Two short-lived rebel "governments", had preceded the arrival of Gbenye in Kisangani.) At the moment of its establishment, the revolutionary government derived continuous succor from its very success and the sense of triumphant momentum. But when the swollen rebel armies encountered a level of resistance with which they could not cope and began to fall back, the aura of invincibility soon vanished. Troubles crowded in upon the Kisangani leadership, and the gossamer fabric of unity was rent. Bitter conflict soon emerged between Gbenye, Soumialot, and Olenga.

By early September, the balance of force had clearly altered. The Tshombe government had reinforced the demoralized national army with a few hundred white mercenaries, and most of the former Katangan gendarmerie had been integrated into the national army. Meanwhile, by late August, the rebel leaders had recognized that European residents in the towns under their control might be a shield against aerial bombardment. Subsequently, the concept of the "white umbrella" was enlarged to include using the nationals of countries aiding the central government, that is, Belgium and the United States, as negotiating counters to halt the columns closing in on Kisangani. The hostage policy led to the Belgian-American parachute operation at Kisangani and Isiro. "Dragon Rouge" began at dawn on 24 November in Kisangani, and on the same day the first national army-mercenary column reached Kisangani. Some two thousand hostages, mainly Belgian and American, were evacuated. Five days later the Belgian paratroopers were withdrawn from the Congo. However, Kindu had already been retaken on 6 November.

The loss of the capital of Lumumbism, the proclaimed seat of the revolutionary government, was a mortal blow to the rebellion in the eastern Congo. The three most important leaders asserting a pan-rebel authority—Gbenye, Soumialot, and Olenga—made their way into exile. The enormous indignation in many African states at the Belgian-American intervention with "Dragon Rouge" was translated into a major flow of military supplies via the Sudan, Uganda, and Tanzania. But the loss of central direction, which had emerged in the period between July and November 1964, shriveled the rebellion into localized pockets. The perspectives of the insurgents had profoundly altered, prospects of success were nil, and demoralization was widespread. Nevertheless, in the zone around Kisangani, in Buta-Aketi, Bafwasende, Opala, and several other areas, rebel groups rendered key roads insecure for many months. The most substantial zone of continued dissidence was the Fulero-Bembe pocket, located in inaccessible mountain terrain. This group (although marked by internal tensions between Fulero and Bembe) received more regular moral sustenance from external insurgent leadership cliques, and had access to arms supplies across Lake Tanganyika.

The bitter factionalism which characterized rebel exile politics, combined with military defeat on the terrain, led to a progressive loss of external credibility for the rebellion, and thereby to diminishing support. The final blow was the removal of the Tshombe stigma by Kinshasa. At the Organization of African Unity (OAU) summit conference in Accra in October 1965, President Kasavubu, fresh from his abrupt removal of Tshombe as Prime Minister, was welcomed back into grace. On 25 November, Kasavubu and Tshombe were both overthrown by General Mobutu, whose political style placed the Congo even closer to the mainstream of African diplomacy. The consequence of this takeover was to compound the isolation, frustration, and internal tensions of diverse rebel exile groups.

Antecedents: Relative Deprivation

The history of the 1964 revolt is thus described in brief. More important than the chronological skeleton is the comparative significance of this drama, seen against the historical regularities in African protest movements and the contemporary patterns of post-independence politics. The first set of questions which arises relates to the emergence of an insurrectionary potential. One of the most striking aspects of the rebellion was the incredible speed of its transmission in responsive areas. Herbert Weiss ably summarized the situation:

> The speed with which the rural population rallied to the rebellion in virtually every region touched by it is probably the most important common denominator of all the local uprisings. It is inconceivable that such massive and rapid support was the result of laborious organization by a trained revolutionary elite. . . . Thus, the only alternative explanation is that a great degree of protest potential already existed and that the rebellion, insofar as it was organized at all, presented a framework within which this protest could express itself.

One useful conceptual prism for examining the emergence of an insurrectionary potential is the sociological workhorse of relative deprivation.   The sense of grievance must have a reference point. Similarly consciousness of deprivation has meaning only in terms of some vision or recollection of non-deprivation. In the Congo, we may suggest that a sense of deprivation was not only widespread, but measured along three dimensions: in temporal space, in vertical social space between strata, and in horizontal communal space between ethnic groupings.

The time dimension had two aspects: the immediate recollection of a more ordered and materially prosperous life situation, and a utopian vision of future well-being briefly generated by the explosion of terminal colonial nationalism. A paradoxical nostalgia for certain aspects of the colonial order was encountered with surprising frequency in the Congo in 1961–64. This was not, of course, a yearning for the myriad vexations of the authoritarian Belgian colonial system—for a restoration of European authority—but simply a faintly gilded memory of an epoch when jobs were more plentiful for the unskilled, when rural marketing mechanisms worked reliably, when roads were kept in good repair, and when local dispensaries had possessed both personnel and medical supplies. Compounding the disappointments of the present was the seismic effect of the electoral promises of 1960. Consider, for example, the following campaign poster widely distributed by the party dominant in Kwilu, the *Parti Solidaire Africain:*

1. Complete elimination of unemployment and work for all.
2. Expansion of school facilities, especially in rural areas. Elimination of all school fees for primary and secondary schools.
3. Salary raises for everybody.
4. Improvement of housing of rural areas.
5. Free medical care for all non-wage earners.

Fatuous as these pledges were, they were outstripped in apocalyptic content by the rhetoric employed at local election meetings. Mechanization of peasant agriculture, price rises for peasant crops, a style of life modeled on that of the Belgian rulers—all of these aims were said to be within reach in the *anno mirabilis* of 1960.

In the best of circumstances, a sense of disappointment would have been inevitable. Independence brought the worst of circumstances to most rural and many urban areas. Except for the poles of relative prosperity in the Kinshasa-Lower Congo and Southern Katanga areas, commercial networks shriveled and the embryonic welfare apparatus of the terminal colonial state atrophied. Diminished well-being opened an enormous chasm between promise and performance, past and present.

The social stratification dimension of relative deprivation refers to the rapid development after independence of a vast differential in access to material rewards between those able to move into the formerly Belgian-occupied roles and those who lacked opportunities for status mobility. Stratification of African society prior to 1960 was primarily on a prestige and educational/occupational basis and was not marked by large disparities in wealth or power.   The highest prestige occupations, in both the public and private sectors, were clerical positions. The very lexicon of stratification is revealing. Prior to independence the Congolese elite was generally referred to as *évolués,* a term descriptive of their educational rather than their economic status. After independence the elites decolonized the vocabulary but preserved the same basis of distinction by relabeling themselves "intellectuals."

Until the eve of independence, a dual reward system had been in effect in the civil service which maintained the remuneration of Congolese petty functionaries at a very modest level, not far removed from the wage levels of the urban worker.   The flight of Belgian functionaries and army officers in 1960 suddenly opened up ten thousand top positions, which were swiftly filled by clerks and noncommissioned officers. In addition, several thousand highly paid "political" positions were created in 1960 at the central and provincial levels. Certain categories of persons, such as the military and police forces and teachers, were in good positions to enforce claims for sharp increases in pay. Finally, the achievement of independence opened up entirely new opportunities to the Congolese commercial sector, through special assistance available from the state. For example, in Kinshasa since independence, the thriving Congolese commercial entrepreneurial group accumulated much of its initial capital either through direct political activity or through favored access to import licenses and foreign exchange quotas—highly profitable commodities during periods of currency instability.

Table I offers a general picture of the pattern of salary increases from the time of independence to the period of the rebellions. During this time, the exchange value of the Congo franc fell to one-seventh of its pre-independence level. In evaluating the relative position of different groups, one must recall that top functionaries had enjoyed a swift

TABLE I   Rise in Salaries by Social Categories, 1960–65 (Indices as of
31 December 1965 have as their base 30 June 1960 = 100.)

Category	Nominal	Real
Civil servants		
Auxiliaries (messengers, etc.)	498	102
Clerks	678-1073	139-219
Bureau chiefs	241	49
Permanent secretaries	153	31
Military		
Privates	414	85
Sergeants	571	117
Teachers		
Teachers	333	68
Primary teachers without		
degree	566	116
Private sector		
Legal minimum (bachelor)	306	63
Legal minimum (married,		
3 children)	255	52

Source: Forthcoming study on economic change in the Congo 1960–65 by the *Institut des Recherches Economiques et Sociales*, Université Lovanium, quoted in Jean Louis Lacroix, *Industrialisation au Congo* (The Hague, 1967), 203.

vertical ascent up the scale, from a clerical position in 1959, drawing perhaps 40,000 Congo francs ($900) annual salary, to a rank earning perhaps five times that figure in 1960. The extent to which the politician-functionary strata monopolized the resources of the state is indicated by the fact that in 1965 payment of political personnel consumed 10 per cent of the operating budget, and an additional 20 per cent of the operating budget went for provincial political sectors or for "irregular expenditures"—political payments occurring outside the regular budgetary channels. Another 29 billion of the 55 billion franc total went to cover central administration, education, and subsidies to provinces. Most of these disbursements were for salary payments.

The rapid polarization of the socio-economic strata was rendered dramatic in its impact by the frequently conspicuous display of new wealth. The opulent life style of the colonial establishment served as a reference point for the administrative bourgeoisie. The very spatial structure of colonial towns tended to enhance the visibility of stratification. The well manicured European quarters had been carefully demarcated from the African quarters by green belts, golf courses, zoos, or other appropriate buffer areas. Politicians and civil servants in large numbers inherited the housing that was attached to ranking position in the state hierarchy and then became removed from the humbler strata by the devices which had once served to preserve the segregated character of colonial society.

A rough estimate of those benefiting materially from independence might total 150,000. Awareness of the new gap between the political-administrative class and laborers, unemployed, and peasantry was general by 1962. The vexations of the deprived were multiple. For urban workers who had jobs, wages did not keep pace with inflation. But mere employment was a blessing, as unemployment rates in the towns shot up. From the depression until 1956, involuntary urban unemployment had been a marginal phenomenon only; the 1957 recession in the Congo produced cyclical unemployment, then assumed to be temporary; the 1960 crisis converted this pressure into massive structural unemployment. Pressure on employment opportunities was exacerbated first by a vast flight to the cities after independence, when administrative controls on this kind of influx were removed, and second by a reduction in the number of jobs available. The population of Kinshasa had at least doubled since independence, some estimates placed it as high as 1,500,000, and most towns had experienced similar growth. The magnitude of the drop in the number of employment outlets is suggested by figures for Kinshasa, although the capital, along with the cities of the Copperbelt, was a center of relative prosperity.

On 31 December 1959, 87,000 were employed; on 15 December 1961, only 58,000 jobs existed. Unemployment rose in that period from an estimated 29 per cent to 58 per cent of the wage earning population. Paradoxically, the unemployment rate was also affected by a trend toward the mechanization of industry; government-imposed minimum wage rates had risen to a point where industrial enterprises could no longer afford to employ a superabundance of unskilled hands.

One apparent outlet for the unemployed was the administration itself. There was an enormous inflation of the lower ranks of government public works and other departments employing the unskilled, particularly in the provinces. However, these were legally on "contract" rather than enjoying civil service status. The number of *sous-contrats* was estimated as high as 300,000; the elasticity of the lower reaches of the administration is suggested by the sixty-three chauffeurs who had been hired in the North Katangan territory of Kongolo to drive the one inoperative administrative vehicle attached to the territory. But such employment was often sheer illusion. Pay arrearages became a general pattern in the provinces, especially in the lower ranks of the administration. By the time of the rebellion, arrearages of up to two years were common. The *sous-contrats* were a large and inflammable group in provincial capitals, particularly receptive to the argument that the political-administrative elite consumed all public resources and thus deprived them even of the modest wage which was their nominal right.

The tensions generated by new stratification patterns were most acute for the young men who were recruited into the rebel armed forces. Students of social stratification elsewhere have observed that a crucial factor reconciling lower strata with their status is a belief in the possibilities of mobility, either inter-generational, or, for the young, within their own careers. The post-war period produced a generation of young men who developed new aspirations through the availability of primary education and the opportunity for migration to the towns. This group was particularly vulnerable to the pressure of diminished employment opportunities beginning in 1957, and was threatened with forcible return to the villages by the colonial administration. The promise of nationalism reopened vistas of mobility for these young men, and they responded with militant enthusiasm. Most parties developed large and volatile youth wings in 1960 which provided paramilitary muscle for the election campaign. Correspondingly intense was the bitterness when, after independence, the youth found that the unlimited horizons of the campaign for independence had suddenly contracted. Boundless hope was replaced by unrelieved despair. It was in this setting that judgment was passed against the members of the new elite who had found fulfillment in independence. It is within this context that the social logic of the extraordinary violence unleashed by the rebellions against "intellectuals" becomes clear,   as does the appeal of a call for a "second independence."

For many in the older generation, "independence" had never had the credibility which it had enjoyed with the youth. Alan Merriam, describing the pre-independence year in a Songye village where he was resident, suggests a pattern that was widespread: "Independence was conceived as something with which the young men were concerned, and the older people were not vitally interested. When they spoke of it, it was with a certain diffidence and even boredom; the problem was simply not theirs to solve and they preferred to give their attention to other matters." For the generation over thirty, one may suggest that the idea of the limited good had taken full hold. For those who endure it, rural poverty begets highly limited expectations. The resource "pie" is constant and small; rural life is a zero-sum economic game.   The actual shrinkage of rural resources after independence was perhaps an unanticipated disappointment, but the sense of relative deprivation which it generated was attenuated by the far more modest expectations of change.

A little explored facet of stratification is that involving sex differences in mobility opportunities. Its potential significance is suggested by the important role that townswomen played in northeastern Congo. *Femmes nationalistes* formations appeared in a number of places, and in Bunia played a central role in driving the national army out in August 1960. In Isiro, Kisangani, and Kindu, women were in evidence, both in the violence and in claiming some share in power. For example, in Kindu Olenga promised the *femmes nationalistes* a place in the governing council for Maniema shortly after the rebel triumph; women apparently participated, particularly when judgments were being rendered against adversaries of the rebel regime.   Young women who had fled the village enjoyed meager prospects. The highly functional colonial educational system had placed little stress on educating girls, who were unlikely to enter the economy as units of production. Thus, only a handful of townswomen possessed the educational credentials which governed access to most high-status roles, or, for that matter, spoke French, the language of the modern sector. A study in Lulua-bourg shortly before independence showed that 25.6 per cent of the males over five spoke French, as compared to 1.08 per cent of the females.   The only occupational outlets in the town were petty trade and prostitution or concubinage. Although it would be misleading to speak of "women" as a categoric group which nurtured collective resentments, the social situation of townswomen did generate a striking degree of female militant action.

The third axis of relativity in the perception of deprivation runs horizontally across the Congolese polity and is cut into ethnic and regional segments. The dynamics of rebellion and, most central of all, the causes of its failure can be understood only when this dimension is appreciated together with the other two. The gradual expansion of social and political consciousness in the cities in the post-war years was marked by the crystallization of ethnic as well as Congolese/African self-awareness. The politicization of the rural areas, which diffused from urban-political nodular points, followed the same pattern. Thus, the cognitive map through which groups evaluated the distribution of social and material rewards gave a prominent place to the ethnic landscape. The new political class, compelled by the electoral time-table to develop a rural clientele at breakneck speed, necessarily relied on the ethnic linkages. The political lexicon which developed was heavily laden with ethnic terminology because the infinite complexity and incomprehensible fluidity of both provincial and national politics could be diminished by the application of ethnic labels to contending groups. The inaccuracy inherent in this process could in turn be reduced by the self-fulfilling prophecy: once labels became current, groups often tended increasingly to resemble their sterotypes. Kwilu is the clearest example. Two important groups, the Pende and the Bunda, came to see provincial and national politics as offering privileged access to other groups in the area bearing the generic label of "Mbala."

The dominant party in the region had been openly split, since 1960, between a faction led by Cleophas Kamitatu, a Ngongo but labeled Mbala, and Antoine Gizenga, a Pende. Mulele, the apostle of insurrection, was a Mbunda. Despite the fact that the Kwilu provincial government was headed by Norbert Leta, a Pende, at the moment of rebellion, it was a Mbala regime in the eyes of most Pende and Mbunda. And this perception in turn meant that the Kwilu insurrection was a "Pende-Mbunda" movement in the eyes of other Kwilu groups, so that despite the fact that rural Mbala shared the same social and material grievances in the name of which Mulele raised his banner, their perception of the movement precluded their rallying to it.

The horizontal segmentation process in the eastern Congo was necessarily far more complex, as the rebellion affected a far greater area. It is nonetheless true that close investigation reveals the importance of the ethnic thread in the texture of revolt. Throughout the eastern Congo, a central place in the rebel elite which became a factor of polarization was held by Tetela-Kusu. In the Uvira-Fizi area, the massive participation of the Bembe generated a hostile response on the part of the Rega in the Mwenga area. Shi in the Bukavu area, who had grown restive under alleged "Kusu" domination during the Kashamura-Omari regimes in 1961, and had in turn purged the Kusu from the Kivu administration when Kinshasan control was reasserted, were, a priori, reserved about a new movement in which Kusu leaders were prominent.

In a broader sense, there were marked disparities in well-being between the two zones of prosperity—Kinshasa/Lower Congo and the Katangan Copperbelt—and the "interior." In geopolitical terms, the poles of prosperity happened to coincide with the two most strategic areas. To the extent that rebellion was also a movement of the "interior" against the "capital," and had some continuities with the 1960–62 uprising of the impoverished north versus the opulent south (Katanga), the people at the prosperity poles saw themselves as threatened and were therefore immune to rebel solicitations.

The tridimensional nature of relative deprivation helps to make clear the pattern of response to the appeal to arms. Insurrectional potential accumulated in most parts of the country during the vicissitudes of the early post-independence years. Response, however, was sharply different from one zone to the next. The fragmented perception of grievance suggests at least a part of the explanation. Deprivation was relative in geographic as well as social space and time.

Antecedents: Power Deflation

To the catalog of grievance must be added the diminishing capabilities of the political system. Chalmers Johnson has offered a useful set of categories for analyzing these aspects of the antecedents to rebellion. Revolution, Johnson suggests, occurs when social systems have become "disequilibrated." As a part of this process, governments experience a "power deflation," sharply reducing their ability to cope with an armed challenge to their exercise of power. The final catalyst to insurrection is an "accelerator," which Johnson describes as "The event which triggers revolution in a society that is disequilibrated and that has a discredited base of authority." "Accelerators are," he continues

> occurrences that make revolution possible by exposing the inability of the elite to maintain its monopoly of force. They are not sets of conditions but single events—events that rupture a system's pseudo-integration based on deterrence. Accelerators always affect an elite's monopoly of armed force, and they lead either mobilized or potential revolutionaries to believe that they have a chance of success in resorting to violence against a hated system.

We have already considered the "disequilibration" of the post-independence social system in the Congo. A profound power deflation occurred in the immediate aftermath of independence with the mutiny of the army and the flight of the European cadres who had operated the authoritarian structures of the colonial system. However, the presence of United Nations forces as a surrogate for the normal governmental monopoly of coercion in a polity, added to the sheer speed of the transformations effected by independence, delayed the period when power deflation became an invitation to insurrection. Further, rebellion could only develop when the full social consequences of 1960, in terms of "disequilibration," could work themselves out. In a compelling metaphor, Parsons has suggested that the coercive sanctions available to governments are analogous to the gold basis of a monetary system. Power, like money, is dependent on confidence, which "implies vulnerability to certain types of disturbances analogous to inflation and deflation in the economic case. A highly developed power system cannot meet all of its presumptively legitimate obligations at once."

The nature of the coercive instruments available to the government after independence led to the capricious, unpredictable, and irregular application of force. This replaced the more regularized colonial practice. Colonial order, of course, reposed upon overwhelming force. This force was frequently used at the local level to quell minor disturbances and the occasional substantial revolts which marked the Belgian period. As an instrument of colonial control, coercion was predictable in its operation. The July 1960 mutiny, and the improvised Africanization which followed, meant that a new random factor of arbitrarily imposed violence appeared. Perpetuation of the colonial practice of distributing troops to every district and territory meant that the army was omnipresent. Brutality was not new to the national army, but the frequent lack of relationship between application of coercion and the requirements for public order was an innovation. The capricious use of force by local commanders, or administrators, or even troops on their own, diminished the effectiveness of coercion as an instrument of government control. Force was arbitrary, unpredictable, and inexplicable. The ability of the army to secure rural co-operation was thereby gravely compromised.

Power deflation also occurred because of the transmission of instability down the various echelons of the administration. The crisis was initially centered at the national level, but the provinces were soon affected. Provincial conflicts were multiplied by the splintering of the six original provinces into twenty-one in 1962. Many experienced paralyzing disputes; divisions within groups surfaced which had never previously even been visible (Tetela of the savannah versus Tetela of the forest in Sankuru and Bena Tshibanda versus Bena Mutu wa Mu-kuna among the Luba of South Kasai). Provincial conflict in turn resulted in frequent purges of district commissioners and territorial administrators; at the lowest level, rivalries over chieftaincies were abetted by the new opportunities for claimants to enlist the support of provincial political factions. Changes of provincial regime then often meant changes in chiefly personnel.

To instability must be added the contraction of the capabilities of the field administration. Administrative vehicles broke down, and re-pair was often impossible in areas distant from Kinshasa or Lubum-bashi. Administrators were consequently confined to their headquarters and lacked the material means to maintain the array of services and controls previously exercised. In 1962 in Gungu territory, later a focal point of the Kwilu rebellion, the local administrative offices had virtually exhausted their supply of paper. There were substantial variations in degree from one region to another; however, as a rule of thumb, the greater the distance from Kinshasa or Lubumbashi, the more substantial was the deflation of administrative power.

The accelerator was an interlocking set of circumstances which offered vivid evidence of the weakness of the government's deterent force. The first aspect was the spectacular success of Mulelist bands in Kwilu in suddenly sweeping administrators, missionaries, and planta-tion operators out of Gungu and Idiofa territories in January 1964. The partisan bands possessed only spears, machetes, and bows and arrows, yet they overwhelmed the police and army detachments in the area. Although the Kwilu rebellion had been contained by April 1964, its capacity to generate massive participation, and to pit spear against firearms, had a major demonstration effect.

More decisive was the rout of the national army in the eastern Congo. The defeat in May of two government battalions in the Ruzizi plain by predominantly Fulero warriors began the process, and events in North Katanga and Maniema in June and July completed it. The national army, terrorized and demoralized, simply evaporated. The fleeing troops explained their headlong retreat with horrifying tales of the prowess of the rebel bands, thus cumulating the terror. A Congolese account of an engagement along the Kabambare-Kasongo road in July is a prototype of national-popular army combat:

. . . The horde continued to advance, inexorably, like the tentacle of an octopus sliding toward a man to seize and strangle him. The soldiers fired, without interruption. Defying the bullets, the "mulele" came toward them, chanting at the top of their lungs: Mulele-Mai [water]! Mulele-Mai! Mulele. . . . Our gendarmes began to doubt the effectiveness of their weapons. The distance diminished: 200 meters . . . 150 . . . and fear built up in our ranks. . . .

At their waist hung all sorts of leaves: banana or palm fronds. These leaves concealed their shorts. Branches placed here and there in their belt gave them an even more savage and ferocious appearance. Their chests were covered with animal skins. . . . As they marched, their headdress, made of feathers and skins, shook like the mane of a lion. At their neck and waist, oscillating at the cadence of their step, were diverse amulettes and packets of "dawa" . . . . The horde approached, like a sinister monster. They were now only 100 meters—very close. A shiver of fear ran through the ranks of the soldiers. Then suddenly, the firing stopped, with only the chants of the rebels breaking the silence. A moment of hesitation—and the same idea came like a flash to the mind of all our gendarmes: "They are invulnerable . . . invulnerable . . . Run for your lives!" The order was not given, but it was executed. . . . The simba   found it beneath their dignity to pursue.

In appearance, despite the magnitude of power deflation, the disproportion between government force and the insurgent arsenal was still overwhelming. A crucial aspect of the accelerator was a supernatural multiplier which at this juncture utterly transformed the balance of force. A faith in magic as a power resource is rooted in traditional cosmology and appears to be a universal attribute of human communities before a scientific viewpoint becomes dominant (and for that matter frequently co-exists with theories of material rational causation). The folklore of African resistance is filled with remarkably parallel responses to the uniform problem: how can men with spears, bows, and arrows overcome the force of enemies with firearms? No material counterforce was available; help could only come from the pantheon of supernatural forces. A superior force within the hierarchy of causation could transform the lethal agent of the rifleman, his bullet, and render it as harmless as a raindrop. The keys to the kingdom of magic were held by those with the specialized knowledge of and access to occult forces; the continuous intercession and collaboration of wizards was indispensable to insurgent power. The utility of magical armament was enormously enhanced by the fact that it was equally plausible to government troops, who shared the same belief system as the insurgents.

The decisiveness of magic as the pivotal component of force during the zenith of the eastern rebellion is underlined by the fact that the only real military defeats suffered at this stage were at the hands of hostile rural bands who could more readily counter this force on its own terms. The defeat of Olenga's August assault on Bukavu was determined to a large extent by the decimation of his forces at the approaches to the city by Mwami Kabare's Bashi warriors. Particularly enlightening is the account given to a popular army council meeting in July 1964 of the stinging defeat suffered by a predominantly Bembe insurgent group attacking Rega irregulars who were defending their home territory of Mwenga; participants in the council were four rebel officers, two "advisers," and two *docteurs-feticheurs*. An officer who had taken part in the Mwenga battle reported that "the war which we carry on with soldiers and that with populations are two different wars . . . when we fight with the inhabitants who utilize Urega fetishes." On the third assault wave against the Rega forces, the insurgents found themselves "fighting against devils, not men." The combat was marked by extraordinary phenomena; the Rega possessed a gigantic dog, which required sixty-one bullets to bring down. When an assistant fetish doctor broke ranks and fled, scattering the *dawa* upon the ground behind him, the young *simba* took fright and fled in turn. Rebel troops, when they discovered that the Rega possessed unknown fetishes and knew the secret of their own, would only resume combat when a fetish of higher quality was brought into play. The popular army war council unanimously decided that a colonel would be dispatched immediately to Kalemie to secure this assistance.

There were other new capabilities offered by the utilization of magic. In Kwilu, the mystique of Mulele's leadership rested in part upon his extraordinary powers. He was said to be invulnerable to bullets and to demonstrate his force by firing blank cartridges at himself. He could move long distances through government lines, by rendering himself invisible, or by transporting himself as a bird, or by using a tiny airplane no bigger than the palm of a hand. Not only could the force of a government bullet be reduced but arrows could be transformed into cartridges in flight.

The potency of magic as force rested upon the universality of its plausibility. For those on both sides, at least partly enmeshed in the traditional belief system, social reinforcement operated through the sharing of these convictions with all the others in the group, and the inadequacy of alternative sources of explication. E. E. Evans-Pritchard gives a lucid summary in his Zande study:

> In this web of belief every strand depends upon every other strand, and a Zande cannot get out of its meshes because it is the only world he knows. The web is not an external structure in which he is enclosed. It is the texture of his thought and he cannot think that his thought is wrong.

The system provided explanations for its own failures. In the popular army in the east, its use was systematized, sanctioned by a range of taboos, many of which had clear social control functions (such as the prohibition against sexual intercourse during a campaign), and administered by a cadre of fetish doctors attached to every unit. An elaborate ritual was developed, including "baptism" of new recruits— a laying on of hands to transmit invulnerabilty from the supernatural domain to the *simba* through the agency of the specialist in wizardry. Thereafter, certain proscriptions such as the prohibition against turning one's head in combat, provided explanation for a reasonable number of failures. Beyond a certain threshold, however, as the Mwenga example suggests, a conviction of collective failure of magic could develop. However, questioning did not extend to the larger issue of the efficacy of magic in general, but rather to the shortcomings of the particular fetishes in hand.   The national army itself, when the rebellion was in decline, became increasingly effective against residual pockets in part because *simba dawa* (although not magic in general) lost its credibility.

Value-Orientations: From Marx to Mama Marie Onema

Thus by 1964 an insurrectionary potential had been realized. The precarious legitimacy of the post-independence regime had been gravely impaired, and the credibility of its coercive power severely devalued. For those persuaded that the construction of a new Congo required the destruction of the existing regime, possible success nurtured hopes which expanded in tandem with the shrinkage of government capability. For rebel leaders, the revolutionary hour was at hand; in July 1964, the road from Kasongo to Kinshasa was paved with dazzling prospects of imminent triumph. We must now shift our focus from cause to process and suggest the essential dynamics of the rebellion in order to seek insight into its decomposition and collapse.

A first part of the answer to the failure of the rebellion lies in the extraordinary internal diversity of insurgent forces. This can be seen through the ideological and value spectrum and through the stratification of participation in rebellion. As a syncretic mélange of ideas and symbols drawn from many sources, the ideology of rebellion displays evident continuities with the multitude of separatist churches, messianic sects, witch-finding movements, and other religious expressions of the tensions of social change during the colonial period.

At the summit, there was an infusion of Marxist-Leninist, and to some extent Maoist, patterns and categories of analysis. To those prepared to accept the premises and the selective use of evidence, this provided an apparently coherent explanation of why the first achievement of independence had gone awry. Reduced to its simplest terms, this analysis argued that the Kinshasa regime incarnated the national bourgeoisie, definitively corrupted by its alliance with imperialist forces. Capitalist imperialism in the Congo was represented by Belgians and Americans; increasingly, the Kinshasa regime was dependent upon the support of its external protectors. The *compradore bourgeoisie* (those who have linked their class status to imperialism in Maoist parlance) joined hands with Belgian and American capitalist/imperialist forces in the systematic exploitation of the impoverished masses and the national resources.

The infusion of Marxist-Leninist-Maoist thought into the ideological panoply of the rebellion came primarily through the agency of a small number of leaders who, between 1960 and 1964, had the opportunity for travel and study in China, the U.S.S.R., and Eastern Europe, and thus gained exposure to revolutionary currents of political thought. As ideology hunters, these young men were favorably predisposed to a system of analysis offering a radical critique of the existing regime which also provided an identification of the enemy that corresponded with their own perceptions. Another source of ideological exposure were the Communist embassies situated in Brazzaville and Bujumbura, the two key sanctuaries for rebel leaders. The Chinese were particularly evangelical in their efforts to improve the ideological sophistication of the rebel elites. Also, in the guerrilla training camps of Congo/Brazzaville, ideological instruction was part of the program, with some participation by Chinese instructors.

Pierre Mulele was probably the most ideological of the rebel luminaries. Mulele had enjoyed only modest visibility in 1960; in the national elections, he had, with only 5,520 votes (compared to 60,511 for Kamitatu and 52,445 for Gizenga), stood ninth among *Parti Solidaire Africain* candidates in the number of preferential votes received. He was Minister of Education in Lumumba's government and then fled to Kisangani with the Gizenga group. However, by December 1960 he was disillusioned with Gizenga and left for Cairo with the designation of ambassador. On 21 March 1961, he wrote to Nkrumah to ask support from Ghana, because he "considered himself the sole person to assume leadership in trying to halt the sad course of events which followed the illegal dismissal of Lumumba." According to Nkrumah, Mulele kept in close touch with the Chinese embassy in Cairo and in 1962 traveled via Prague and Moscow to Peking, where he underwent a training course in guerrilla warfare. Upon his return to Kwilu in mid-1963, Mulele soon assumed the dimensions of a regional prophet. Curiously, he never put his political philosophy in writing, nor did he publish a manifesto or program. As reconstructed from numerous accounts of those who lived in the forest camps which he and his lieutenants organized, Mulelist ideology had three main themes. There were two main classes in society, capitalists and impoverished masses. In the Congo, the capitalist class was divided into foreigners and those associated with the Kinshasa government—the "reactionaries." Two sorts of struggle existed: reformist, to be avoided as only alleviating and not rectifying the sufferings of the mass; and revolutionary, whereby the masses assumed control over their own destiny. Thirdly, in tactical terms, the revolutionary struggle had to be conducted by partisans whose relationship to the villages had to be "as fish in water"; village support and integration of partisans into the village milieu were the indispensable prerequisites to success. Mulelist partisans had as their tactical primer a document entitled "Ordre de mission des partisans." This partisan bible was largely inspired by the classic writings of Mao on guerrilla warfare; Benoit Verhaegen demonstrates the point-by-point literal correspondence between Mulele's text and Mao's military thoughts.

The Marxist-Leninist contribution to the rhetoric of insurrection in the eastern Congo was much more fragmentary. The fabric of rebellion was far more complex in design, and no charismatic leader enjoyed the ascendancy which Mulele had in Kwilu. The only close equivalent to the partisan training camps deep in the forested valleys of Kwilu were centers of political instruction organized by Antoine Marandura, son of the sometime Mwami Musa Marandura, in the mountainous part of Fulero country. A few second-rank leaders, such as Laurent Kabila in North Katanga, or Tony Nyati in Kisangani, had studied in Eastern Europe, and had formulated their thoughts with some concern for ideological sophistication. Also, in the predominantly Bembe redoubt in the Uvira-Fizi area there were a large group of Cuban ideologists and military technicians during much of 1965, when the rebellion was in decline; included in this latter group, the evidence suggests, was the late Ernesto "Che" Guevara.

The next layer of political thought was the radical but vague nationalism epitomized by Lumumbism in 1960. Areas in which widespread response to the call of rebellion occurred were all dominated by parties displaying an aggressive response to terminal colonial rule. Militant nationalism at this stage, however, was largely measured in terms of style and tone. The only really defined goal was unitary government and immediate and total independence, and degrees of militance were measured by the level of commitment to these simple aims, whose consequences and further implications went largely unexplored. Most of the leadership in the eastern Congo spoke primarily in the Lumumbist idiom. The destruction of the Kinshasa regime, a vigorous reassertion of Congolese control over its own destiny, and a vague socialist commitment were recurrent themes. But at bottom it appeared far more a frame of mind and a style of expression, than an interrelated set of ideas.

Finally, there was incorporated into the value spectrum a range of ill-defined norms and orientations which rendered the movement intelligible to the audience of rural and urban youth to which it appealed. Characteristic was, in Kwilu, the curious extension of Maoist logic, to extol the pristine virtues of the rural village; the working class, as a revolutionary force, disappeared altogether. Vehicles of acculturation such as the Christian missions, European artifacts, and the use of French were rejected. Indeed, the Mulelists also proscribed the "state Kikongo," a simplified, detonalized version of Kikongo used by the administration and in primary schools in the Kwilu-Kwango area, in favor of Lingala (an equally deformed, river-trading lingua franca which had been standardized and simplified by the colonial administration). The new society, Renée Fox and others suggest, "is conceived as a gigantic village, composed of smaller villages where people will recover their own authentic identity, the satisfaction of all their material needs, justice, creative activity, and joy in working the soil in common." The importance of traditional cosmologies has been described previously. Of particular interest is the effort to systematize and employ in a uniform manner a composite of beliefs and practices borrowed from a variety of groups. The North Katanga rebellion of 1960–62 and the Luba refugee camp in Lubumbashi in 1961–62 saw frequent exploitation of magic as a control mechanism; Balubakat *jeunesse* played some part in south Maniema before and during the rebellion, and one of the two most renowned fetish doctors was a Luba. The *simba* initiation rites were similar in a number of respects to Kumu ceremonies, and this may have been a source of the technology of magic. But traditional cosmologies were specific to given cultural areas in their detail, even if broadly similar in outline. Thus, the effort to standardize magic in the popular army was, in its context, a radical innovation.

Skill Groups and Diversity in Participation

Functional and social stratification in participation also played an important part in the rebellion. The rebellion was a multi-dimensional drama enacted in many different ways at different levels of society.

Each category of participant differed in perspective, political resources, and action capabilities. The simultaneous pursuit of varying aims by interlocking and overlapping circles of participants lies at the very heart of the process of violence.

At the top was the rebel elite, composed predominantly of political leaders spawned in the tumults of 1959–60. They had in common a thorough hostility to the political formula which had emerged in 1961 in Kinshasa national politics, even though some, such as Gbenye, had held ministerial posts. Most had been associated with the Gizenga regime in Kisangani in 1960–61, although not with Gizenga's subsequent adventure at the end of 1961. Most had committed themselves to national politics since 1961. This group launched the *Conseil National de Libération* in October 1963 in Brazzaville. From the outset, it was rent by debilitating factionalism. The significance of simple personal incompatibilities is impossible to overestimate; the messiah complex was common to the 1960 political generation. Mulele mistrusted Gizenga; Egide Bocheley-Davidson detested Gbenye, who was in turn sharply critical of Gizenga's leadership in Kisangani in 1960–61. Anicet Kashamura, who never rallied to the rebellion despite his apparent ideological sympathy for its cause, published highly unflattering views of Gbenye and Thomas Kanza, among others. Soumialot split with Gbenye and Olenga; Olenga in turn had a violent altercation with Gbenye in Khartoum in mid-1965 and promised a Uganda Commission of Inquiry that he would reveal the "whole truth" about other rebel leaders before he was forcefully rusticated by Ugandan police in 1966. Neither a sense of shared political goals nor a common ideology was sufficient to generate sustained collaboration among the elite.

The rebel elite had differing audiences. Kanza, designated "Foreign Minister" of the revolutionary government in Kisangani in September 1964, had a slender domestic base among university students and intellectuals, and a much more important constituency in the African diplomatic sphere, where, during his period of service, he was a persuasive advocate. However, his commitment to rebellion only came after he had agreed to enter the Tshombe government as Foreign Minister, and the appointment had been vetoed by President Kasavubu, with whom the Kanza family had a personal vendetta. Mulele refused to take any part in exile politics in Brazzaville, and operated from his Kwilu redoubt. Bocheley-Davidson remained in Brazzaville, and operated from the *Conseil* secretariat which was situated there; the *Parti Solidaire Africain* Gizenga group for the most part did likewise.

The rebel elite did have in common their aspiration to operate at a national level. They were thus, of necessity, coalition builders, seeking to aggregate regional pockets of discontent. As regional auxiliaries, the elite worked with a set of leaders whose aspirations and operations were more local. Most belonged to the 1960 political class, and many had served as provincial ministers or even national deputies, but had failed to achieve prominence. At the time that insurrection broke out, many found advantage in an alliance which offered to reverse existing provincial power arrangements. Virtually all had been associated with the "Lumumbist bloc" of parties in 1960, and so found congenial the symbols and rhetoric of rebellion. What is striking about this group, however, is the extent to which the structure of provincial conflict as it stood in 1964 tended to shape their options. In North Katanga, Ildephonse Massengo and Roger Kabulo established their links with rebel leaders at a moment when the province was literally paralyzed by the bitter Sendwe/Mwamba-Ilunga struggle. In Sankuru, Louis Lumumba, brother of the late Prime Minister, served as a reluctant and ambiguous ally of the rebels during their five-day occupation of Lodja in August. The provincial government established for Maniema after the rebel conquest of Kindu was, according to Verhaegen, "by its composition neither a People's Government, nor a revolutionary one. It could perfectly well have been elected by the provincial assembly of the preceding regime. Its principal characteristic was to be drawn from the 'counter elite'—that is, that fraction of the politico-administrative elite which, while possessing the same characteristics as the group in power, had previously been thrown into opposition." In Kisangani, François Sabiti played a similar role; his father and grandfather had served as chiefs of the *arabisé* quarter of the African town.

From July 1964 on, a distinctive military elite emerged in the eastern Congo, as the popular army became a substantial organization replicating the national army in structure and nomenclature. The popular army took shape in the Fizi area in the first part of June when three columns were formed under the command of Jean-Bosco Kalisibe, Victor Tshombaz, and Olenga, all three Tetela-Kusu. Soumialot, also identified as a Kusu (although his father was a Songye), initially invested the officers with their functions, but by late July Olenga had become the dominant and autonomous force within the insurgent constellation, deriving his authority from his relative control of a potent political resource, the popular army. There was a marked predominance in the insurgent officer corps of Tetela-Kusu. A number had once served in the national army, but had been purged, as members of Lumumba's ethnic group, for suspected disloyalty to the Kinshasa regime. The homogeneity of the rebel officer corps no doubt contributed to the cohesiveness of the popular army, and to its effectiveness as a pressure group. At the same time, as the possible instrument of Tetela-Kusu ethnic hegemony, this homogeneity ultimately rendered the army suspect in areas outside the Maniema core.

The popular army rank and file were of a very different origin. Initially, the troops were heavily drawn from certain groups, above all the Bembe of Fizi. Fulero and Rwanda Tutsi refugees were also numerous at first. As the insurgent columns marched through Maniema, many others were enrolled, with Ngubangu of Kabambare and Zimba of Kasongo particularly numerous. Subsequently, as the rebel force snowballed in size, its composition became rather more diffuse, but at bottom it was a Maniema army. Once outside the areas in which the predominant groups had local attachments, it became an alien force, with its separation from the civilian population reinforced by its own taboos. It was a crusade of rural youth, mainly in the twelve to twenty age group.

The organization of Mulelist partisan bands was sharply different. These were structured into small teams, each team led by "political commissioners" and based in a village, or a forest camp. Not every villager was integrated into the teams, but every village in the core areas of the Mulelist movement had a team. There was no effort to constitute larger units, and no distinctively military elite emerged; the partisans remained more firmly linked with the political apparatus.

The urban-based "youth" groups were both an asset and a liability to rebel elites. The Kisangani situation was the prototype. The *Mouvement National Congolais*/Lumumba "youth" had been given major responsibilities in party organization in 1960; flying squads of young men had seen to the establishment of the party in the Orientale-Maniema hinterland of the Lumumbist capital by achieving the co-operation of chiefs and local leaders where possible, and by intimidation where necessary. By 1964, Kisangani was full of very angry young men, cheated in their own eyes of the birthright of independence; their leaders had been in and out of prison as successive weak administrations in Kisangani tried to maintain a tenuous social peace. For a time after independence, the *Mouvement National Congolais*/Lumumba "youth" had been led by Bernard Salumu, "boss" of Kisangani city in the Gizenga period. He had been succeeded by Victor Benanga and Alphonse Kingis; the latter was also a Kitawalan pastor, leading a religious community on the left bank of the Congo River at Kisangani. Benanga and Kingis were ruthless, violent, and sanguinary, and their "youth" gangs were responsible for much of the indiscriminate slaughter of "intellectuals" which occurred during the rebel administration. They belonged to a *tsotsi* subculture, and were never brought under the control of the rebel leadership. The first

"revolutionary provincial government" constituted at Kisangani at the time it was first captured by rebel forces was led by Kingis and Benanga; Olenga, upon his return from the unsuccessful assault on Bukavu, sacked the "youth" leaders, declaring: "Well-founded complaints had been registered denouncing actions in violation of the most elementary notions of the rights of man, such as arbitrary arrests, killings; in a word barbarity and vandalism have made their appearance."
(Olenga at the same time personally executed the army commander he had left in charge, Col. Kifakio, in front of the leading hotel.)

Competing rural elites were an important part of the mosaic of rebellion at local levels. The Belgian version of local administration, although officially based upon respect for traditional criteria in the selection of the chiefs who were the capillaries of rural governance, placed a higher value on efficiency and productivity. Consequently, there was a substantial reservoir of potential claimants to official investiture when competitive provincial politics injected new opportunities for ousting incumbents. Rival claimants to chieftaincies frequently had a significant clientele and were, in the context of electoral politics, attractive allies for town-based politicians. The sharp conflicts which arose at the provincial political level after independence further complicated many local situations, as ephemeral regimes used chieftaincies as a reward for their followers and removed those conspicuously identified with rival factions. The rebellion provided an opportunity for those deprived of office to reverse their status.

In Opala territory, southwest of Kisangani, a local chief who had been ousted by Belgian officials the year before independence had, initially in 1960, become a rural organizer for the *Mouvement National Congolais*/Lumumba "youth." When the Lumumbist regime in Kisangani was displaced in 1961, he found himself again excluded from office. When the Opala region was overrun by insurgent forces, he had a new opportunity to recover power. Indeed, at this stage he enlarged his ambitions by proclaiming himself paramount chief of the entire Mbole ethnic group, which was dominant in Opala territory. To assure the permanence of his new title, he assassinated eight of the nine incumbent local chiefs in the area. The acephalous Mbole tradition lent no sanction to his claim, but the invocation of fidelity to Lumumbism provided a partial surrogate.

Another specimen of the interaction between local leadership conflicts and the rebellion lies in the chieftaincy struggle among the Fulero. The Fulero had a relatively centralized traditional political structure, which initially had a royal caste of alien origin, in common with many kingdoms in the interlacustrine area. However, the Belgians had deposed this group, when it proved insufficiently pliable. At the end of the colonial rule, Henri Simba, the invested *mwami* of the Fulero chieftaincy, claimed his office on the basis of customary sanction, but the traditional rules had undergone a major mutation. Simba chose to oppose the militant nationalist parties, *Centre de Regroupement Africain* and *Mouvement National Congolais*/Lumumba "youth," which sought to organize the Uvira area in 1960. The foremost Fulero spokesman of the politically militant was Musa Marandura, who was elected provincial councillor from the area. Under the Kashamura-Omari regime in Bukavu in early 1961, Simba fled to exile in Burundi, and Marandura was declared "President" of the chieftaincy; he immediately proceeded to purge most of the subordinate chiefs and replace them with the politically faithful. Simba, however, had his revenge when Jean Miruho came to power in mid-1961; he was reinstalled as *mwami* and chased the Marandura men. By late 1963, Marandura, aided by his son Antoine, began organizing the residual political "youth" branches of 1960 vintage, and isolated attacks upon subordinate Simba chiefs began at the end of the year. Soumialot already had close contacts with Marandura. When he arrived in February 1964 to organize an insurrection in the east from Bujumbura, he had little difficulty in hitching the local purposes of the Marandura faction to the broader aims of the *Conseil National de Libération*.

The importance of magic in the rebellion made those specializing in its invocation and control a skill group of some importance, especially in the eastern Congo. Wizards from certain cultural groups had particular reputations extending far beyond their own ethnic areas; fetish-manipulators did not need to come from the group whose needs they were serving. (Kusu-Tetela have a particular notoriety in this regard.) The high priestess of the eastern rebellion, Mama Marie Onema, had a reputation throughout the Maniema-Kisangani area even before the rebellion offered her new opportunities. She was a wizened, one-breasted woman of very short stature whose startling appearance enhanced her effectiveness. She was resident at Kindu at the moment of the rebellion, and General Olenga, after the capture of Kindu, sought her out immediately to enlist her services. She held court in Kisangani during the period of the revolutionary government. After the fall of the rebel capital, she was captured by forces of the central government. Sûreté chief Victor Nendaka induced her to change her allegiance, and in early 1965 the former rebel zones were saturated with government posters announcing Mama Onema's switch. The specialists in magic operated within the popular army; every unit was anxious to have a technician of occult forces in order to be able to offer continuous protection from the dangers of combat.

The multiplicity of values and elites helps to clarify the complex molecular structure of the rebellion. At any given time and place, the valence of the component value and elite elements could vary within a considerable range. No single group or belief system could dominate the rebellion across the whole area in which the insurrection occurred. Further elucidation of this point requires some consideration of symbols of rebellion, orbits of influence of particular groups and individuals, and arenas of conflict.

Symbols and Diffusion of Rebellion

In general, one may suggest that, particularly for rural populations, modern politics required translation into locally meaningful symbols if the populace at large were to be able to relate thereto. In the Congo, the three most important types of symbols were heroes, ethnic labels, and political parties. The diffusion of the rebellion, and the attraction of the local population to it, depended upon local populations finding within the symbolic language which announced the insurrection a basis of identity with the rebellion. Conversely, symbols can be negative; where the labels by which the option of rebellion was presented evoked hostility, resistance occurred.

The memory of Lumumba, the martyr, and the luminous living legend of Mulele were the two most conspicuous hero symbols for rebellion, although they operated in a somewhat different fashion. In 1960, Lumumba had, in most parts of northeastern Congo, become the human incarnation of the inchoate hopes and aspirations of the first independence. His name had infused with a palpable, human symbolism both the dominant party (the *Mouvement National Congolais*/Lumumba "youth") and the visceral nationalism which swept the area (Lumumbism). Lumumba, Lumumbism, and Lumumbists were omnipresent in the catechism of the eastern rebellion. The new party cards issued in 1964 contained a red spot, symbolic of the blood of the patron saint. The centrality of Lumumbism helps to clarify the boundaries of rebellion. In North Katanga, rural populations which rose against the Tshombe regime in Lubumbashi in 1960–62 were quiescent in 1964, even when rebel warriors arrived, because neither Lumumbism, nor any of the other symbols of rebellion, had a binding appeal. But when the rebel columns reached the fringes of the Ubangi district, sharp resistance was encountered as they left the radius of Lumumbist appeal. The possibility of a rebel push toward central Kasai was abandoned because of the necessity to pass through territory of the Luba of Kasai; here the Lumumba symbol evoked not just indifference, but violent antipathy. The Lumumba symbol was peculiar to the eastern rebellion; it was not utilized in Kwilu.

Mulele was a new entry in the symbolic lexicon. His role in 1960 was too slight to achieve wide public visibility; his personality was invested with legendary attributes only when the Mulelist maquis exploded into view at the beginning of 1964. For Kwilu, he was a charismatic guerrilla leader, with prophetic, superhuman qualities. In the eastern Congo, Mulele was less a person than an omnipotent force. Rebel forces marching into battle chanted "Mulele mai! Mulele mai!" (Mulele water); the chant reinforced the potency of the ritual immunizations provided for the troops by the unit *docteur-feticheur*, with the terrible powers of the man-spirit, Mulele. Gbenye, when he reached the eastern Congo in late August, ordered the popular army to chant "Lumumba mai!" rather than invoke Mulele. However, this order was not fully executed, presumably because of the specific symbolic properties which the name of Mulele had come to incorporate, even though as a real person he was wholly unknown in the eastern Congo.

Political party labels also offered a mechanism for relating peasant populations to the rebellion, as well as determining the boundaries of the rebellion's appeal. Party as a symbol was not much used in Kwilu, where the zone of the Mulele maquis was roughly co-terminous with the Gizenga wing of the *Parti Solidaire Africain*. Mulele, because of the far more thorough infusion of a whole new symbolic system in his forest training camps, did not need the 1960 symbols. But in the east, party labels served to objectify both friend and foe. *Mouvement National Congolais*/Lumumba was the principal party symbol of the rebels, possession of a paid-up party card was indispensable to personal security, and prior association with the party was a requisite criterion for appointment to political office in Kindu, Kisangani, Isiro, and Bunia, where "provincial" administrations were established. Other parties of the 1960 Lumumbist coalition, *Centre de Regroupement Africain* (Kivu), Balubakat and Cartel (North Katanga), served as accessory symbols. The enemy bore the *Parti National de Progrès* (PNP) label after the 1960 administration-supported moderate movement which had, by the time of the May 1960 elections, been literally liquidated in the Lumumbist zones. (Those labeled for execution were "PNP," which was virtually a residual category for functionaries, politicians, and chiefs identified with the Kinshasa regime, or for those who failed to establish their *Mouvement National Congolais*/Lumumba *bona fides*.) Radeco, the short-lived national coalition which former Prime Minister Adoula sought to erect, was also a designation of the "social enemy" and identified as a functional equivalent of the "PNP."

Ethnic labels as symbols of conflict were also crucial to the pattern of diffusion. The importance of ethnicity in the cognitive process converted the abstract idea of insurrection into the specific message "group X is in revolt." Reaction to the opportunity of rebellion then depended, in part, on whether or not group Y saw itself threatened by group X. In Kwilu, the perception of Mulelism as a Mbunda-Pende movement rendered it self-containing, although fragments of some other neighboring groups took part in the early stages, when, among other things, they had to consider the greater risks of not joining a movement which might prove victorious. In North Katanga, rebel columns were largely composed of Bembe, with an infusion of Rwandan refugees and Fulero. Although some Luba leaders, such as Ildephonse Massengo and Laurent Kabila, played a part, the government briefly constituted in Kalemie was not rooted in North Katangan ethnic realities. In Kalemie itself, the dominant townsmen, the Tumbwe, played almost no part in the bitter factionalism of provincial politics, nor were they represented in the rebellion. Both the Luba-dominated factions of Sendwe and Mwamba-Ilunga, and the insurgent government, were equally alien.

In Kivu and Maniema, Fulero, Bembe, Ngubangu, Zimba, and Kusu-Tetela participated heavily. Rega found themselves cast in the role of enemies, of Bembe in Mwenga, Zimba in Kasongo, and Kusu in Kindu, and were thrown into opposition. For Kivu, Olenga's invading column was a Maniema force, and both major Shi factions, Kabare and Ngweshe, resisted. In North Kivu, provincial politics was dominated by a conflict between Rwandan immigrants and Nande, embittered by a dispute over the territories of Goma and Rutshuru. The sympathies of Rwandans for the rebellion rendered it a threat to the Nande.   In northern Maniema, the Kumu initially rallied to the rebellion. Kumuhood was bound up with the syncretic movement of Kitawala, which had been absorbed into the segmentary structure of Kumu society. Kitawala had been the object of repressive measures by the colonial administration and the post-independence government. Rebellion initially offered the possibility of support to Kitawala, and therefore Kumu identification with the movement was strong. However, Kitawala came into sharp conflict with rebel leaders and the popular army and Kumu support for the insurgents melted; the national army had little difficulty reoccupying the Kumu area.

The Tetela-Kusu label played a pivotal role in the dialectic of rebellion in the east. From the earliest days of the colonial period, a Tetela-Kusu myth had developed. Tippu Tip claimed to have received the keys of the Maniema kingdom from Kasongo Rushie, whom he described in his memoirs as the "Sultan of Utetera." Subsequently,

Tippu Tip's legendary lieutenant, Ngongo Lutete, led marauding bands of Tetela-Kusu on raiding expeditions throughout the Maniema-Sanguru-Lomami areas. A large percentage of the *wangwana* (free men) who settled around the Swahili outposts of Kasongo, Nyangwe, Kibombo, and Kisangani, and were labeled by the Belgians as *arabisés*, were of Tetela-Kusu origin. Ngongo Lutete allied himself with Congo Independent State forces in 1892, and many of his men joined the *Force Publique*. Two major mutinies, in 1895 at Luluabourg and in 1897 in the Ituri forest, were described as "Tetela revolts." The group was divided by colonial administrative boundaries, with those in Maniema labeled "Kusu" and those in Sankuru (Kasai) as "Tetela." A congress called in March 1960 asserted the cultural unity of the group, designated it "Ankutshu-Anamongo," and pledged its support to the party of its favorite son, Lumumba. The ethnic solidarity of the Tetela-Kusu, and its affinities with the eastern portion of the much vaster Mongo culture cluster, was one pillar of the electoral success of the *Mouvement National Congolais*/Lumumba "youth" in 1960.

In 1960, a tract appeared which played a major part in establishing the political legend of the Tetela-Kusu. Entitled "Parchemin que tout Ankutshu doit avoir et connaitre par coeur," the document is a statement of extravagant ethnic chauvinism. Its origin is obscure, but the improbable extremism it expressed led most observers to believe it to be a forgery. In 1964, the "Parchemin" reappeared throughout rebel areas in the eastern Congo. Its concordance with the fears and suspicions evoked by the striking pre-eminence of Tetela-Kusu in rebel leadership ranks, and above all in the popular army officer corps, gave it a subjective authenticity. Whatever its origins, it came to be widely believed in intellectual circles.

The tendency to identify the rebel elite with Tetela-Kusu became more pronounced with the establishment of a revolutionary government in Kisangani. Gbenye, president of the revolutionary government, was a Bua, but the other two designated ministers actually in Kisangani, Soumialot and François Sabiti, were both identified as Kusu. In Kindu, the designated provincial regime had eight of twelve Tetela-Kusu ministers who dominated the government. Gbenye was led to communicate an order to the commander of the "3rd Groupement" of the popular army at Kisangani warning, "There could be no question of being Mutetela to be promoted, and we must not limit the success of our citizens because of their ethnic origins." Particularly in the northeast, mutterings about the "foreign" character of the revolutionary regime were frequent.

Curiously, the Tetela-Kusu saliency in the eastern rebellion did not achieve massive support for the rebellion in Sankuru. Provincial politics in Sankuru had catalyzed a division between Tetela "Eswa" and Tetela "Ekonda" which had not previously been perceptible to students of the area. The "Eswa" group, roughly speaking, lived in the savannah lands, and had experienced some acculturative contact with the Arab-Swahili trading states of the nineteenth century. The "Ekonda" were forest dwellers who occupied a more inaccessible area where opportunities for economic and social change had been less. By 1963, bitterness between the two reached the point where a large part of the principal town of Lodja was burned. The legacy of this dispute appears to have precluded a unified response to the rebellion, despite the identification with all of its symbols. Rebel operations in Sankuru were ephemeral and superficial.

Structure and Leadership: Political Resources and Radius of Influence

There were a number of instances where ethnic communities did not respond as a single group to the rebellion. In these instances, a dialectic of local factionalism frequently operated. The choice of a given leader or faction tended to be determined by the choice made by the alignment of the local faction with whom conflict was most salient; it was in terms of this symbiosis of hostility or alliance that the rebellion would be perceived. (A similar pattern has been widely remarked upon in choosing between co-operation and resistance in the initial phase of colonial penetration, and in the diffusion patterns of rebellious movements such as Maji Maji.) By adding this factor, one may complete the analysis of diffusion in Kwilu. The Mbunda and Pende wholly identified with the symbols of the rebellion, and rallied en masse. The Mbala and Ngongo were so threatened that they opposed as communities. In other small groups in the area, neither attracted by nor totally repulsed by the ethnic identifications of Mulelism, the local dialectic prevailed—examples of this reaction were found at least in some degree among the Ding, Lori, Nkutshu, Shilele, Suku, Wongo, and Yanzi.

At the leadership level, the rebellion was far too diverse for any single man to assert personal ascendancy; the most prominent individuals, such as Gbenye, Soumialot, Olenga, Bocheley-Davidson, Mulele, and Gizenga, each had orbits of influence determined by their range of activities. Gbenye had two key assets: regional support from the Bua area, in the Aketi-Buta zone of Uele, and an intimate familiarity with the complex social relationships in Kisangani deriving from pre-independence prominence in the city. Soumialot had a radius of activity with Kindu as its hub, and Maniema, South Kivu, and part of North Katanga enclosed within its circumference. However, he had never lived in Kisangani so that when the Lumumbist capital became the central place of the eastern rebellion, Soumialot was partly eclipsed by Gbenye. François Sabiti could be effective within the Kisangani urban area, but nowhere else. Bocheley-Davidson held as his precarious political resource the Brazzaville exile machinery, but could not have challenged Gbenye, Soumialot, or Olenga on the ground in the eastern Congo.

The rebellion produced a growing number of structures which served as resources in the matrix of interpersonal rivalry. The Mulelist maquis possessed its own infrastructure, not linked to any other. The *Conseil National de Libération* in Brazzaville was split into Gbenye and Bocheley-Davidson factions within a month after its foundation. When Soumialot established operations in Bujumbura, he set up a "CNL-East." After the establishment of the revolutionary government in September 1964, Gbenye and Soumialot quickly came into conflict over their respective prerogatives. Gbenye argued that the revolutionary government had superseded the *Conseil*, while Soumialot maintained that his responsibilities as head of "CNL-East" gave him separate sanction for his exercise of authority. At the same time, at the OAU summit conference in Addis Ababa which took place simultaneously with the proclamation of the revolutionary government in Kisangani, Bocheley-Davidson reaffirmed that the *Conseil National de Libération*/Brazzaville was the sole representative of the Congolese revolution and that Gbenye had been expelled from his office in the Conseil. The *Mouvement National Congolais*/Lumumba "youth" re-emerged as yet another structure, with two committees, led by Victor Benanga and Gustave Ifefeko, respectively, appearing in Kisangani the day after the *simba* conquest. In Kindu, a Conseil des Sages was constituted as a quasi-provincial assembly, as well as a new provincial government. *Mouvement National Congolais*/Lumumba "youth," and the *femmes nationalistes* were other structures offering organizational resources to local leaders. Finally, the popular army under Olenga was to all intents and purposes an autonomous body.

The organizational picture became even more complex in the declining phase of the rebellion, when much of the activity was carried on in the vacuum of exile. Brazzaville, Accra, Conakry, Algiers, Cairo, Khartoum, Kampala, Dar es Salaam, and Bujumbura provided the changing loci for shifting alignments of rebel personalities and their diminishing clientele. In April 1965, Soumialot established in Cairo a *Conseil Suprême de la Révolution* which included Gabriel Yumbu and some other members of the Bocheley-Davidson wing of the *Conseil*

National de Libération, but excluded Gbenye and Olenga. Bocheley-Davidson himself at this juncture had a temporary reconciliation with Gbenye. Col. Vital Pakassa, a former national army officer who had been a close associate of Gizenga, rallied to the Gbenye camp and was assassinated in Cairo by Soumialot's men. Gizenga, driven by a curious obsession as the self-anointed successor of Lumumba, in 1965–66 became an important part of the mosaic. After his release from prison by Tshombe in July 1964, he declined to join the *Conseil National de Libération;* instead, he sought to organize his own United Lumumbist party, repeating an unsuccessful initiative of 1961. In September 1966 in Cairo, he formed a *Front Congolais de la Révolution,* which won over some of the exile clientele. The remaining pockets of internal rebel resistance had their choice of soliciting external support from the Gbenye, Soumialot, or Gizenga factions.

The arena of conflict determined what political resources could be brought to bear. In 1964, when the decisive action occurred on the sundry battlegrounds of insurrection within the Congo, leaders able to provide direction and relative control within this framework were predominant. The metamorphosis into the murky world of exile politics compelled rebel elites to base their actions upon other foundations. Access to moral backing and financial support from states committed to at least covert support of Congolese revolutionaries was one key. In this type of world, Olenga was simply unable to compete. On the other hand, Gizenga by 1965–66 could appear as the most plausible revolutionary alternative to external supporters. His absence of grass roots revolutionary capability was less important than it had been at the peak of rebellion.

Rebellion in Power

The dilemmas of the deprived in the Congo were illuminated by the record of the rebellion in power. A paradoxical aspect of the rebellion was that its greatest success was its greatest disaster. The capture of Kisangani led to the erection of the form and structure of a regular government, but the rebel regime in its three months of power demonstrated that, although it might make things worse, it had neither the ideas nor the capacity to make them better. The surfacing of latent personal tensions, the multiplicity of organizational structures, the unleashing of the most violent and dangerous rebel support groups, and the vaguely politicized urban youth, all combined to lead to an inevitable and disastrous result.

The Kisangani problem was foreshadowed by the train of events in Kalemie, the first significant town under prolonged rebel administration. At the beginning of the two months of insurgent rule in late June, Soumialot imposed a tenuous order upon the town, and popular army units kept themselves and the terrorist groups under some control. Soumialot, who had never lived in Kalemie, tried to maintain his version of personal rule; his days were passed in continuous audience, listening to the complaints and pleas of the unemployed, functionaries, schoolmasters, pastors, thieves, and company representatives. But personal rule and improvisation were inadequate to sustain the city. After a little more than a month, Soumialot left in despair, and the town sank into total chaos. It was described by one witness: "There is no longer any authority whatsoever in Kalemie; the so-called rebels have barely heard of Soumialot, who has in any case left for Kindu. Everyone has equipped himself with a scrap of paper, bearing the title he has given himself. Colonel, Chief of Special Branch, Police Commissioner, etc. It is the most total anarchy, which encourages theft and pillage, the ultimate aim of these disoriented young men, transformed for the instant into insurgents."

In Kisangani, the insurgent regime was initially sustained by the euphoria of success, the new hopes for a genuine second independence which had been generated, and the confiscation of the liquid capital available in bank vaults, company cash boxes, and shop inventories. The first rebel authority was a triumvirate of "youth," which proved to be literally a *tsotsi* regime; "youth" power was turned to the task of unrestrained vengeance against all who were labeled as "PNP." The installation of the revolutionary government under Gbenye saw an effort by an older generation of politicians to assume charge and to reassert social control over the forces unleashed by the rebellion. What is striking about the Gbenye period is the effort to restore precisely the patterns of administration which had prevailed before. Aside from new personnel and an alteration in rhetorical style, the rebel regime came empty-handed to its rendezvous with the millennial dreams of its following. The only innovation was the further diminution of administrative capabilities, produced by the purge of "PNP" elements from the public service and the assassination of others, the rupture of supply routes, and the confusion resulting from multiple claimants to the various segments of authority. The seriousness of the deterioration of the situation was concealed by the depletion of stocks of all sorts —monies, vehicles, fuel, and other goods. In Kisangani and Isiro, "People's Co-operatives" were opened and confiscated goods were sold at 1960 prices. The supplies, obviously, did not last long, and there was no possibility of replenishment. The devastating impact of these destructive policies was not fully felt until after the rebel authority had evaporated from the towns of the northeast. Even the modest pre-rebellion level of economic activity in this vast area has been impossible to restore, and in 1968 the prospects were dreary.

Concluding Remarks

Strategists of rebellion for the Congo would appear to be faced with an insoluble dilemma. At the present stage in the evolution of society and polity, there would appear to be no navigable channel between the Scylla of ethnic encapsulation and the Charybdis of incapacity to govern urban areas. The Mulelist strategy, despite its far greater sophistication in formulating ideology and exploiting the technology of guerrilla warfare developed in China, Vietnam, Algeria, and Cuba, was in the last analysis a failure when judged against its presumed goal of overturning the Kinshasa regime. Mulelism defined its own orbit of action. Once the movement had set its limits, the government could at its leisure wear it down by slowly breaking the crucial links between partisan teams and village support bases. The village populations could not indefinitely withstand the tremendous hardships caused by their forcible relocation in the forest with the partisans; little by little they succumbed to the blandishments of the government to leave the encumbering presence of the guerrilla units. The process took a heavy human toll, as both the government and partisans directed their reprisals at the most vulnerable group, the villagers. In the eastern Congo, the whole flimsy superstructure centered on Kisangani was extremely vulnerable to counterattack by even a modest military force. An illusion of omnipotence tottered upon incorporeal pillars of magic. The sorcerer's apprentices of terror and demoralization swept away the national army units and the legal administration in front of the advancing *simba*. But the process was halted where the attainment of the perimeter of insurgent appeal was combined with the injection of a small but decisive counterforce of mercenaries who were impervious to the primary weapon of the insurgent army. The effective force of white mercenaries which went into action at the beginning of September was four hundred; in addition, the capabilities of the national army were enhanced by a modest number of Belgian military advisers, and a handful of aircraft secured through the good offices of the United States. The added force input was infinitesimal when contrasted to the 500,000 French troops in Algeria, or a similar number of American in Vietnam. Presumably the warnings of Debray to Latin American revolutionaries concerning the illusions of liberated zones, and the dangers of false analogies with the Chinese situation, are germane.

The conclusion to be drawn from the Congo rebellion would seem to be an empirical invalidation of Chou En-lai's classic observation that "Africa is ripe for revolution." More germane is Zolberg's penetrating observation:

> . . . it is unlikely that movements such as these will be able to translate their revolutionary aspirations into the institutionalization of a new regime and of new social structures. African society does not have a center; its syncretic character insures that it cannot be turned upside down, or that if an attempt is made to do so, some groups will shift their relative positions but the society as a whole will remain very much as it was before.

The very lack of integration of a polity as vast and diverse as the Congo means that all roads to rebellion lead to the same impasse. Neither China nor Cuba—nor Zanzibar—can serve as a political model for the Congo. The millennial dreams of the deprived have given way to renewed despair, as the devastation and destruction remaining from the aborted rebellion are visible to all in the affected zones. A post-rebellion song from the Pende areas of Kwilu which gave strong support to Mulele suggests that those who paid the enormous price of embarking upon unsuccessful revolt will be reluctant soon to repeat the experience:

Quand je vous vois, la honte me prend
Oh vraiment, quand je vous vois
la honte m'etreint;
Car nous avons été
Trois années entières dans le bois
Parce que Mulele avait donné
de mauvaises directives.
Pour avoir donné de mauvaises directives
Gatshinga fit périr une multitude d'hommes
et à sa suite
Funji avait aussi montré
une mauvaise voie
Qui fait périr une multitude d'hommes.

The very disparities which created the insurrectionary potential in the first place are redoubled; nothing could be more vivid than the contrast between the relative opulence of the Lower Congo, and the hopelessness of Kisangani. No doubt the illusion of the apocalypse will be reborn, and new prophets will bear the message. Only the most consummate leadership can forestall yet another rendezvous with rebellion.

THE AUTHORS

ROBERT I. ROTBERG is associate professor of political science and history, The Massachusetts Institute of Technology, and a research associate of the Center for International Affairs, Harvard University. A graduate of Oberlin College, Princeton University, and the University of Oxford, he previously taught at Harvard University. He is the author of: *The Rise of Nationalism in Central Africa: The Making of Malawi and Zambia, 1873–1964* (Cambridge, Mass., 1965), *A Political History of Tropical Africa* (New York, 1965), *Christian Missionaries and the Creation of Northern Rhodesia, 1882–1924* (Princeton, 1965), and *Joseph Thomson and the Exploration of Africa* (London, 1971). He edited and introduced George S. Mwase, *Strike a Blow and Die: A Narrative of Race Relations in Colonial Africa* (Cambridge, Mass., 1967). He is the editor of *The Journal of Interdisciplinary History*.

LEON CARL BROWN, professor of Near Eastern history and civilization, and Director of the Program in Near Eastern Studies at Princeton University, has spent several years in the Middle East and North Africa, first with the United States Foreign Service and recently in independent research under the auspices of the Ford Foundation and the Institute of Current World Affairs. He is coauthor with Charles A. Micaud and Clement H. Moore of *Tunisia: The Politics of Modernization* (New York, 1964), editor of *State and Society in Independent North Africa* (Washington, 1966), and author/translator of *The Surest Path* (translation with commentary of Khayr al Din al-Tunisi's *Aqwam al masalik li ma'rifat ahwal al mamalik*) (Cambridge, Mass., 1967).

247

ELIZABETH HOPKINS, associate professor of anthropology at Smith College, was a research associate of the East African Institute of Social Research from 1961–63 and did field work in Ankole and Kigezi. She is the author of several articles on East Africa.

SHULA MARKS received her Ph.D. from the University of London and is lecturer in history with special reference to South Africa at both the School of Oriental and African Studies and the Institute of Commonwealth Studies, University of London. She is the author of *Reluctant Rebellion: An Assessment of the 1906–8 Disturbances in Natal* (New York, 1970).

AUDREY WIPPER is a Canadian who teaches sociology at the University of Waterloo. She received her Ph.D. from the University of California, Berkeley and previously studied at McGill University. She was a research sociologist at the Institute of International Studies, Berkeley and a research associate of the East African Institute of Social Research. She is presently completing a study of syncretist sects in Kenya.

M. CRAWFORD YOUNG teaches political science at the University of Wisconsin, where he has been a member of the faculty since 1963. He is the author of *Politics in the Congo* (Princeton, 1965), and, in collaboration with Charles Anderson and Fred von der Mehden, *Issues of Political Development* (Englewood Cliffs, 1968), as well as a number of articles concerned with Congolese, Ugandan, and African politics. He served as chairman of the African Studies Program at the University of Wisconsin from 1964 to 1968, and, beginning in 1968, as associate dean of the Graduate School. In 1969 he became chairman of its Department of Political Science. During 1965–66, he was visiting lecturer in African Studies at Makerere University College.

INDEX